# Gabrielle's Time Tale

JEFFREY HIGGINSON

Illustrations by
Jeffrey Higginson

To my precious wife (Stacie), my 2 precious children (Emily and Eric), and a precious baby daughter on the way

# CONTENTS

# ACKNOWLEDGMENTS

Just like my first book, a big thanks again to my dear wife, Stacie, for everything she did to allow time for me to write this book. She's still the best wife in the world!

Thanks to my daughter, Emily, for all the trouble of posing for not only the cover photo, but also for many illustration photos for this book. Posing for some of these photos was not fun for her.

Thanks to two of my sisters, Melissa and Rebecca, for proofreading and helping to make needed changes for improvement.

# 1
# LOST AND FOUND

        Gabrielle was a young, sweet girl who was good at making new friends. Everyone called her Gabby. At five years of age, she had many friends that she had gotten acquainted with in the time period of less than a year. She was always honest and friendly. However, she wasn't like anyone else. Everyone else had parents—at least at some point in their lives. In addition to not knowing if she ever had any parents, nobody knew where she came from, nobody knew her full name, and nobody knew when she was born. Comparing her to other children, it was everyone's best guess that she was currently at the age of five. Although she was always completely honest, her curiosity as to why she had no parents would later make everyone question her honesty.

        It started one year ago when Gabby was presumptively at the age of four. It all happened in River City, Tennessee with a population of over twelve thousand residents.

        On a spring day in the month of May in the year 2019, Mr. and Mrs. Felding were driving to the grocery store. They were both close to the age of fifty, and their two sons and two daughters had all grown up and moved away. For several months, they both wished they were a bit younger with kids in their house to raise again, but they both knew that time was only making them older by the minute.

        When they were only half a mile away from the location of the grocery store, Mrs. Felding looked to the left across the street where there was a field of many trees. "Pull over," she said.

"What?" Mr. Felding asked.

"Pull over!" repeated Mrs. Felding, still looking out the car window to the left.

"What's wrong?" asked Mr. Felding while pulling over to the side of the road.

"Why is that little girl walking all by herself?"

Mr. Felding looked to the left where Mrs. Felding was looking, but he couldn't see anyone besides the people traveling in their cars. "What are you talking about? What little girl?"

Mrs. Felding pointed towards the little girl across the street who was walking in the field along the outskirts of the trees not too far from the road. "Right over there."

With cars passing by in both directions, although there were not too many to block his view, Mr. Felding took another look. "I still don't see anyone. Maybe we should continue on our way to the store."

"But how can you not see her? She's just over there not too far from the road," said Mrs. Felding, pointing towards the little girl again.

Mr. Felding took one more look. A semi truck then passed by, traveling in the opposite direction from where they were heading. As soon as the semi truck was out of the way, he finally saw her. "Oh, there she is. And why is she wearing that dress? Today is only Tuesday. Is she coming from or walking to a special event?"

"I don't know, but in a city this big, she shouldn't be walking alone by herself."

"Yeah, maybe we should go find out where her parents are before something happens to her."

Mr. Felding turned off the car. He and Mrs. Felding got out and stood beside the street while they waited for traffic to pass. When the street was cleared, they walked swiftly toward the little girl.

As soon as they got across the street, they walked slower as to not scare away the girl.

"Excuse me," Mrs. Felding said to her, but the girl just kept walking with no response. Mrs. Felding turned to her husband. "I'm sure I spoke loud enough. Can she not hear me?" She turned back to the little girl. "Excuse me," she said again. The girl looked over to them and stopped walking. Mrs. Felding faced her husband. Speaking quietly, she said, "It looks like she heard me this time." Facing the girl again, she spoke a little louder. "Where are your parents?"

"I don't know," the girl said.

"What's your name?" asked Mrs. Felding.

"I'm Gabrielle."

"Are you going somewhere?" Mr. Felding asked.

"I'm trying to find my house," answered Gabrielle. "I think I'm lost."

"Where did you come from?" asked Mr. Felding.

"From over there," Gabrielle said, pointing towards the middle of the field of trees.

Mrs. Felding started feeling quite worried for Gabrielle. She turned back to Mr. Felding and said quietly in a worried tone of voice, "There's nothing in that field besides a forest of trees."

Mr. Felding started feeling worried as well. He walked over to Gabrielle through the short distance of the few feet that had been spacing them apart. "I think you should come with us," he said while reaching out his hand. "Maybe we can help you find your house along with finding out where your parents are. It's not good for a little girl to be alone outside in a big city."

While cars were passing by on the busy, paved street, Gabrielle looked around, and she wondered what the old man was talking about concerning a big city. All she could see was a dirt road that was empty, which ran through a huge, grassy field with spaced-out trees on both sides, and there were no buildings anywhere. She remembered being told to not go places with strangers, but as lost as she felt, she decided to trust the old couple in hopes that they could lead her back home, so she took ahold of the old man's hand.

The three of them walked to the edge of the road and stopped. Mr. and Mrs. Felding waited for both ways to be clear of traffic before crossing. "Why are we standing here?" asked Gabrielle.

"We need to wait for both ways to be clear before we cross," replied Mr. Felding.

Gabrielle looked down the street in both directions, and all she could see that was moving on the road were a few leaves slowly being blown by a slight wind. *Maybe they don't want the leaves to hit us,* she thought.

As soon as the traffic was clear, they started walking across the road back to Mr. and Mrs. Felding's car. On their way, Gabrielle was fascinated that the rocky, dirt road was the least bumpy road she had ever walked on.

When they approached the car, Gabrielle pointed to it and asked, "What's that?"

"That's our car," answered Mrs. Felding.

Gabrielle looked down at the tires. "Is it like a buggy?" she asked. Then she looked around in all directions. "Where's the horse?"

Still feeling worried, Mr. Felding turned to face his wife, and he spoke quietly to her. "She obviously knows some history, but she doesn't even know what a car is," he said, pausing to glance over to Gabrielle before turning back to Mrs. Felding. "Maybe she's been lost for longer than we thought."

Mrs. Felding led Gabrielle to the passenger side of the car away from the traffic, and she opened the back door for her. "We don't have a baby seat or a booster seat for you, so you'll just have to sit right here on the back seat for now." Gabrielle got in, and Mrs. Felding helped her with the seatbelt.

As soon as Mr. Felding started the car with no sound of any other cars on the street, Gabrielle felt scared. "What's that noise?" she asked in a tone of fright.

"I started the car," Mr. Felding said, "and the noise right now is the motor."

"Oh," responded Gabrielle. She immediately calmed down and assumed the car was like a small train that didn't need any train tracks.

Knowing that keeping Gabrielle at home with them would most likely result in receiving a criminal record as a kidnapper, Mr. Felding headed to the police station to report the situation. On the way there, Gabrielle constantly looked out the windows while she enjoyed the smooth ride.

After a while, she noticed a building that she had never seen before, located close to the street. "Wow! I've never seen a building like that before!" she exclaimed.

"Which building?" Mrs. Felding asked.

Gabrielle pointed towards the building. "The only one over there."

Mrs. Felding turned around and looked to see where Gabrielle was pointing, but there were too many buildings along the busy street to know exactly which one she was referring to. Mrs. Felding assumed that what Gabrielle said about the *only* building meant the only one in the exact direction to wherever she was pointing. "Yeah, there are lots of buildings everywhere like that," she responded, pretending she knew which building Gabrielle saw.

While they continued to travel, Gabrielle looked out the windows in all directions, and there was only the one building that she could see, which happened to be the oldest building in the entire city. *Maybe she thinks one building is a lot of buildings,* Gabrielle thought.

Approaching an intersection up ahead, Mr. Felding started slowing down to a red traffic light, needing to turn left.

When they came to the intersection, the left turn light turned green, so Mr. Felding proceeded. Gabrielle looked out the window to the left while they were turning, and it appeared that they were turning off the dirt road onto the grassy field. "Why are you turning off the road onto the grass?" she asked.

"Onto the grass?" asked Mr. Felding. Immediately, he assumed that Gabrielle must have seen a few grass clippings on the road. "I'm turning off that road because we need to take this other road to get to where we're going."

"Oh," said Gabrielle. *Well, he's either taking a shortcut through the grass to another road, or someone forgot to make a road that goes to where we're going,* she thought. However, she was surprised at how smooth a ride on a grassy field could be.

Not understanding why they had to stay tied to the seat, Gabrielle figured out how to unbuckle her seatbelt. Having sat beside the window on the passenger side for long enough, she moved over to the window on the driver's side. Looking outside to the left, wanting to see what made the ride feel so smooth, she looked downwards at the ground, and she was immediately astonished when she saw the grass-covered ground that they were traveling on turn quickly into a dirt road. Gradually, it turned into a paved road, and she watched while the road grew wider and wider.

A minute later, she looked across the street and noticed another building, then another, and then another. The entire street was soon filled with numerous buildings on both sides. In addition to what she was seeing, she saw a car passing them in the other lane, heading in the same direction and, after a short moment, several cars were coming on the other side of the road, heading in the opposite direction. *I hope we're not too far from home,* she thought. *I don't remember this city.*

After Mr. Felding parked the car close to the entrance of the police station, Mrs. Felding took ahold of her purse and got ready to open the car door. Looking at the unorganized contents of her purse, it looked like a jumbled-up mess, and she didn't want to wait for a time when she would immediately need something and have to spend time to find it. "You two go ahead," she said. "I'll be there as soon as I get things organized here."

After entering the police station, Mr. Felding noticed a service desk located halfway down the hallway. Sitting behind the desk, a policeman named Officer Gunwell was doing some paperwork. Gabrielle followed Mr. Felding over to the desk.

When they approached the desk, Gabrielle wondered what they were doing inside an empty building. "Why are we walking over here?" she asked.

"We need to talk to this nice police officer," replied Mr. Felding. Then he turned to Officer Gunwell. "Pardon me, officer."

While Gabrielle looked around the empty building, the officer looked up from doing his paperwork and saw Mr. Felding standing there. "What can I do for you, sir?"

"There's nobody here," Gabrielle said to Mr. Felding. "Who are you talking to?"

Mr. Felding looked at Gabrielle. "I'm talking to this policeman right here behind the desk."

Officer Gunwell was a little confused. He looked at the man who was standing at his desk while he waited for an answer to his question and wondered whom the man was talking to.

Gabrielle looked at the empty desk. "But there's no policeman here."

"Of course there is. He's sitting right here," said Mr. Felding, pointing behind the desk.

Officer Gunwell's confusion soon led him to assume that the man who appeared to be talking to nobody was talking into the speaker of a small, hidden cell phone. *Oh, I hope this is not another one of those cases,* he thought, referring to several other crazy people who had come into the police station in the past.

Mr. Felding turned to Officer Gunwell. "I'm sorry, officer. I'm just talking to this little girl here. My wife and I found her walking along the street all by herself. She doesn't know where her parents are, and she said she's lost."

"Who are you talking to?" asked Gabrielle at the same time the officer asked a question.

"I can't hear two people at once," said Mr. Felding. "What were you saying, officer?"

"I asked you how old she is," repeated Officer Gunwell.

Mr. Felding looked downwards at Gabrielle. "Oh, I'd say she's about three or four." Then he turned his head back towards the officer.

Officer Gunwell wondered why the man needed to look at the floor to answer the question. "And what's the girl's name?"

Mr. Felding looked at Gabrielle. "Would you like to tell him your name?" he asked her, not knowing that she and the officer could not see or hear each other.

"Tell who?"

"The policeman."

"But nobody's here."

Mr. Felding assumed that Gabrielle must have been pretending that everyone was invisible. "Just say your name."

Gabrielle assumed that Mr. Felding must have been pretending to talk to a ghost. "Gabrielle," she said to the invisible ghost.

Officer Gunwell waited several seconds to hear the girl's name. "I can't hear her, sir. Could you turn up the volume on your phone?"

"What phone?" asked Mr. Felding.

"Well, whatever you're talking into. Could you turn up the volume or just tell me the girl's name?"

"I'm not talking into anything, and she just told you her name."

*How long do we need to play ghost?* Gabrielle thought.

"Where is she?" asked Officer Gunwell.

"She's standing here beside me," answered Mr. Felding.

Officer Gunwell looked to both sides of the man. Then he looked carefully again. Seeing nobody there, he stood up from his desk. "I need to go grab some more paperwork," he said. "Just wait right here, and I'll be back shortly."

While the officer headed down the hallway away from the entrance doors towards one of several office rooms, Mrs. Felding entered the building. She saw Mr. Felding and walked over to him.

In the office room, Officer Gunwell grabbed a paper to file another case of a lunatic needing psychiatric treatment. A fellow officer noticed what he was getting. "Another one of those cases, huh?" the fellow officer asked.

"Yep . . . another one," said Officer Gunwell.

"Did you get his name?" asked the other officer.

Officer Gunwell realized that he hadn't asked the man's name amidst the squabble of trying to find out the name of a girl who didn't seem to exist. "No. I'll go do that right now."

As soon as Officer Gunwell opened the office door to return back to the service desk, Gabrielle turned to face the office, and she saw him coming out. She pointed to him and said, "There's the policeman!"

*At least she finally stopped pretending that everyone is invisible,* thought Mr. Felding.

While walking back down the hallway from the office room, Officer Gunwell looked towards the service desk and noticed a lady and a little girl standing next to the man who had been acting peculiar.

After arriving back at the desk, the officer faced the man and said, "Sir, I need to get your name." He placed a guest sign-up sheet and a pen down on the desk in front of Mr. Felding. "Please sign here." Next, he turned to face the lady. "And you're the wife?" he asked while Mr. Felding signed his name.

"Yes, officer. I'm Mrs. Felding."

Officer Gunwell faced the little girl who he assumed was brought into the police station by Mrs. Felding. "And who do we have here?"

"I'm Gabrielle," the girl said.

"Well, that's a good name for a pretty girl like you!" said Officer Gunwell. "And that's a pretty dress you have on! It looks a lot like the dresses shown in some ancestry photos." The officer turned to Mr. Felding. "Is this the lost girl you were talking about?"

Mr. Felding assumed that the officer didn't have good vision in his eyes before heading to the room down the hallway, and perhaps had put contacts in his eyes before coming back to the desk. "Yes, this is the girl."

Officer Gunwell faced Gabrielle. "So, little lady, I understand you're lost?"

"Yes, sir."

"Do you know where you live?"

"No, sir."

"Who are your parents?"

"I don't know."

"How long have you been lost?"

"I can't remember."

"What's your last name?"

"I don't know."

Officer Gunwell sat down at the desk. After setting aside the file of psychiatric cases, he grabbed a paper on which he started to file a missing-child report.

After filling out what little information he was given, he turned to Mr. and Mrs. Felding. "Are either of you licensed for foster care?"

They both shook their heads. "No, we're not," Mr. Felding said.

Officer Gunwell turned to Gabrielle. "Well, Sweetheart, our only option right now is to put you in foster care while we do some investigation as to where your parents are."

"Okay," Gabrielle said, trusting the policeman, but unsure and a little scared about what they were going to do with her.

Gabrielle stayed at the police station while Mr. and Mrs. Felding headed to the grocery store where they were heading to earlier that day.

After they were done shopping, they headed home. On their way, they thought about their experience with Gabrielle. "She sure was a sweet girl," said Mrs. Felding.

"Yeah. If only our kids could be that age again," Mr. Felding said, "it sure would make me feel a lot younger."

"It's too bad that we can't just grow younger every day. Wouldn't it be nice if we *could* have someone like Little Gabby to raise again?"

"Well, the only way for *that* to happen is to wait for grandkids to come along. And even then, our kids will be raising them most of the time."

A few seconds of silence passed before an idea came to Mrs. Felding. "Oh, Honey, I have an idea! What if we could get licensed for foster care like the officer mentioned? That way, we won't have to wait for grandkids to come along, and it will be like raising kids of our own again!"

Mr. Felding thought about it for a moment. "We don't know what child or children we will be getting. And by the time we get licensed, Gabby will probably be in another foster home."

"But what if we can get someone just as sweet as Gabby was? I'm sure we can say no to any foster placement that doesn't feel right for us."

"I guess we could try," agreed Mr. Felding.

# 2
# A HOME FOR GABBY

Over the course of the next four months, Mr. and Mrs. Felding took every necessary step to get licensed for foster care, which included finding a foster-care agency, filling out an application, going through several weeks of training, and much more. After the approval and licensing were completed, they waited for a placement call from the agency.

Two days passed, and they hadn't yet received a phone call. They knew it could be any length of time before receiving a call, but, during those two days, Mr. and Mrs. Felding wondered how things worked out with Gabby in the foster-care program.

"I wonder how long it took to find a foster home for her," said Mrs. Felding.

"Or maybe they found her parents by now. It's already been four months."

"Well, no matter what happened to her, I guess we'll never know."

After a few seconds, Mr. Felding thought of an idea. "If we really want to know, which I kinda would like to, then maybe we could go back to the police station where we last saw her, and the officers might know what happened."

"Yeah, Honey, that's a good idea!"

Later that day, they entered the police station once again. They walked toward the service desk, and there they found the same policeman.

They stopped at the desk. "Pardon me, officer," said Mr.

Felding.

Officer Gunwell immediately recognized the voice, and he looked up from his paperwork. "Well, Mr. and Mrs. Felding! What a surprise! It's been a while, but how could I forget you? So what brings you back? How can I help?"

"We just came to see if you had any information about what happened to Gabby," Mrs. Felding said.

"Oh, yeah, the little girl you brought in," Officer Gunwell added.

"Yes," continued Mrs. Felding. "We were just curious to know how long it took to find a foster home for her, or if you've found her parents yet."

"No," responded Officer Gunwell, "we haven't found her parents as of yet. We've knocked on several doors in the city as well as several neighboring cities and towns, we've hung thousands of flyers, and we also had it announced on television news channels and several radio stations. Not only does no one seem to know anything about the little girl, but there's also not one single trace of evidence anywhere in finding her parents . . ."

"And so she's in a foster home?" interrupted Mr. Felding.

"That's what I was getting to," said Officer Gunwell. "She's not exactly in a foster home right now. We haven't had any luck with that either. We tried taking her to foster-care agencies, which didn't work out, and then we took it upon ourselves to introduce her to several licensed, foster-care couples that we found, but everyone that we've taken her to—every licensed couple as well as the agencies—all claimed that they couldn't see her. She was always standing in front of them, but they kept asking where she was. And not just that, but she couldn't see them either. She thought I was talking to ghosts. I assumed the reason why everyone said what they said was because the licensed couples didn't want to take her in as their foster child, and she didn't want them either. I was even referred to as a crazy officer by a few of them."

"That sounds strange," said Mrs. Felding with an odd look on her face. "Who wouldn't want Gabby?"

Mr. and Mrs. Felding looked at each other. After that, they each sensed that they both had the same thing in mind, which turned odd expressions into partial smiles. Mr. Felding turned to Officer Gunwell and said, "We're both licensed for foster care now. We've been working on that ever since we left Gabby here. So we'd like to take her with us if it's okay."

"Where is she?" asked Mrs. Felding.

"Well, I can't hand her over to you yet," said Officer Gunwell. "First, I need to talk to the agency that you're licensed through." From his pocket, Mr. Felding pulled out a business card that he had gotten from the agency, which included the phone number, and he handed it to the officer who took a brief look at it. "Okay. Let me go make a quick call, and I'll be right back."

Officer Gunwell entered into another office room where there were telephones for making certain types of outbound calls.

After dialing the number, a secretary from the agency answered. "Hi. Thanks for calling Downtown Foster Care. How may I help you?"

"Hi. This is Officer Gunwell."

"Oh, yes, the crazy officer! Do you have another invisible child that you'd like to bring over?"

"Ha-ha," Officer Gunwell said sarcastically. "I'm calling to check on the licensing of Mr. and Mrs. Felding."

The agency secretary looked though the computer files and found the last name of Felding. "Yes, here they are. And it looks like they've completed the entire course, so they're good to go! However, foster children need to be placed in homes through foster agencies. Are you calling for the purpose of settling a foster dispute, or do you have a foster child you're trying to place into the home of the couple you mentioned?" she said, unsure about the mentality of the crazy officer.

"This is confidential police business," said Officer Gunwell, knowing that sending Gabby through the agency was impossible, "but thanks for the information!"

Officer Gunwell returned to the service desk and handed the business card back to Mr. Felding. "Your license through the agency has now been verified. We've been keeping Gabby here at the police station with us. She's been taken care of by some other officers who will bring her out after they help her get ready. And after she's ready, she's all yours." The officer briefly paused. "But before they bring her out, I need to warn you about her. I don't know how easy it will be for you to have her in your home."

"What do you mean?" asked Mrs. Felding. "Has she been misbehaving, not cooperating, throwing temper tantrums, fighting with anyone . . ."

"No, nothing like that," interrupted Officer Gunwell. "She's actually one of the sweetest little girls I've ever seen."

"So what's wrong with her?" Mr. Felding asked.

"Well, several things," replied the officer. "After you brought her here, we found out she didn't have any extra outfits. We then got her some outfits including a new pair of shoes, but after we showed them to her, it took a while to get her to want to change out of her dress. When she saw the pants we got for her, she thought they were clothes for boys, and she said girls only wear dresses. She also didn't know what a t-shirt was, and she didn't know how to put it on once we finally convinced her to change out of her dress. Not only that, but she also asked us where the outhouse was. And for the next two weeks, she kept acting surprised that the restroom—she still called it an outhouse—was inside the building. In addition, she asked us where we keep the candles and lanterns. She had never seen a flashlight, a light switch, an outlet, an electric cord, a telephone, a radio, a refrigerator, a microwave, and several other things, so we had to do a lot of explaining of what things were and how they work. And she kept wondering how the ink of a ballpoint pen doesn't spill out while shaking it."

"Being as young as she is," said Mrs. Felding, " she sounds like a normal child with most of what you said. I'm sure there are many children around the age of four who don't know what things are or how they work, especially since she probably had been lost for a long time."

"Then how do you explain the outhouse, the candles, and the lanterns?" asked the officer. "Most kids her age don't even know what an outhouse is."

"It sounds like she probably knows some history," said Mr. Felding. "It reminds me of when she asked us about a horse and buggy."

"It doesn't sound like there's anything wrong with her," Mrs. Felding said. "And with knowing some history, she might be smarter than most kids her age."

At that moment, another officer brought Gabrielle out from down a nearby, side hallway, and Officer Gunwell turned to see them coming. "Here she is," said Officer Gunwell, seeing her dressed in one of her new outfits.

As soon as Gabrielle saw Mr. and Mrs. Felding, she recognized them, smiled, ran over to them, and gave them each a hug.

"Would you like to come home with us?" Mrs. Felding asked her. Gabrielle faced Mrs. Felding, smiled, and nodded her head. Mrs. Felding turned to Officer Gunwell and asked, "Is there anything else we need to do before we take her with us?"

"Nope. She's all yours," said Officer Gunwell.

Mr. Felding took ahold of Gabrielle's belongings including a teddy bear that the officers had gotten for her, another new outfit, her dress, a pinafore, a pair of bloomers that she had worn underneath her dress, a pair of black stockings, a bonnet, and a pair of old-fashioned boots with laces that appeared to be in good condition. "Okay. Let's go," he said.

This time, Mr. and Mrs. Felding had a booster seat on the back seat of their car. After they got to where their car was parked in the parking lot, Mrs. Felding helped Gabrielle climb onto the booster seat, and she helped buckle her in. "We need to stay buckled in until we get home," she told Gabrielle.

While traveling, Mr. Felding thought about what the officer told them. Speaking quietly to his wife, he asked, "Remember what the officer said about them taking Gabby to some foster agencies and foster couples?"

"Uh-huh," voiced Mrs. Felding.

"After he told us that Gabby thought he was talking to ghosts, I thought about the day when we took Gabby to the police station. After I took her inside while you stayed in the car, we went to the service desk where the officer was at, and Gabby kept saying she couldn't see him. But I knew she could see him because she saw him after you came in, so I thought she was just pretending he was invisible. Do you think she was also pretending that the agents and foster couples were invisible just so she could be with us? After all, you saw how she ran over to us and gave us a hug right after she saw us today."

"If that's the case," said Mrs. Felding, "then how do you explain the agents and foster couples not seeing Gabby anywhere? Who wouldn't want a sweet, little girl like her?"

"Well, when I took Gabby into the police station, it wasn't just her who couldn't see the officer. He couldn't see her either. At the time, I figured he had bad eyesight before he went to another room, and he must have somehow fixed his vision in the other room because he saw her after he came out. So the only explanation I can come up with is that the agents and couples must have all had bad eyesight."

"*Everyone* having bad eyesight?" Mrs. Felding asked in disbelief.

"What other explanation could there possibly be?"

"In that case, how do you explain the time when you couldn't see her walking beside the street on the outside of the field of trees? Did you have bad eyesight? And why didn't she hear me the first time when I tried to get her attention?"

"Maybe I couldn't see her because I wasn't looking in the exact direction where she was, and maybe it seemed like she didn't hear you the first time because she thought you were talking to someone else," Mr. Felding explained.

During the ride home, Gabrielle's full attention was focused on the view of the city outside the car windows, so she didn't know what Mr. and Mrs. Felding were talking about.

After finally arriving, they walked into the home of Mr. and Mrs. Felding. "First thing we'll do," Mrs. Felding told Gabrielle, "is show you your room. Come this way." Gabrielle followed Mrs. Felding to the bedroom. Mr. Felding tagged along, carrying Gabrielle's belongings.

"This will be your bedroom," Mrs. Felding said to Gabrielle after entering the room while Mr. Felding placed Gabrielle's things on top of the chest of drawers. "It used to belong to my two daughters before they moved away. I've been working on cleaning, arranging, and organizing in here during the past four months, and now it's all ready for you."

Gabrielle looked around the room. It was the most elegant bedroom she had ever seen. "Wow!" she said. "This is my bedroom?"

"Yep, it's all yours," said Mrs. Felding. Then she walked over to the chest of drawers after Mr. Felding was out of the way. "And you'll need some extra outfits." She opened the top drawer and pulled out some toddler-size clothes. "I've been saving these for many years," she told Gabrielle, showing several outfits to her. "My daughters used to wear these when they were your age."

After looking around the bedroom for a while, everyone returned back to the living room. "What's that?" asked Gabrielle, pointing at a large, black, rectangular object.

"That's our television," said Mr. Felding.

*Television?* Gabrielle thought. Having never heard the word, she was left in a state of wonder. "What's a television?"

"You've never seen a television?" Mrs. Felding asked in surprise while trying to find the remote.

"No, I haven't," Gabrielle said.

"Honey, where's the remote?"

Mr. Felding turned his head to the nearby armrest of the couch. "Here it is," he said while reaching down and taking ahold of it. "I'll turn it on." Then he sat down on the couch and pushed the power button, which turned on the television.

"I hear someone," said Gabrielle. Looking at the television screen, she felt scared. "Someone's in there! How do they get out?"

Mr. and Mrs. Felding both laughed. "Nobody is inside the television," Mr. Felding said. "It's just a video that was recorded with video cameras."

Still in a state of wonder, Gabrielle asked, "What's a video camera?"

"You've never seen a video camera either?" asked Mrs. Felding.

Pushing the power button on the remote, Mr. Felding turned off the television, and he stood up from the couch. "I'll go get ours to show you," he told Gabrielle. He placed the remote back onto the armrest of the couch right before he started heading to the closet of the master bedroom where the video camera was stored.

As soon as Mr. Felding was gone from the living room, Gabrielle went over to the armrest of the couch, curious to know how the television was turned on and off with a device that didn't appear to be connected to it. She picked up the remote, pointed it at the television just like Mr. Felding had done, and started pushing random buttons. "It doesn't work anymore. Is it broken?"

Mrs. Felding responded, "You need to push the red button at the top of it."

Gabrielle pushed the red button, and the television came back on. She closely examined the remote, and there still didn't appear to be any hidden wires or anything else connecting the remote to the television. She pointed the remote back to the television, pushed the red button, and the screen turned completely black again. "Hey, I'm a magician!" she said. "I did some magic!"

Right at that moment, Mr. Felding came back with the video camera. He walked over to the couch and sat down next to Gabby. "This is a video camera," he said, showing her the camera. "This is the on-and-off switch. When you move the switch up like this," he said while he demonstrated, "it turns on."

Gabrielle watched the camera while the black screen suddenly began to show the part of the living room that the camera was facing towards. "Hey, that's part of the room that we're in!"

"That's because the camera is facing over there. Wherever it faces, it shows up on the screen," said Mr. Felding. "Now, do you see this red button?"

"Uh-huh."

"When I push this, it will start recording anything that I point the camera at, and it will also record any sounds." Mr. Felding pushed the record button. "And now it's recording." He turned it around to face Gabrielle. "There you are! Would you like to say something?"

"Hi. I'm Gabrielle," she said with a smile while facing the camera. Then she looked over to the television, and all she could see was a black screen. "Why am I not on the television like the other people were?"

Mr. Felding pushed the record button to stop recording. "Because I don't have the camera connected to the television," he said.

"But *this* thing isn't connected to it!" said Gabby, looking at the remote that she was still holding. "Maybe the camera isn't magic like this thing is."

Mr. Felding turned the camera around, switched it from the record mode to the play mode, and said, "Look on the camera screen, and you can see yourself." Then he pushed the PLAY button.

Gabrielle not only saw herself on the screen, but she also heard her own voice coming from the small speaker. "Hey, that's me! I can see myself!" she exclaimed, fully enthralled with what she saw and heard.

Much of the day passed by, and it was nearly time for dinner. Mrs. Felding headed to the kitchen to prepare dinner, and Gabrielle followed.

After entering the kitchen, Gabrielle noticed more unfamiliar objects. "What's that?" she asked, pointing to the toaster.

"It's a toaster," responded Mrs. Felding.

"What's a toaster?" asked Gabby.

"It heats things up such as bread for making toast."

While Mrs. Felding worked on gathering the needed ingredients for making dinner, Gabrielle stood close to the counter, stared at the toaster, and tried to think of any logical answer to her curiosity.

A minute later when Mrs. Felding was getting the last ingredient, Gabrielle decided to give up on trying to figure it out all by herself. "How do you put the wood in the toaster when it's so small, and where does the fire go?"

"Huh? We don't put wood in the toaster. What are you talking about? What fire?" Mrs. Felding asked. Suddenly, it dawned on her. "Oh, you're probably wondering how it heats up. It doesn't heat with fire. It's made of heating elements that get hot after you put something in it to get toasted."

"Oh," said Gabby. Then she looked all around the kitchen. "And what's that? And that? And that? And that? And that?" she asked, pointing at several other strange-looking objects.

The rest of the day rushed by. Mrs. Felding put Gabrielle to bed. Afterwards, she came out from the bedroom into the living room and sat on the couch beside her husband. "It's been quite a day!" she said while she rested her head against the back of the couch, facing the ceiling.

"It sure has!" agreed Mr. Felding.

Mrs. Felding turned to face her husband. "Do you know what Gabby said in the kitchen?"

Mr. Felding shook his head. "What did she say?"

"She thought there was fire in the toaster, and she wondered where we put the wood in it to burn. After I explained how a toaster works, she didn't know what an electric can opener was, and she had never seen a dishwasher, an electric hand mixer, a blender, or an electric griddle. It seemed like I had to explain the entire kitchen to her. Do you think the officer was right? What if it's not going to be easy to have her here?"

"It seems like she doesn't know what a lot of things are right now, but that's probably the same with other kids her age. After we teach her what different things are, I'm sure it will be easier. But I'm surprised at how much history she knows—the horse and buggy, the outhouse, the candles and lanterns, the dress that she was wearing when we found her, and now the heating of food with fire. It makes me wonder who taught her these things."

"What if she came from another country?" suggested Mrs. Felding. "Maybe she came from a poor country that doesn't have electrical things. After all, she never asked us about anything that doesn't run on batteries or electricity."

"And if she came from another country," added Mr. Felding, "then how did she get here? And whoever brought her here, why would they just drop her off?"

"I don't know," said Mrs. Felding. "But if that's what happened, then it probably happened when she was a baby, being that she doesn't know who her parents are. And if that's when it happened, then who's been taking care of her ever since then? And who bought her the dress and boots that she was wearing?"

Mr. Felding thought for a moment. "We'll probably figure it out over a course of time," he said while he picked up the remote to turn on the television.

"And speaking about time," added Mrs. Felding who had been teaching piano lessons at home for a few years, "I have two students coming tomorrow—one at eleven, and one in the afternoon at two-thirty. So we should watch our shows before it gets too late."

After turning down the volume of the television enough to not wake up Gabby, Mr. and Mrs. Felding quietly watched their late shows before heading to bed.

# 3
# MAKING NEW FRIENDS

The next morning, Gabrielle came out of her bedroom, wearing one of the outfits that the Felding daughters had worn at her age. She walked to the kitchen where Mrs. Felding was cooking breakfast.

While stirring the scrambled eggs in the pan on the stovetop, Mrs. Felding turned to see Gabrielle entering the kitchen. "Good morning, Sweetheart!" she said, immediately noticing the outfit that Gabrielle had put on all by herself. "My, my, don't *you* look nice today!"

Gabrielle smiled while she positioned herself into a few different poses for showing off her outfit. Then she walked closer to Mrs. Felding. "What are you making?" she asked.

"I'm making scrambled eggs. We're also having hash browns that are in the oven, and toast that's on the plate by the toaster," answered Mrs. Felding before she resumed stirring the scrambled eggs.

Gabrielle turned to look around the rest of the kitchen. She soon noticed some clean dishes on the corner of the countertop close to the table that was located several feet behind Mrs. Felding—three plates, three drinking glasses, three forks, and three butter knives—that looked like they had been taken out of the cabinets and drawers to be used for breakfast. She walked over to that part of the countertop, carefully grabbed some of the dishes, placed them into position on top of the table, and continued until the table was all set.

As soon as the eggs and hash browns were finished, Mrs. Felding turned off the oven and the burner on the stovetop. Not knowing what Gabrielle had been doing, she took ahold of the handle of the pan of scrambled eggs. While carrying the pan, she turned around and started walking towards the table. She looked ahead of her, and she saw Gabby looking at her with a smile while standing next to the table that was all set with every dish put into their proper place.

Mrs. Felding finished walking the remainder of the distance to the table. While placing a hot pad and the pan onto the middle of the table, she looked over to Gabrielle. "Did you set the table?" With a smile still on her face, Gabrielle nodded her head. Then Mrs. Felding added, "Oh, Gabby, that was so sweet of you! Thank you!" Afterwards, she headed back to the oven to grab the pan of hash browns while Gabrielle headed to the countertop to grab the plate of toast.

After all the food was on the table, Mrs. Felding grabbed a container of orange juice from the refrigerator while Mr. Felding walked into the kitchen for breakfast after getting ready to head off to work. "Something smells good!" he said.

"And it wouldn't quite be ready if it wasn't for Gabby," said Mrs. Felding.

"Oh, really?" said Mr. Felding while taking a seat at the table. He turned to face Gabby, wondering what she did. "What did *you* do to help?" he said in a friendly tone.

Gabrielle smiled once again. "I set the table!"

While Mrs. Felding took a seat after setting down the container of juice, Mr. Felding looked around the top of the table and saw how orderly and meticulous every dish was placed. "Wow! Good job!" he told Gabrielle. He and Mrs. Felding looked at each other, both with expressions of wonder about who taught Gabby how to set the table, knowing she hadn't seen the process of the table being set for dinner the previous day.

After breakfast, Mr. Felding headed off to work at the local furniture store where he had been working as a salesman for several years. Mrs. Felding started working on clearing off the breakfast dishes from the table while Gabrielle left the kitchen.

Two minutes later, having only a handful of dirty dishes still on the table to clear off, Mrs. Felding started hearing something that she never would have expected to hear. Coming from the living room was the sound of "Twinkle, Twinkle, Little Star" being played on the piano. She looked at the time on the clock, and it was only eight-thirty. *That can't be Molly coming more than two hours early,* she thought. *I didn't even hear the doorbell!* Feeling suspicious, she walked into the living room where she caught the sight of Gabrielle sitting at the piano, playing two notes at a time—one note with each hand. "Where did you learn that?" she asked while walking closer to the piano.

20

Gabrielle stopped playing. Immediately, she turned to see Mrs. Felding walking                    towards her. "I don't know," she answered.

Standing beside the piano, Mrs. Felding asked, "Did you learn that all by yourself, or did someone teach you?"

"I don't know," Gabrielle repeated. "It's just a song that I know how to play."

"But how did you learn it?"

"I can't remember."

Without asking any more questions in her attempt to satisfy her curiosity in regards to how the song was learned, Mrs. Felding decided to consider it as a mystery in addition to the other mysteries about Gabby, but she also wasn't going to let the beginning of Gabby's musical talent go to waste with no chance to improve. Being a piano teacher, she decided to help Gabby learn more, seeing she already had an obvious interest in playing the piano. "Could I sit here next to you?" she asked. Without hesitation, Gabrielle moved over to make room for Mrs. Felding on the piano bench.

After thirty minutes of the regular length of time for beginners, Gabrielle not only wanted to learn more, but Mrs. Felding also wanted to teach more. They ended up spending two hours at the piano. Then Mrs. Felding worked on getting ready for her next student while Gabrielle headed to her bedroom to be mesmerized once again by the new things that she had.

At exactly eleven o'clock, the doorbell rang. Mrs. Felding

headed to the front door.

After opening the door, she found five-year-old Molly Robinson standing next to her mom. Mrs. Felding looked at Molly and greeted her with a smile. "Hi, Molly! Are you ready for another lesson?"

"Uh-huh!" said Molly with a smile while she nodded her head, and she stepped through the doorway into the house.

"I'll be back in thirty minutes," her mom told her.

Mrs. Felding and Molly both sat on the piano bench. "Today," said Mrs. Felding, "we're going to work on our fingering while we learn scales, triads, and arpeggios."

A few minutes later, Gabrielle came out from her bedroom, wondering what was being taught at the piano.

As soon as she stood beside the piano, Mrs. Felding noticed her. "Oh, Molly, this is Gabby. Gabby, this is Molly."

"Hi," said Molly.

"Hi," said Gabby. "What are you learning?"

"I'm learning what fingers to use when I play sails."

"No," said Mrs. Felding, looking at Molly, "they're called *scales.*"

"Yeah. And then I'll learn triads and . . ." said Molly, trying to think of the other word, "apple joes."

"They're called *arpeggios*," said Mrs. Felding. "And I think we've done enough on scales, so let's learn some triads. A triad is a group of three notes," she said while she played a triad. Then she raised her fingers off the keys. "For some of these triads and arpeggios, your hands might need to be bigger for your fingers to reach some of the keys, but like my piano teacher told me many years ago, it's never too early to learn. So I'll just show you on some of these, and I'll let you practice what you can reach."

Gabrielle stood beside the piano for the remainder of the lesson while watching Molly practice. Eager to learn, she paid close attention to everything that was being taught.

After thirty minutes, the lesson was done. Mrs. Robinson hadn't yet returned. "She should be here shortly," said Mrs. Felding, "especially since you live only three houses away."

"Where is your house?" Gabrielle asked Molly.

Molly pointed in the direction where she lived. "Down that way," she said. "I live in the brick house with the white fence.

"Do you have a piano in your house?"

"Uh-huh," said Molly while she nodded her head. "I practice fifteen minutes every day."

"You do?" asked Gabrielle in total surprise. Feeling excited, she turned to Mrs. Felding. "Could I practice every day too?"

"I was hoping you would," answered Mrs. Felding, "especially since you already have a head start."

Just then, the doorbell rang. "Is that your mom?" Gabrielle asked Molly.

"I think so," said Molly.

Mrs. Felding headed to the front door while Molly and Gabrielle followed.

Realizing that Molly was about to leave, Gabrielle wondered if she would ever see her again. "Will you be coming back?"

"I come here for a piano lesson every Saturday, so I'll be here next week," Molly replied.

Mrs. Felding opened the door, saw Mrs. Robinson, then turned to Molly and said, "Here's your mom, Molly. We'll see you again next week."

"Okay," said Molly while she walked past Mrs. Felding.

Gabrielle followed Molly until she came to the doorway. She stood beside Mrs. Felding while she watched Molly leave the house. "Bye," she said.

Molly stepped out of the house and turned around to face Gabby at the doorway. "Bye," she replied.

While taking ahold of her daughter's hand, Mrs. Robinson started walking away slowly while she briefly waited for a response. In a matter of seconds, Mrs. Felding closed the door.

After walking away from the house, Molly's mom spoke in a tone of disappointment. "Well, that wasn't nice of her to ignore you like that."

Immediately, Molly was confused. "What? Who ignored me?"

"Mrs. Felding didn't say anything after you said bye to her."

"I didn't say bye to her," Molly explained calmly. "I said it to the other girl, Gabby, who told me goodbye."

"Who's Gabby? I didn't see another girl. What are you talking about? Was she far into the house where I couldn't see her?"

"She was right beside Mrs. Felding at the doorway. How did you not see her, Mom?"

"Molly, there was nobody standing next to Mrs. Felding. You need to stop pretending!"

"But I'm *not* pretending! Gabby even watched me during most of my lesson."

"Well, if I just didn't see her somehow, then I would have heard her say goodbye to you if she was really standing that close to us, but I didn't hear anyone either. And I know you spoke loud enough for Mrs.

Felding to hear, so if she wants to ignore you like that, then I'll just get on the phone when we get home and find you another piano teacher."

Suddenly, thinking about Gabby, Molly broke into tears. "No! Please! I like Mrs. Felding!"

"Yeah, you must like her enough to be making excuses for her ignorance by mentioning an imaginary girl. I'm not going to allow you to be taking lessons from someone who ignores her students. And just for the excuses that you're trying to make, you're going to practice for a whole hour every day, starting today, until I can find you another teacher."

Not having seen Molly's mom either, Gabrielle assumed that she must have been standing on the other side of the wall by the doorway or perhaps on the driveway while waiting for Molly to come.

At exactly two-thirty, Mrs. Felding heard the sound of her doorbell. Her next student for the day was a fourteen-year-old girl named Sophie Jackson who had been taking piano lessons ever since the age of twelve. She lived several houses away on another street in town. Her dad had been taking her to piano lessons up until a few weeks prior to her latest ringing of the doorbell, but ever since then, she had been walking to her piano appointments alone by herself.

While Mrs. Felding started the piano lesson with Sophie, Gabrielle stayed in her bedroom, not wanting to wait an entire week to see Molly again. *What does her piano look like?* she thought. *I wonder if she has any toys to play with.*

After a few minutes of thinking about Molly, Gabrielle started feeling lonely and bored. This time, forty-five minutes for a more advanced piano lesson seemed to be taking forever, and she didn't want to interrupt what sounded like a more advanced lesson being taught. Having nothing to do inside the house, she headed to the back door to see what was outside. Walking through the kitchen where the back door was located out of sight from where the piano was at, Gabrielle tried to be as quiet as possible to not disturb Mrs. Felding and her student.

Standing in the back yard, looking around, there still didn't appear to be anything to do. Three apple trees, a small shed with a lock on the doors, a garden hose attached to a portable sprinkler lying next to the back of the house, and a fence around the property were the only things she could see. She walked over to the apple trees and gazed upward, but there were no tree houses and no swings hanging from any of the branches. Starting to feel bored once again, her thoughts returned back to Molly, but that only made her feeling of loneliness increase.

Suddenly, she remembered what Molly said in regards to where she lived. *Three houses down the street in a brick house with a white fence?* thought Gabrielle. Then it dawned on her that she wouldn't need to wait until next Saturday if she could go see Molly at her house, and it didn't take any time at all for the idea to seem too good to pass up. Without hesitation, she started making her way along the side of the house towards the front yard. She was used to walking a good distance away by herself outdoors just as she had done on the day when she first met Mr. and Mrs. Felding, unaware of what could happen to children who aren't with an adult. However, approaching the sidewalk that stretched along the side of the road, everything was quiet and peaceful. The streets were completely empty with no cars coming from any direction, and there was nobody else anywhere in sight.

Meanwhile, Mrs. Robinson was going down the list of piano teachers, making phone calls, trying to find someone else who would be available, experienced, and affordable for being Molly's new teacher. Up to this point, she had dialed four phone numbers—three of which she couldn't get ahold of anyone, and the other one being a wrong number.

After hanging up on the fourth try while sitting in the living room, her attention was drawn to the lack of hearing the piano being played. "Molly!" she hollered. Molly had been in her bedroom with the door closed, not wanting to experience any disappointment by listening to her mom on the phone with other piano teachers.

A moment later, after hearing her mom calling for her, Molly entered the living room from the hallway. "You found another teacher?" she muttered softly in a tone of gloom with a desolate look on her face, not knowing any other reason why her mom would be needing her.

"Not yet," said Mrs. Robinson while turning to look at Molly. "And stop looking like it's the end of the world! You haven't started your hour of practice. I suggest you go do that right now," she said sternly, pointing in the direction of the piano room.

Immediately, Molly turned in the direction of the piano room and started walking away. She was always taught to obey her parents, so she wasn't about to argue.

Molly sat on the piano bench and started practicing while her mom started dialing the next number on the list. At that moment, a knock was heard at the door. Using it for an excuse to temporarily get out of practicing, Molly quickly plopped off the bench and hurried to the front door. "I'll get it!" she shouted while the next phone call was ringing. Just then, the phone call was finally answered.

"Hello. Sally's Piano Lessons. How may I help you?"

"Hi," said Mrs. Robinson, talking on the phone. "I'm looking for a piano teacher who can teach beginner lessons to a five-year-old. Do you teach students in that age range?

25

"Yes, I do," said Sally. I can teach as young as toddler age, and my oldest student is eighteen."

"Would you have some time in your weekly schedule? And how much do you charge?"

Right at that moment, Molly opened the door. "Hi, Molly!" said Gabrielle in a cheerful tone of voice while standing outside the doorway.

Feeling excited to see Gabrielle again, Molly turned to her mom. "Hey, Mom, it's Gabby!"

"Well, that sounds like a fair price. How long have you been teaching?" Mrs. Robinson said while still on the phone. And having heard Molly, she stood up to see who was at the door.

"I've been teaching for almost eleven years," said Sally. "If you'd like to schedule an appointment, I have some free time on Tuesdays and Wednesdays anytime after two o'clock. Would any of those days work for you?"

Mrs. Robinson looked to see who was at the door. As soon as she made eye contact, Gabrielle spoke with a smile. "Hi. I'm Gabby."

"Um . . . it looks like something has come up. I'll have to call you back," said Mrs. Robinson on the phone right before she hung up and turned to face the doorway. "Come in." Gabrielle stepped inside, and Molly closed the door.

"See, Mom?" said Molly. "This is the girl who I was talking about."

"Yes, I see. It looks like I owe you an apology, Molly. And you don't have to practice for an hour each day anymore." Then she turned to look at Gabrielle and said, "So *you're* the one who said goodbye to Molly. I don't know how I couldn't see you or hear you." Trying to think of any logical explanation, she added, "Maybe the brightness outside made it look too dark inside, and you must have told Molly goodbye right when cars were passing by. And speaking about cars on this busy street out here, did you come here by yourself?" she asked, not knowing that any other piano lessons were being taught in the Felding home at that time, and assuming Mrs. Felding must have known where Gabby had gone.

"Uh-huh," answered Gabrielle while nodding her head. "But the street was empty. I didn't see any cars."

"What? How could you not see any cars?" Mrs. Robinson asked in a tone of unbelief. "This is the busiest street in town! There's never a minute of the day when there's not a car on this street."

Gabby shrugged her shoulders, not knowing why she didn't see or hear any cars on a busy street. Mrs. Robinson then assumed there had to be a logical explanation just like when she herself didn't see or hear

26

Gabby at the doorway of Mrs. Felding's house. Perhaps Gabby didn't recognize any cars because her full attention was focused on something else. Perhaps she was losing both her hearing and her eyesight, and maybe had to slowly feel her way down the sidewalk until coming to a fence. Perhaps everyone in town decided not to travel during the time when she was walking from one house to another, which would have been an extremely rare moment. Or perhaps there was another unknown reason why she thought the street was empty.

Suddenly, Molly remembered being asked by Gabby if she had a piano. She turned to Gabby and asked, "Do you want to come see our piano?"

Gabrielle grew excited. "Yes! Yes!" she said, immediately starting to follow Molly to the piano room. "Do you have any toys?"

While leading the way to the piano room, Molly replied, "I have lots of toys in my bedroom. I'll let you play with them after I show you the piano."

A few minutes later, Sophie walked out the door after having finished the piano lesson. Mrs. Felding sat down on the living room chair that was next to a small table where a book of crossword puzzles had been placed. Going on the assumption that Gabby was still in her bedroom, she picked up the book, opened to where she had left off, and worked on the puzzles while she waited for Mr. Felding to come home from work.

Shortly after four o'clock, Mr. Felding returned home. Mrs. Felding heard the front door open, looked up from her puzzle book, and said, "Welcome home, Honey. How was business today?"

Carrying a small stack of papers, Mr. Felding closed the door after stepping inside. "It was better than average. We made several sales today. And how were things here at home?" he asked while heading to the couch to take a seat.

"Everything went well this morning with Molly. Gabby even stood by the piano and watched us for most of the lesson. And did you know *she* not only has an interest in learning to play the piano, but she also knew how to play 'Twinkle, Twinkle, Little Star'?"

"Oh, really? Did you . . ."

"No, I didn't," interrupted Mrs. Felding. "She already knew."

"Then who taught her?"

"I don't know. And she also didn't know. She couldn't remember how she learned it. Either someone taught her and she doesn't have a good memory, or she's just musically talented."

"Well, there's another mystery to add to the rest of them," said Mr. Felding while turning his head from side to side in a motion of trying to look for something. "And speaking about Gabby, where is she?"

"She went to her bedroom right before Sophie came, and she's been in there ever since then. She hasn't come out."

During a moment of silence, Mr. Felding listened closely to any sounds from down the hallway, but he couldn't hear anything. "I can't hear anything. Are you sure she's in there?"

"The last time I saw her, she was heading to her bedroom. She probably had a big day, so she's probably taking a nap," said Mrs. Felding after trying to come up with a reason as to why the house was so quiet.

For the next thirty minutes, Mrs. Felding worked on her puzzle book while Mr. Felding looked through his small stack of papers, working on going through the sales for that day.

A few minutes after four-thirty, Mrs. Felding set her puzzle book aside and headed to the kitchen to start preparing dinner.

While she gathered all the needed pans, utensils, and ingredients, Mr. Felding finished going through the stack of sales. He then set the papers down and headed to Gabby's bedroom, curious to see why her nap was taking so much time, and knowing that it wouldn't be long before he would need to wake her up for dinner.

Right after arriving at her bedroom with the opened doorway, he quietly looked inside. It didn't appear that Gabby was on her bed, so he looked everywhere around the room, but he couldn't see her anywhere. *Maybe under her bed?* Mr. Felding thought. He got down on his hands and knees and looked under the bed, but there was no sight of her there either. Then he looked in her closet before coming to the conclusion that she was definitely not in her bedroom. *Is she sleeping on our bed?* he thought. He went to the master bedroom and looked around, but there was not one single trace of Gabby anywhere. *Did she sneak past us and wait for us in the kitchen?*

Mr. Felding walked into the kitchen. Seeing Mrs. Felding, he asked, "Is Gabby in here? She's not in her bedroom, and she's also not in ours."

Mrs. Felding immediately placed down the ingredients that she was holding. Her eyes grew wide in a worrisome manner of despair. "No, she's not in *here*. If she's not in her bedroom, then where is she?" she expressed while heading to the back door and reaching for the doorknob to look outside.

"I'll go look out front," Mr. Felding said right after seeing Mrs. Felding making her way towards the back yard.

Two minutes later, Mr. and Mrs. Felding met up in the living room. "Did you find her?" asked Mrs. Felding.

"No. She's not out there."

"She's not behind the house either."

Afraid they might never see her again, and knowing she must have left the house by herself, they tried thinking of any reason as to why she would want to leave. "Did she finally remember who her parents are?" asked Mr. Felding, knowing there could be a million other possible reasons. "Maybe she left to go find her house."

"And suppose she gets lost while trying to find it. What if she's never found?" added Mrs. Felding. "Maybe we should call Officer Gunwell to report a missing child before she gets *too* lost."

"Unless she's just one or two roads off the street in one direction or another. And what if she comes back home right after we finish talking to Officer Gunwell? In that case, we'll have to call him right back to tell him she's already home, and then he might call *us* crazy just like the foster-care agencies called *him*."

Mrs. Felding took a deep sigh of desperation. "Where could she be?" she asked with great concern while shaking her head. At that moment, her cell phone rang. "I wonder who that could be," she said while reaching for her phone in her pocket.

"If we're lucky," said Mr. Felding, "maybe it's Officer Gunwell calling to tell us that Gabby is there at the police station."

Mrs. Felding answered the call. "Hello."

"Hi, Mrs. Felding. This is Mrs. Robinson. What time were you planning on coming over to pick up your daughter?"

"Daughter?" asked Mrs. Felding in a tone of confusion. "Both of my daughters live out of town. What are you talking about?"

"This little girl named Gabby. Molly said she saw her at your house."

Mrs. Felding's eyes grew wide again, but this time in joyful surprise. "Gabby is over there?"

"Over where?" asked Mr. Felding, having listened to what his wife was saying.

"Shhh," whispered Mrs. Felding to her husband, trying to listen to what Mrs. Robinson was saying.

"I thought you knew she was here," said Mrs. Robinson.

"No, I didn't. I was teaching a lesson to another student, and I thought she was in her bedroom. She must have snuck out for some reason."

"Then who's Gabby if she's not your daughter?"

"It's a complicated story," replied Mrs. Felding, "but I guess you could say she's our foster daughter. And we'll have to start teaching her that she shouldn't go outside by herself, especially living right by a busy street."

"Yeah, I know Main Street is always busy," said Mrs. Robinson, not believing what Gabby had told her, "and you probably won't believe this, but she said there were no cars on the street when she was coming over here. She said the street was empty."

"Oh, I think I can believe it," Mrs. Felding said.

"How can you believe something like that?"

"Well, like I told you, it's complicated. And by the way, what is she doing now?"

"She's outside with Molly in our front yard. I'm watching them through the window. They're playing a new game that Gabby taught Molly. And after Gabby told us what was needed for the game, it's a good thing we had two small hoops and two long, wooden rods that we had to cut in half to make four of them. She said the game is called *Graces*."

"*Graces*?" repeated Mrs. Felding, recalling what she had heard when she was much younger. "I don't think it's a new game. I remember my grandma talking about it a long time ago. But anyway, I appreciate the call, and I'll come over now to pick her up."

"Okay, we'll see you when you get here."

Right after the phone call, still curious to know, Mr. Felding asked, "Where is she?"

"She's three houses down the street at the Robinsons' house. She's playing with Molly right now, so it's my guess that she left during the lesson with Sophie so she could go play with Molly. After all, she stood at the piano during most of Molly's lesson, and I didn't see her at all ever since I started the lesson with Sophie."

"And what was the talk about *Graces*?"

"Mrs. Robinson told me that Gabby taught Molly how to play it."

"What!?" asked Mr. Felding in a state of wonder. "Who taught Gabby how to play *Graces*? I don't think a four-year-old could make up a game that was already invented about two centuries ago."

"I don't know, but I need to go get her now."

A few minutes later, Mrs. Felding came back home with Gabrielle. While they walked through the doorway of the front door, they continued their disagreement that was started before returning home.

"Yes, there were," said Mrs. Felding.

"No, there weren't. I didn't see them," said Gabrielle.

"I pointed them out to you. Didn't you look?"

"I looked, but there was nothing there."

Curious again, Mr. Felding wanted to know what the disagreement was about. "What wasn't where?" he asked.

Mrs. Felding turned to him and said, "Oh . . . Gabby says she didn't see most of the cars on the street that I pointed out to her when we were walking back home."

"They weren't there!" exclaimed Gabby.

Mrs. Felding looked at Gabby, turned to look towards the kitchen, and then turned back to Gabby. "Well, no matter if they were or weren't, I need to go continue preparing dinner," she said while starting to head to the kitchen. Gabby started to follow.

"Hey, Gabby. Come here," said Mr. Felding in a gentle tone, sitting on the couch.

"Huh?" asked Gabby while turning to walk towards Mr. Felding.

"Here. Take a seat." Gabby sat next to him. "I heard you taught Molly the game of *Graces*."

Gabby smiled. "Yeah, it was fun!"

"Who taught you how to play it?"

"I don't know."

"The last time you played it before today, who did you play it with?"

"I can't remember."

Later that night after Gabrielle was put to bed, Mr. and Mrs. Felding sat in the living room on the couch, getting ready to watch their late shows on television. "Once again, it's been quite a day," said Mrs. Felding.

"Yeah, it sounds like it," agreed Mr. Felding. "What happened while you were bringing Gabby back from the Robinsons' house?"

"After Mrs. Robinson had told me on the phone that Gabby didn't see any cars on Main Street out here, I started pointing out some cars to her that were passing by, and she told me she couldn't see them. But what was strange was that the street was not completely empty, according to her. On the way home, she ended up seeing two cars. One of them was that old 1967 Ford that drives by every now and then, and the other one looked like an older car from the 1950s that was remodeled. There were no other cars as old as those two, and even though there were numerous other vehicles that drove by, she said she couldn't see any other ones."

"I think there's a simple explanation for that."

"Huh? What kind of an explanation could there be?"

"Well," explained Mr. Felding, "she probably likes the looks of classic cars. And maybe she was pretending to ignore the other ones just like at the police station when she pretended Officer Gunwell was a

31

ghost."

Mrs. Felding thought about what Mr. Felding said. "Yeah, that could be it. I should go explain it to Mrs. Robinson tomorrow. Right now, she thinks Gabby is crazy."

"It seems like everyone is starting to think that everyone else in River City is crazy. And before we start being crazy enough to stay up half the night, we should start watching our shows now."

# 4
# MYSTERIOUS MYSTERIES

Nobody knew just how crazy River City would soon become. Gabrielle was starting to think everyone else was crazy by pretending to see things that weren't there. Everyone else who had already met Gabrielle was starting to think of her as being crazy for pretending to not see things that were plainly visible. Molly even started to wonder why Gabby would say that everything was quiet and peaceful during times while they played outside when the traffic was so loud, why she had never seen an airplane or a helicopter, and why she never heard of the game of *Monopoly*.

On a school day towards the end of September, Mrs. Robinson took Molly to the Feldings' house after school. Gabby had previously asked Molly to come over to her house, and Molly had gotten permission from her mom.

Just seconds after the doorbell was heard, Gabby opened the door and invited Molly inside. "I'll be back later to bring you home," Mrs. Robinson said to Molly. "Have a fun time!"

"Okay, Mom."

Gabrielle shut the door. "My bedroom is back this way," she told Molly. "Follow me."

After entering the bedroom, Molly briefly looked around. "Where's all *your* toys?"

Gabrielle grabbed her teddy bear. "I have this teddy bear that I got at the police station, and a few toys are in the bottom drawer," she said while turning to look over at the chest of drawers. "Those are older toys that Mrs. Felding's daughters used to play with, but the daughters

33

are adults now."

"You said *Mrs. Felding?*" asked Molly. I thought she was your mom."

"She said she's called a foster mom."

"What's a foster mom? Is Foster your last name?"

"No. A foster mom just takes care of kids who don't have other parents to take care of them."

"Oh," replied Molly. "Then what's your last name? You never told me."

"I don't know."

"Do you have a last name?"

"Not that I can remember."

Molly looked at the teddy bear that Gabrielle was still holding. "Why were you at the police station?"

"Because Mr. and Mrs. Felding took me there so the officers could try to find my parents, and they also tried to find a home for me, but they kept taking me to empty houses and talking to nobody."

"Why did they do that?"

"I don't know. I think they were just crazy," said Gabrielle. Then she became somewhat excited about the thoughts of playing games. "Do you want to play a game now?"

"Yeah!" said Molly with a smile. "How about hide-and-seek?"

"Okay," agreed Gabby. "You count, and I'll hide."

When dinnertime was starting to approach, Mrs. Robinson came to pick up Molly, the Felding household had dinner, and Gabrielle was later put to bed.

Once again, Mr. and Mrs. Felding sat on the couch for preparing to watch their late shows on television. Mr. Felding thought about the day when Gabby taught Molly the game of *Graces*. "I've been thinking about the old days when my grandparents told me about the game of *Graces* that Gabby somehow knows," he said to his wife.

"Yeah, I had heard about that game too," added Mrs. Felding. "I heard about it from my grandma, and even though it's been so long ago, I remember her teaching me how to play it when I was a little girl."

"Talking about our grandparents, we haven't been to the River City Cemetery in quite a while to visit their gravestones."

"Maybe we could do that tomorrow, and this time we can take Gabby with us."

The next day while Mr. Felding was gone to work, Mrs. Felding started explaining the plans for the day to Gabrielle. "We're going to the city cemetery after Mr. Felding gets home from work," she said. "And did you know that the game of *Graces* was invented a long time ago?"

"Uh-huh," said Gabby while thinking fifty years was a long length of time.

"The other day when Mrs. Robinson told me that you were playing it with Molly, it brought back memories of when my grandma taught me how to play it, and Mr. Felding's grandparents told him about it, so we're going to the cemetery to see their gravestones. We haven't been there in a while, and we wanted you to come with us."

"Is that the cemetery on Maple Street?"

Immediately, Mrs. Felding was struck with an intense feeling of wonder. "Where did you hear about Maple Street?"

"I don't know."

"You must have heard it from *someone*! From what I learned, it was almost one hundred years ago when they changed the name of Maple Street to Cherry Street. And how do you know about the cemetery?"

"I remember being there," Gabrielle replied.

"Who took you there?" asked Mrs. Felding.

"I don't know."

"Did you go there by yourself?"

"I can't remember."

"But if you can remember being there, then why can't you remember who took you there?"

"I don't know."

"Did the police officers take you there when you were staying at the police station, and did they tell you about Maple Street?"

"No."

"Well, do you remember anything else about the cemetery besides being there?"

Gabrielle thought for a short moment. "I remember it was a small cemetery with thirty gravestones."

"Only thirty gravestones?" repeated Mrs. Felding. "Then you must be thinking about another cemetery in another city—maybe one that's still on Maple Street somewhere. The River City Cemetery is the only one in River City, and there are hundreds of gravestones."

Gabrielle had no response. She wondered what other city she had been to, but she couldn't remember being to any other cities or towns.

After Mr. Felding stepped into the house upon returning back home, not seeing anyone in the living room, he hollered, "Let's go!" Mrs. Felding and Gabrielle soon entered the living room and were ready to go.  Then they all headed on their way to the cemetery that was located on the other side of the city.

When they arrived at the opened entrance of the gated River City Cemetery, Gabrielle looked through the car windows, and she was astounded at the vastness of the cemetery.  She knew she had been there before, and supposedly being only four years of age, assuming she was there sometime within the previous four years, she couldn't understand how the number of gravestones could expand so quickly in such a short amount of time.  She wondered if River City was crazier than she thought.  Had everyone in the entire city been digging holes for coffins and caskets?  And how was everyone dying so quickly to enlarge the cemetery so much?  Was there a war that she didn't hear about?  Whatever the case, something seemed strange.

Driving slowly in the cemetery, Mr. Felding found the section where both sets of grandparents were buried.  He parked the car along the side of the section.  They all got out, and Gabrielle followed until they found the gravestones of their grandparents that were located only a short walking distance apart.

While at each gravestone of deceased grandparents, both Mr. and Mrs. Felding told memories about them from what they could remember.  Gabrielle could hear that something was being said, but most of her attention was constantly focused on wondering why the cemetery looked so enormous, and how it rapidly increased in size.

Gabrielle's attention suddenly turned back to Mr. and Mrs. Felding right when they were finished telling their stories of family history. "Do you have any questions?" Mrs. Felding asked Gabrielle, referring to questions about anything that was mentioned, assuming she was listening to what they had been saying.

"Yeah," answered Gabrielle. In preparation for her upcoming question, she turned in all directions to quickly look around at the entire cemetery. "How many shovels were used to dig the holes for all these graves? Does everyone in the city have to dig in the cemetery?"

Mrs. Felding chuckled. "No. The gravediggers who work in the cemetery are the only ones who dig out the graves."

"Are there a lot of gravediggers?"

"Oh, there are probably a few gravediggers for this cemetery with how big it is."

Gabrielle quickly looked around the entire cemetery again. "They must be very strong to dig out all these graves with a shovel, and it must have taken them forever!"

"They don't just use a shovel," responded Mrs. Felding. "They use excavation equipment including a backhoe, and it doesn't take forever like it used to take a long time ago."

"Machines can dig holes too?" asked Gabrielle in a tone of great surprise, already having learned about so many other technological devices.

"Yeah. And not every kid your age knows that. As long as you keep asking any questions you have, you'll keep getting smarter and smarter!" explained Mrs. Felding. Then she turned her head to face Mr. Felding who appeared to be staring at something. "Is something wrong, Honey?"

Unsure about what he thought he was looking at, Mr. Felding continued to stare. "I don't know."

"Well, what are you looking at?"

"Two sections over," he said while he pointed at the location of what he was looking at. "That looks strange."

"What are you talking about?"

"Uh . . . just to make sure I'm seeing what I think I see, let's take a walk over there."

Nearing the mentioned section of the cemetery after a matter of seconds, it was now clear to see that what he thought he saw was true. Surrounded by many gravestones was an empty area with nothing besides grass. The area was large enough to have another gravestone, but there were no gravestones there, no tree stump to indicate that a tree was there, and no disturbance of the ground to indicate that any gravestone had been removed. All other areas of that size that were visible from that spot in all directions had a gravestone, and Mr. Felding wondered why that spot was empty. "I've been here several times before, and I thought the cemetery was all filled with gravestones around this area. I don't remember seeing an empty spot here."

*You don't remember one spot?* Gabrielle thought to herself. *And I don't remember the entire cemetery!*

Throughout the time at the cemetery, looking at any individual gravestone never crossed Gabrielle's mind. The wonder of how a small cemetery could expand so quickly had taken her full, constant attention.

In the morning of the following Saturday, Gabrielle started feeling excited as soon as she woke up, knowing that she would soon be seeing Molly again. The excitement gradually increased through breakfast time, and it grew more afterwards. She kept feeling more excited with every minute that passed.

At eleven o'clock, the excitement reached its peak when the doorbell was heard. "She's here!" yelled Gabrielle from her bedroom while she immediately ran to the front door to open it. Also on her way to the front door from the kitchen, Mrs. Felding was surprised at how quickly four-year-old legs could run.

Practically two seconds after the ringing of the doorbell, Gabrielle opened the door. "Hi, Molly!" she said with a big smile.

"Hi, Gabby!" said Molly with just as big of a smile.

Mrs. Felding arrived at the doorway. "Come in, Molly. Let's get started," she said, referring to the next piano lesson.

Molly stepped into the house. "I'll come pick you up at one o'clock. Have a good time!" said her mom.

Gabrielle stood by the piano throughout the thirty minutes of the lesson. Not only did she want to be with Molly as much as she could, but she also wanted to learn what was being taught.

When the piano lesson was done, Molly followed Gabby to her bedroom to play. Before getting out any toys, Gabby's continued bewilderment about the cemetery was too great to remain silent without resolving the mystery. "Have you been to the city cemetery?" she asked Molly.

"The city cemetery?" repeated Molly, thinking it was a strange topic to discuss at the beginning of playtime. "Why do you ask?"

"I was there earlier this week with Mr. and Mrs. Felding, and it was way bigger than it used to be. Have you been there?"

"My parents took me there a few times, but it always looked like the same size."

"Really? You were never there when there were only thirty

gravestones?"

"Only thirty?" repeated Molly. "You must have been to another cemetery."

"But I don't remember being at a cemetery outside River City, and Mr. and Mrs. Felding said that's the only cemetery in the city."

With a confused look on her face, Molly didn't seem to have an answer. Then an idea suddenly came. "Maybe you had a dream about being in a small cemetery, and maybe your dream seemed real."

"Maybe," said Gabby, taking Molly's idea into consideration.

After playing for a while, Mrs. Robinson came to pick up Molly at one o'clock.

At two-thirty, Sophie arrived for another piano lesson. The doorbell rang. "I'll get it!" yelled Gabrielle from her bedroom while she started running to the door, unaware of what time it was, and assuming Molly was coming back for something. From the kitchen, Mrs. Felding headed to the front door, knowing who had come, aware of the time, and was once again surprised at how fast Gabby could run.

Gabby opened the door. Sophie saw her, and not having seen her before, she introduced herself. "Hi. I'm Sophie. Is Mrs. Felding here?" she asked, knowing that Mrs. Felding's children were all grown up, and not knowing whether the young girl was related.

"I'm here," said Mrs. Felding, arriving at the doorway. "Come in."

Sophie stepped inside. "Who are you?" she asked Gabby in a friendly tone.

"I'm Gabrielle."

"Oh, that's a pretty name!" said Sophie before looking at Mrs. Felding with an expression of wondering who the girl was.

"This is my foster daughter," said Mrs. Felding.

"Oh, I didn't know that you had any foster kids!" exclaimed Sophie. Then she turned back to Gabby. "Good to meet you!"

"Shall we get started?" asked Mrs. Felding.

Sophie nodded her head. She sat on the piano bench in front of the bass section of the piano. Curious to learn something more advanced, Gabby stood beside the piano by the treble section while Mrs. Felding sat next to Sophie who then turned to look at Gabby.

Mrs. Felding began. "The first thing that I'll show you today is how to . . ."

"It looks like I have an audience this time," interrupted Sophie while smiling at Gabby.

Mrs. Felding turned to look at Gabby while assuming she would be a distraction for Sophie's lesson. "Hey, Gabby, why don't you go play with . . ."

"No, that's okay," interrupted Sophie again. "I don't mind."

After forty-five minutes, the piano lesson was done. Facing Sophie, Gabby exclaimed, "You're very good at the piano! It would take me a million years to play like you can!"

"Thank you!" said Sophie. "But I've only been taking lessons for two years ever since I was twelve. I got a late start. If you start learning now, then you'll be playing better than me by the time you're my age."

Speaking to Sophie, Mrs. Felding added, "She's already been taking lessons. She's been practicing every day for a while, and she almost has 'Twinkle, Twinkle, Little Star' all mastered."

"Ooh, wow!" Sophie told Gabby. "Good job! Keep it up!"

In the morning of the following Wednesday on the 2nd day of October, Gabrielle awoke to the smell of breakfast being cooked, yet it was still a little while before the food would be ready. She went to the entryway of the kitchen and saw that breakfast wasn't going to be ready anytime soon. Not having seen Molly or Sophie ever since the previous Saturday, Gabrielle started feeling kind of lonely. She quietly walked into the living room, went to the front window, and looked outside. Still, not many cars were passing by on the road, but she noticed that cars were coming a little more often than before. She then turned to look at the piano. Not seeing Molly or Sophie on the piano bench, her feeling of loneliness remained. She turned back to the window to look outside once more, turned her head to the right to look down the road, and noticed Sophie walking on the sidewalk, coming towards them.

Suddenly, every sense of loneliness departed, and Gabrielle grew excited. She dashed into the kitchen. "Hey, Mom!" she hollered.

Ever since the previous Sunday morning, Gabrielle had been referring to Mr. and Mrs. Felding as Dad and Mom. Having lived with them for as long as she had been, it had started to seem to her like they were her real parents, and being called Dad and Mom was something that both Mr. and Mrs. Felding had been looking forward to for a while.

"Whoa!" said Mrs. Felding as soon as Gabrielle entered the kitchen. "You startled me! What's wrong?"

"Nothing's wrong. Sophie's coming!"

"Sophie's coming? How do you know?"

"I saw her outside when I looked through the window."

Mrs. Felding looked over at the clock that was hanging on the wall close to the back door, and it was a few minutes before eight o'clock. "No, I don't think she's coming, Sweetie. It's almost time for school to start. She always walks past our house on school days on her way to and from school."

"May I go to school too? I can go catch Sophie and walk with her!"

"I think you're a little too young right now. You're old enough for preschool, but we didn't even bring you home from the police station until after the school year started. You'll be starting school next year when you go to kindergarten."

Gabrielle felt a little disappointed that she couldn't be with Sophie more often, and it was all because of her age. However, she knew she had no control over her age. She knew she couldn't grow one or two years older in just one or two days.

While gloomily walking around the kitchen for a minute, Gabrielle thought about not being old enough to see Sophie at school. Wanting to be with a friend, another thought eventually came. She turned back to Mrs. Felding and asked, "Can Molly come over today?"

"I don't know. We'll have to ask her mom."

"Then may I go to Molly's house?"

"Maybe later today if they aren't busy."

"May I go right now?"

"If you go right now, then Molly won't be there. It's a school day for her too."

Gabrielle continued to feel disappointed while she slowly walked back to the front window through the living room. She looked outside again, and there was no sight of Sophie anymore. She knew she would have to wait until sometime after school got out in order to see Molly again. She imagined school would be lasting the majority of the day, but she didn't know how many hours it would take, and she felt too disappointed to ask.

At eight o'clock, Mr. Felding walked out from the hallway into the kitchen. Expecting to be the last one into the kitchen as usual, he couldn't see Gabby anywhere. "Where's Gabby?" he asked.

"She's in the living room," said Mrs. Felding.

"What's she doing there? Does she not want to help prepare breakfast?"

Mrs. Felding grabbed on to the handle of the hot pan of scrambled eggs, picked it up from the stovetop, and started taking it to the table along with a hot pad. "I think she's a bit disappointed that she doesn't get to go to school to see her friends more often."

Mr. Felding looked through the entryway of the kitchen that faced the living room, and he saw the back of Gabby who was facing the front window. "I'll go try to cheer her up," he said while starting to leave the kitchen.

"And tell her that breakfast is ready," Mrs. Felding added.

Mr. Felding walked up to the front window and stood beside Gabby. He faced the window and looked outside, pretending to see whatever Gabby was staring at. "I heard you're not having a good morning," he told her.

"I want to be older," Gabrielle said in a tone of sadness.

Mr. Felding looked downwards at Gabrielle and saw a tear streaming down her cheek. He knelt down and gently put his arm around her shoulders. "You know what?" he said while he looked at her. "A long time ago when I was a boy about your age, I wanted to do everything that the bigger people did. I wanted to go to school, drive a car, get a job, and buy a house. When I got older, lots of the homework from school was too hard, learning how to drive a car was frustrating, trying to find a job took a long time, and I eventually found out that buying a house would later include paying all the bills along with doing lots of repairs whenever something broke or didn't work like it should. So don't be in a hurry to grow up. Otherwise, you'll miss out on lots of good times while you're young because wanting to be older will just make you feel discouraged. And when you get old enough to go through the harder times, you'll look back and wish you were younger." Mr. Felding paused. Then Gabrielle turned from the window to face him. He looked into her eyes and spoke in a gentle, sincere tone of voice. "You're precious. And you have a precious heart. Don't ever let anything take that away from you."

Gabrielle smiled. "I love you, Daddy!" she said, giving him a big hug.

"I love you too, Precious! Now let's go eat some breakfast before the food gets cold."

Later that day, Mr. Felding returned home from work. As soon as Gabrielle knew that his time at work was done, she wondered if school was also done. She walked into the kitchen where Mrs. Felding was starting to prepare dinner. "Mom," she said, "is school done yet?"

Mrs. Felding looked at the time on the clock. "It should be done by now. You're still wanting to see Molly?"

Gabrielle smiled. "Yeah!" she said cheerfully.

"Okay. I need to call Mrs. Robinson first to make sure they're home and to make sure they aren't busy with other plans." Mrs. Felding placed down the ingredients and utensils onto the countertop. She grabbed her cell phone and dialed the number.

"Hello."

"Hi, Mrs. Robinson. This is Mrs. Felding. Gabby has been wanting to be with Molly all day, so I was wondering if I could bring her over if you don't have any other plans."

"Yeah, please feel free to bring her over. Molly has been on my case about wanting to see Gabby, so now she can stop pestering me! But I'll need to start dinner soon, and we'll need to eat in one or two hours."

"Same here. I just barely started preparing dinner too. We'll be there shortly."

"Okay. See you when you get here."

A few minutes later, Mrs. Felding and Gabrielle were approaching the front door to the Robinsons' house. With only a few feet remaining in the distance to the door, they heard a shout from inside the house. "Mom, Gabby's here!" And before Gabrielle would have rung the doorbell, the front door opened.

"Molly!" shouted Gabby while she dashed the short distance through the doorway into the house, feeling so excited.

"Gabby!" expressed Mrs. Felding in a tone of disappointment. "Where are your manners? You don't just run into someone else's house like that!"

"Sorry, Mom," said Gabby.

Mrs. Robinson showed up at the doorway right after hearing what was being said. "That's okay. If I was her age, I'd probably do the same if I was that excited to see someone."

"Well, I'll be back after a while," Mrs. Felding said before heading back home.

The two girls entered Molly's bedroom. "What do you want to play?" Gabby asked.

"I have a princess matching game we could play," said Molly.

"Okay," agreed Gabby. "Did you go to school today?"

"Uh-huh," answered Molly.

"Did you see Sophie?"

"Who's Sophie?"

"She's an older girl who goes to school."

"Everyone in my class is my age . . . besides the teacher. The older kids go to a different building."

"There's more than one school?" Gabby asked surprisingly. "But I thought all the kids met in one room."

"Where did you get that idea?" asked Molly. "There are way too many kids to fit in one room!"

"How many kids go to school?"

"Twenty kids are in my class, and there are two other kindergarten classes about the same size. And with all the other grades, that's too many for anyone to count!"

While the two girls played the matching game, Gabrielle was left to wonder how the school got so big in addition to the size increase of the cemetery. Although she had never been a student at school, she remembered being there for something, and she thought every student in every grade met together in one room.

After playing for one hour, the doorbell was heard. "That must be your mom," said Molly, still in her bedroom with Gabby. "Now I need to clean up before my mom sees this mess."

"Before I go," said Gabby, "I have a question."

"What's your question?"

"Are we in River City?"

"Why do you ask that?"

"Because everything is so big! I thought everything was smaller in River City. There's the cemetery, and now there's the school."

"The school's been this big for a long time, even when my older cousins were in kindergarten," said Molly. "Maybe you had another dream about a small school."

Gabrielle shrugged her shoulders, still left in a state of wonder.

The next morning on the 3rd day of October, Gabrielle awoke to the quiet sound of dishes being taken out of cabinets and drawers in the kitchen. She got out of bed, got dressed for the day, quietly walked to the entryway of the kitchen, and noticed Mrs. Felding starting the preparation for breakfast with nothing being cooked yet. Not knowing how to tell time, and based upon the looks of the kitchen, she assumed it was earlier than when she awoke the previous morning. She remembered where she had last seen Sophie, and she knew this was another school morning. She walked through the living room to the front window and looked outside. Hardly any cars were passing by. Although she had been told by Mrs. Felding to not wander off outside by herself, she wanted to be with Sophie again, and she knew she wouldn't go too far. Making her decision on what to do, she walked to the front door, slowly opened it, and quietly went outside, gently closing the door behind her. She walked away from the house, turned to the right, and walked down the sidewalk along the street.

Within two minutes of leaving the house, she saw Sophie coming. "Sophie!" she cried out while she hurried over to her.

Carrying a backpack that contained schoolbooks, Sophie heard her name, looked down the sidewalk ahead of her, and saw Gabby running towards her. It appeared that Gabby had a smile, so it didn't look like anything was wrong. "Hi, Gabby! What are you doing out here?" Sophie asked loud enough to be heard. Then she momentarily looked around while Gabby arrived at her side. "Where are your parents?"

"They're at home. I wanted to come see you," Gabby said while walking with Sophie who continued on her way.

"Aww, that's so nice of you to come see me, but it's better for smaller kids who are outside to be with an adult. What if someone in a car comes to take you away? Or what if they don't look where they're driving and run into you?"

Gabrielle looked down the street. "But there aren't many cars on the road."

Sophie looked at all the cars passing by, and then she expressed a different opinion without knowing that Gabby couldn't see or hear most of them. "It looks like enough cars to be dangerous out here all by yourself."

Gabby looked down the street in both directions, and she wondered what was dangerous about only four or five cars on the entire stretch of Main Street. She turned to Sophie and asked, "Are you walking to school?"

"Yeah, that's where I'm going."

"I saw you out the window yesterday."

"Oh, you did?"

"Uh-huh. That's why I wanted to come outside. I also have another friend named Molly who goes to school."

"Molly? I don't think I know anyone named Molly."

"She's in kindergarten."

"Oh. That's why I don't know her. I go to the high school."

"Is it far away?" asked Gabby.

"No. It's right next to the elementary school."

"Oh. Did you know there are three kindergarten classes? That's what Molly told me. How many classes are in your grade?"

"I'm in ninth grade, and we don't stay in just one classroom all day like we did in kindergarten. We move to a few different classes throughout the day. Each student has a class schedule, and each class is a different subject. And most of the classes have a mixture of students in the different grades.

"You still meet in the same room with students of other grades?" asked Gabby.

"What do you mean *still*? That's how high school has always been."

"But I thought every student in *every* grade all met in one room."

Sophie chuckled. "If all students of every grade met in one room, then nobody would have any room to breathe! Either that, or we'd have to meet in the biggest room in the world! Just in my grade, there are over one hundred students. And then if you add the rest of the students from kindergarten through the 12$^{th}$ grade, there's just not a room big enough for everyone at the same time unless everyone met in a football stadium or a basketball arena."

After walking for two minutes, Sophie stopped on the sidewalk in front of the Feldings' house. "Here's your house," she told Gabby while pointing to it. "I need to keep walking to school. I'll see you another time."

"But I want to come with you!" declared Gabby.

"If you come with me to my more advanced classes, then you won't understand anything that we're learning. And it won't be good if your parents wonder where you went."

"Okay," agreed Gabby with a heart full of gloom. "Bye."

"Bye," said Sophie, proceeding to the school.

Gabrielle quietly entered the house. Having been no more than a few minutes ever since leaving, the house was still quiet. Mrs. Felding was still cooking breakfast, and the smell of food was starting to spread throughout the house.

Later that morning, Gabrielle decided to practice going to school. Since she couldn't go to a real school, she turned her bedroom into a school. Imaginably, she and her teddy bear took turns being the student and the teacher. However, after teaching and learning from her teddy bear about letters, numbers, colors, and shapes, she ran out of things to teach. *What else do they teach in school?* she wondered.

In the morning of the following day, Gabrielle awoke early again, but she didn't know what time it was. Because sunlight was shining through the window, she knew it wasn't too early. But was it too late to see Sophie again? She got out of bed and opened her bedroom door, but there was no smell of breakfast food flowing through the air. *It's either not too late to see Sophie,* she figured, *or we're having cold cereal or something else that doesn't need to be cooked.* Curious to know what was for breakfast, she quietly stepped out of her bedroom into the hallway and slowly headed towards the kitchen. Trying to be as quiet as a mouse, she didn't want to make even the slightest sound for fear that Mrs. Felding would know she was awake and ask her to help prepare breakfast, which would eliminate any chance of seeing Sophie if it wasn't already too late.

Gabrielle stopped beside the kitchen entryway that faced in the direction of the hallway. She listened closely. She could hear quiet footsteps coming from inside the kitchen, so she knew that someone was in there. She paid attention to the smell of the air once more, but she couldn't detect any smell of food. *If I peek into the kitchen,* she thought, *what if someone sees me?* Standing as still as can be, she continued to listen to any possible sounds and what the sounds could be.

For the next twenty seconds, she couldn't hear anything. She started to wonder whether someone had gone to sleep in the kitchen. Finally, she heard the quiet sound of a cabinet door being shut just seconds before she heard the sound of a pan being placed onto the stovetop. Standing on the other end of the kitchen from where the oven range was located, she figured there would be no better time to peek into the kitchen. Quietly, she peeked her head around the corner and noticed Mrs. Felding from behind who was breaking some eggs into a bowl. Then Gabrielle quickly hid behind the corner again, giving no chance for Mrs. Felding to turn around to see her.

According to the evidence of the breakfast preparation stage that Gabrielle had witnessed, she presumed that she must have awakened that morning no more than five minutes before the time of morning of the previous day. However, what were the chances that Mrs. Felding had slept in a few minutes later? Was she starting breakfast later than the previous day? With no way to know exactly what time it was, Gabrielle scurried back to her bedroom fast enough to waste no time, yet slow enough to remain completely silent in every movement through every inch of space.

After getting dressed for the day, she left her bedroom in a noiseless manner. She softly crept into the living room, walked to the front door, slowly opened it, and found herself outside once again. Walking away from the house, she turned to the right just like before, and she walked down the sidewalk by the street, hoping she could meet up with Sophie one more time.

Three minutes after leaving the house, there was still no sight of Sophie. Gabrielle wondered what to do. She knew it was Friday. *It's gotta be a school day,* she thought to herself. *Did school get cancelled today for some reason? Did Sophie decide to skip school? Is she sick today? Or did I leave too late to catch her?*

Not letting go of the hope of seeing Sophie, Gabrielle continued walking a few more seconds until she stopped on a corner where the sidewalk headed off to the right alongside another road that headed in the same direction, and the only way to continue straight would be to cross the road. She remembered Mrs. Felding and Sophie both talking about a lot of cars on the road. *What if they saw some invisible cars, and what if an invisible car runs into me?* she thought while she continued looking straight down the sidewalk on the other side of the road to see if she could see Sophie coming.

With no sight of Sophie as well as not wanting to cross the road to continue any further, Gabrielle decided to head back home. Suddenly,

47

right at that moment, she heard her name. "Hi, Gabby!" Sophie said aloud from thirty feet away. Gabrielle turned her head to the right where the sound of Sophie's voice was coming from. When she saw Sophie walking towards her, she smiled.

Sophie came to the corner and arrived at Gabrielle's side. She felt a bit concerned about Gabby walking away that far from home all by herself at her young age, afraid that something could eventually happen to her if she continued to leave home without an adult. "What brings you out this far?" she asked while she turned to her left and continued down the sidewalk. Gabby walked beside her.

"I wanted to ask you a question."

"Oh, sure," Sophie said in a friendly tone. "What's your question?"

"So I was playing school with my teddy bear . . ."

"With your teddy bear? Aww, that's so cute!" interrupted Sophie with a smile.

Sophie's smile seemed to be contagious. "Yeah," said Gabby, returning the smile, "and then I ran out of things to teach. I didn't know what else to teach besides letters, numbers, colors, and shapes. What do your teachers teach?" asked Gabby, not knowing at that moment that her simple question was the beginning of what would lead up to a big discovery in her life.

"I think you might want to ask Molly what her teacher teaches," answered Sophie. "You wouldn't understand what my teachers teach. My classes are much harder and a lot more advanced than kindergarten."

"How is it harder?" asked Gabby.

"Well, for example, we're learning about prepositions in my English class."

"What's a preposition?"

"It's part of a sentence just like a noun, a verb, an adjective, and an adverb."

"Huh? What are those?"

"You'll learn about those after you learn the more basic things. And those aren't the only parts of a sentence. There are also direct objects, indirect objects, interjections, conjunctions, and too many other things about sentences to mention them all. That's why you need to start with the basics."

"But isn't there *anything* you're learning at school that I could learn too?"

"Uh, let's see . . . we're learning about the United States presidents in my American History class. Do you know who the first president was?"

"George Washington."

"Wow!" Sophie exclaimed, amazed that a kid younger than the age of kindergarten would know something like that. "How did you know?"

"I don't know."

"Did your mom or dad tell you?"

"No. I can't remember where I heard it," said Gabby. "Was he a good president?"

"Yes, he was," said Sophie. "He was one of the Founding Fathers of our country."

"Did we ever have a bad president?" Gabrielle asked, wanting to know as much as she could for teaching her imaginary class in her bedroom.

"There have been a lot of good ones and a lot of not-so-good ones," replied Sophie, "but the worst president in the history of our country was President Linstrom."

Immediately, Gabby was struck with a sense of familiarity. She had heard many names before, which included the names of many presidents, but hearing the name of President Linstrom, there was something about that name that was more than just a name. However, she wasn't familiar with any United States president by that name. Was there someone else by that name who was the president of something else such as a club or a committee? Whatever the case, Gabby seemed to be engrossed in thought.

After a few seconds of walking in voiceless silence, Sophie was drawn to the prolonged lack of conversation. "Any more questions?" she asked, looking downwards at Gabby. But there was no response. *Is she mad at me for some reason? Maybe she has a different opinion of who the worst president was,* Sophie thought. "Are you mad at me?" she asked, but still no response. "Hey," she said while she reached up and gently ran her hand along the top of Gabby's head, "what's wrong?"

Gabrielle's attention shifted back to Sophie. "Huh?" she asked while she turned to face upwards at Sophie.

"Is something wrong?"

"I don't know. I heard the name of Linstrom before, but I never heard of a president with that name."

"Well, you're *only* four years old," said Sophie. "I don't think there's anyone your age who's heard about every president."

"But how did I hear about President Linstrom before today?"

"I don't know. Maybe you were told his name when you learned about George Washington. Or maybe you overheard someone else mentioning his name in another conversation."

"Why was he the worst president?"

"Because he created the worst economy in history that resulted in the first of the two Great Depressions, and he didn't even keep one of his campaign promises."

"What were the Great Depressions?"

"They were both periods of time when everyone was starving because the food prices were either too high or there wasn't enough food to go around to everyone. The food prices were much lower in the second Great Depression, but nobody had any money, so the sales of food were no different than the first one. Money wasn't circulating like it should. Lots of people lost their houses and jobs, and the ones who still had a job didn't get paid enough to afford anything."

"Then how did they live?"

"I guess they managed somehow until the economy improved," answered Sophie, "but you'll learn about this when you get into high school." Then she stopped on the sidewalk and looked to the left. "Here's your house. Your parents might be wondering where you are. I'll see you tomorrow when I come for my piano lesson."

"Okay," said Gabby.

After entering the house, Gabrielle heard her name. "Gabby!" hollered Mrs. Felding from the kitchen. "Time to wake up! Breakfast will be ready soon." With the smell of French toast in the air, Gabby walked through the living room to the kitchen entryway that faced in the direction of the hallway for making it appear to Mrs. Felding like she was coming from her bedroom, not knowing how many times Mrs. Felding had been calling for her.

As soon as Gabby got to the entryway, Mrs. Felding saw her and noticed what she was wearing. "Well, that was fast!" said Mrs. Felding. "Seeing that you're already dressed for the day, you must have been awake when I called for you." Then she looked downwards at Gabby's feet. "And since when do you wear shoes for breakfast?"

Gabrielle suddenly realized she hadn't had any time to take her shoes off after coming back in from outside, so she quickly thought of an excuse. "I thought that if we go anywhere today, then you won't have to wait for me to put my shoes on."

"Well, I don't know if we're going anywhere today. You should have asked me first."

The next morning, after Molly arrived at the usual time for another piano lesson, Gabby stood beside the piano once again throughout the thirty minutes of the lesson. Knowing she had seen Sophie twice ever since the last time she had seen Molly, she decided she wanted to spend more time with Molly that day.

When the doorbell rang, Mrs. Felding walked to the door and opened it. Standing on the outside of the doorway was Mrs. Robinson who had come to take Molly home.

Still wanting to spend more time with Molly, Gabby turned to Mrs. Felding. "May I go with Molly to her house?" she asked.

"It depends on if it's okay with her mom."

Gabby turned to Mrs. Robinson. "May I come with you?"

Molly grew excited. "Yeah!" she said in the process of growing a smile on her face.

Not wanting to be pestered by Molly again, Mrs. Robinson said to the kids, "Okay, but we need to find out from Mrs. Felding when she wants us to bring Gabby back home."

Having heard what Mrs. Robinson said, Mrs. Felding replied, "There's no specific time. And I have another student coming this afternoon. If it's fine with you, I'll call you when I'm ready, and then I'll come get her."

"That will work," Mrs. Robinson told Mrs. Felding. "Okay, come on, kids!"

Later that afternoon at Sophie's usual time, Mrs. Felding answered the door after hearing the doorbell. She invited Sophie inside and began to teach another piano lesson.

After forty-five minutes of having no audience, the piano lesson was finished. "Where's Gabby?" asked Sophie.

"She's at Molly's house," said Mrs. Felding. Knowing she had never told each of her students about each other, she added, "She's my other student."

"Oh, the little girl in kindergarten?"

"Yes. You know her?"

"No, I don't. Gabby told me about her."

*Where was I when Gabby told her?* thought Mrs. Felding. "I don't remember Gabby telling you about Molly, and it was just last Saturday when you and Gabby met for the first time. When did Gabby tell you?"

"Two days ago. I was going to talk to you about it. I found her down the sidewalk towards my house when I was walking to school in the morning. She said she wanted to come see me, and I told her she needed to be with an adult. When we got back to your house, I made sure she went back home. Then I found her even farther down the sidewalk all the way to the corner yesterday," explained Sophie, pointing in the direction of the corner that she was referring to, "and she was all by herself again. I felt a little worried, especially with so many cars that are always on Main Street out here."

"Oh, that little girl of mine!" said Mrs. Felding in great disappointment. "I told her to not wander off by herself. I'll have to have another talk with her."

"I hope she doesn't hate me for telling."

"No, I'm sure she won't. If you didn't tell me, then something terrible might have eventually happened to her. She's lucky to have a friend like you."

After Sophie left, Mrs. Felding called Mrs. Robinson.

"Hello."

"Hi. This is Mrs. Felding. I'm ready to come get Gabby now."

"Okay. I'll tell her you're coming."

Minutes later, Mrs. Felding rang the doorbell at the Robinsons' house. Mrs. Robinson opened the door, and Gabby was standing next to her, ready to go.

On their way home, Mrs. Felding asked Gabby, "What did you do with Molly today?"

"We played with her Barbie dolls and her Barbie dollhouse."

"Did you have any lunch?"

"They gave me a sandwich and some yogurt that I ate with Molly."

For the remainder of the walk back home, Gabby told her mom all about her time with Molly that day.

Following their return back home, Mrs. Felding brought up another topic while standing in the living room. "When was the last time you saw Sophie?" she asked, wanting Gabby to be the one to confess.

Gabrielle thought for a short moment. "Don't you remember? I saw her outside through the window."

"Yes, I remember. And that was last Wednesday. Did you see her again after that?"

"Uh . . ." voiced Gabby, afraid to confess that she had gone against what she had been told. "And then I looked outside and saw her two more times."

"Did you see her through the window again?"

*Oh, now I'm busted!* Gabrielle thought. Wanting to be honest, there was no other way to beat around the bush. "No," she confessed. "I went outside to see her."

"Oh, you went outside?" Mrs. Felding asked calmly. "Did you stay close to the house and wave to her?"

"No. I walked down the sidewalk until I found her."

At that point, Mrs. Felding knew that Gabby was telling the truth, especially since Gabby didn't know that Sophie had explained the situation. "Come here," said Mrs. Felding while walking over to the couch. "Let's take a seat." Wanting to test her one more time to see whether she would remain truthful, Mrs. Felding asked her one more question. "How far down the sidewalk did you go?"

"I walked down to the corner . . . but I didn't cross the road!" said Gabby in a tone of innocence.

"All the way down to the corner?" said Mrs. Felding in a disappointing way. She paused for a brief moment. Then she added, "Did you know it takes three minutes to walk that far?"

Gabrielle was speechless. All she could do was give a facial expression that said she didn't know. *I don't know what to say,* she thought. At that point, she began to feel very bad for what she had done—not the act of going outside to be with a friend, but going against what her mom had told her. "I'm sorry, Mom," she said.

Mrs. Felding looked into her eyes that were starting to form a tear. Then she smiled at Gabby, hoping that by seeing a smile, it would keep her cheerful heart from becoming too saddened. "Thank you for telling the truth. But you need to understand why we don't want you to go outside alone," she said. "If you go outside without me, your dad, or another trusted adult, there are bad things that can happen. Someone could take you away, or no telling what else could happen. We don't live in the days when it was safe for young children to walk far distances alone. And even short distances now days could be dangerous. We live in a wicked world with bad things happening everywhere. Your dad and I both love you, and we don't want anything bad to happen to you."

Later that night after Gabrielle was put to bed, Mr. and Mrs. Felding sat on the couch once again. "How did the day go around here while I was gone to work?" asked Mr. Felding.

"Well, let's see . . ." said Mrs. Felding, trying to put the events all together in her head. "After Molly's piano lesson, Gabby wanted to stay with Molly, so she went with the Robinsons to their house. This afternoon, Sophie stayed for a few minutes after her lesson to tell me what Gabby did."

"What did Gabby do?" asked Mr. Felding out of curiosity.

"Sophie told me that Gabby went outside to go meet her in the morning on Thursday while she was walking to school, and then again yesterday morning."

"And that was after Wednesday when she was standing at the front window and wishing she could be with her friends more often."

"Yeah. It must have been while I was cooking breakfast. And she walked all the way down to the corner. I felt disappointed when I heard about that because I had already told her to not go outside by herself, and Sophie was worried that Gabby would hate her for telling me. After Sophie left, I picked up Gabby and brought her back home. I didn't want her to be upset at Sophie, so I didn't mention anything about being told. I just asked Gabby when she last saw Sophie, and I let her confess it herself."

"Did she confess it, or did she lie to you?"

"At first, she tried to avoid the answer, but she ended up telling me everything Sophie told me. She didn't tell me any lies. And then I had another talk with her about why we don't want her to go outside alone without one of us or another trusted adult."

"Well, at least her biological parents or the person or people who started raising her taught her to be honest."

"And that's one reason why she's so precious. A precious heart is filled with honesty."

Eventually, Mr. and Mrs. Felding watched their late shows on television before going to bed for the night.

# 5
# WHO'S THAT PRESIDENT?

"Mom!" shouted Gabby from right outside her bedroom
doorway immediately after coming out of her bedroom into the hallway.

"I'm here in the living room, Sweetheart."

It was Monday afternoon on the 14th day of October. For more
than a week, Gabby had been thinking about her conversation with
Sophie regarding President Linstrom, and she had been wondering if he
had any other name like all the other presidents. As soon as she heard
her mom, she went to the living room where her mom was sitting on a
chair while starting the process of making a crocheted doll. "Hey, Mom,
does everyone have a first name and a last name?" she asked,
remembering the time at the cemetery when her mom encouraged her to
keep asking questions.

"Almost everyone. Why do you ask?"

Gabby walked over to the couch that faced the chair, and she sat
down. "Because I remember President Washington's first name was
George, President Jefferson's first name was Thomas, President
Lincoln's first name was Abraham . . ."

"Where did you learn their names?" interrupted Mrs. Felding.
"Did Sophie tell you?"

"No, she didn't. I don't know where I learned it. But I think I
know the first names of every president besides President Linstrom. Did
he have a first name?"

"Yes, he did. His name was Harold." Suddenly, Gabby grew an
expression of familiarity on her face that Mrs. Felding had never seen
before and was unsure of what the expression was for. "Is something

wrong?" asked Mrs. Felding. Gabby seemed to be deep in thought, and Mrs. Felding waited for a response. "Hey, Sweetheart, what's wrong?" Seeing that Gabby was still not responding, Mrs. Felding knew that her last hope of getting Gabby's attention was to use her full name while speaking somewhat louder. "Gabrielle Felding!"

Gabrielle's attention was immediately turned back to her mom. "Huh?"

"What was that look for? All I said was President Linstrom's first name. What were you thinking about?"

"There's something familiar about that name."

"Well, of course it's familiar. If you know the names of the other presidents, then I'm sure you also heard the name of President Linstrom and just forgot."

"No, I didn't forget," said Gabby. "I never heard of a president with that name."

"Then how did you know his last name?"

"Sophie told me."

"At least you know the name of one more president. Other kids your age don't even know the other ones you mentioned."

"But it's not just the name. I can't explain it, but the name doesn't just sound familiar. It also *feels* familiar."

"How can a name feel familiar?" asked Mrs. Felding.

Gabby thought for a moment. "I don't know. It just does. If I heard someone else say *your* name, then it would be more than just sounding familiar."

"That's because you know who I am. So maybe you learned something about President Linstrom that happened before he got elected as the president," suggested Mrs. Felding.

"I don't remember hearing anything about him," said Gabby. "But if I know all the presidents besides him, then when did he get elected?"

"Hmm . . . I don't know. Let me find out." Mrs. Felding placed her yarn and crochet tools onto the end table that was next to her. She grabbed her nearby cell phone with built-in Wi-Fi, got on to the Internet, and began to research the presidents.

After a few seconds, Mrs. Felding found the answer to Gabby's question. "He won the presidential election in 1876, and he took office as president in 1877.

Not being familiar with historical years, Gabby asked, "How many years before President Johnson was that?"

Curious to know why Gabby mentioned President Johnson instead of a more recent president, Mrs. Felding asked, "Why do you want to know how long before Lyndon B. Johnson?"

"What?" said Gabby. "I thought President Johnson's name was Andrew."

"There were actually two presidents with the last name of Johnson. Andrew was the president right after Abraham Lincoln. But President Linstrom wasn't before him. He was the president right after President Grant."

"But I thought President Grant was the current president."

"Oh, no," said Mrs. Felding. "Ulysses S. Grant got elected almost 151 years ago. Donald Trump is our current president."

With a confused look, Gabby asked, "Who's Donald Trump?"

Suddenly, it dawned on Mrs. Felding. "Oh, I think I know why you haven't heard about some of the presidents. If you thought President Grant was the current president, then you probably only learned about the first eighteen presidents because it doesn't sound like you've heard about any president who got elected after him."

"There were more than eighteen presidents?" asked Gabby.

"Several more," answered Mrs. Felding. "President Trump is the 45th president."

From then on, in addition to wondering how the cemetery immensely increased in size in such a short amount of time, Gabby also wondered how the country could go from eighteen presidents to forty-five presidents in only a few months.

For the next two hours, questions poured into Gabrielle's head while she thought about what she learned. Why did President Linstrom's name feel familiar? Why did he run for president? What did he promise to everyone? Why didn't he keep his campaign promises? Was he married? What was his wife's name? Where did he live before he was elected? Who ran against him in the presidential election? If he's known as the worst president in history, was he also a bad guy? Gabrielle also wondered who taught her about the first eighteen presidents, why she hadn't heard about any president who got elected after President Grant, and why River City seemed to be getting even crazier than before.

After two hours of being haunted by mental curiosity with an abundance of questions, Gabrielle heard the opening of the front door. Mr. Felding had come back from work. With two parents now at home, she wondered if it was a good time to start hounding them with questions. *I can't keep this many questions trapped in my head,* she thought. But knowing that her dad had just come home, she wanted to give him some time to settle down just in case he had a hard day at work.

A while later, the preparation for dinner was done. "Dinner is ready," announced Mrs. Felding. Mr. Felding and Gabrielle sat down at the table while Mrs. Felding took the hot casserole pan out of the oven. Wearing oven mitts, she brought it over, placed it onto some hot pads on the table, and sat down. The delicious smell of homemade casserole seemed to increase everyone's hunger.

After everyone started eating, Mr. Felding asked, "How was everyone's day?"

Mrs. Felding looked at Gabby while answering, "I was given a lot of questions to answer from Little Miss Wonderer." Then she turned to face Mr. Felding and continued. "Apparently, she knows the first eighteen presidents up through President Grant, and I don't know who taught her. It didn't sound like she had ever heard about any other president, but Sophie had told her about President Linstrom, and most of her questions were about *him*."

Mr. Felding looked over at Gabby. "Oh, really?" he said. "Why do you want to know about President Linstrom? Did you know he was the worst president our country ever had?"

"Yeah, Sophie told me," replied Gabby.

"Then why did you want to know more about him?" Mr. Felding asked.

"Because his name isn't just a name. Somehow, his name felt familiar, but I don't know why." With the conversation on the subject, Gabby figured there was no better time to start pouring out her questions. "Was President Linstrom married?"

"Uh . . . I think he was," said Mr. Felding.

"What was his wife's name?" asked Gabby.

"I don't know," Mr. Felding said. "I'll have to research to find out."

"Where did he live before he was the president?"

"I don't know. That's another thing to research."

Gabby turned to her mom. "Do you know, Mom?"

"No, I don't."

"What promises did he make before he was elected?" Gabby asked while turning to look at both her mom and her dad who both shrugged their shoulders with blank looks on their faces. "Did anyone else try to run for president when he did?"

"Now, Gabby," said Mr. Felding, "I think we've had enough questions. But I'll tell you what I'll do. In the next day or two, I'll try to find some books or websites about President Linstrom, and I'll see if I can answer your questions."

When Mr. Felding was gone to work the next day on the 15th of October, Gabrielle's curiosity continued. In the afternoon, she found her mom sitting in the living room, doing some more crocheting. She walked over to the couch again and sat down. "Mom," she said.

"Yes, Sweetheart."

"When was President Linstrom born?"

"I don't know."

"Is he still alive?"

"No way! He was elected almost 143 years ago, and he would be older than that if he was still alive."

"Then how old was he when he died?"

"I don't know."

"Do you know where he was buried?"

"No, I don't, Sweetie. You ask too many questions!"

"But *you're* the one who said I could get smarter if I keep asking questions."

Mrs. Felding thought about that for a second. "Oh, yeah," she said. "I *did* say that. But let me work more on my crocheting, and then your dad and I will do our best to find out anything you want to know."

When Mr. Felding returned back home, he carried with him a book that he had checked out from the city library.

"Welcome home, Honey," said Mrs. Felding who was still crocheting in the living room.

"Is Gabby here, or is she with Molly?" asked Mr. Felding.

"She's here," said Mrs. Felding. "Gabby!" she hollered. "Your dad is home!"

"Gabby!" hollered Mr. Felding. Seconds later, Gabrielle came from the hallway into the living room. "I took some time off work to go to the library today, and I found this book that might answer most of your questions," he said while he showed her the front cover of the book that was titled *The Life of President Linstrom*. Then he walked over to the couch and sat down. "What would you like to know first?"

While Gabrielle took a moment to think of what she wanted the first question to be, Mrs. Felding spoke. "Earlier this afternoon, she wanted to know when President Linstrom was born, how old he was when he died, and where he was buried."

"Okay," said Mr. Felding. "It won't be hard to find the answer to the first of those questions." He opened the book to the first page of the first chapter. In the first paragraph, he found the answer. "He was born on June 2, 1838."

"Why did he want to be the president?" asked Gabby.

Mr. Felding turned back to the Table of Contents and looked through the list of chapter titles. With so many chapters, he was unsure about where to find the answer to Gabby's question. "With a book this thick, it might take a bit of time to find the answers to every question, so what I'll do is skim through the book, and then I'll let you know when I find something."

"Okay," said Gabby.

Mrs. Felding walked to the kitchen to start cooking dinner. Wanting to help, Gabrielle followed. Mr. Felding stayed on the couch and started skimming through the book to try to find anything that Gabby wanted to know.

Immediately after dinner, still sitting at the table, Gabrielle turned to her dad. "Did you find anything yet?" she asked him.

"I found several things that might answer some of your questions," he replied. Gabby followed him into the living room, and they both sat down on the couch while Mrs. Felding stayed in the kitchen to do some cleaning.

Seeing her dad reaching for the book and taking ahold of it, Gabby repeated her most recently asked question. "Why did President Linstrom want to be a president?"

"I haven't found that answer yet," said Mr. Felding. "What else did you want to know?"

"Did anyone else run for president when he did?"

Mr. Felding turned to the page that listed the presidential candidates of the 1876 election. "The election of 1876," Mr. Felding read, "was a close call between three candidates. The candidates included Harold Linstrom of the Equality Party, Rutherford B. Hayes of the Republican Party, and Samuel J. Tilden of the Democrat Party. Due to an extremely close race between Harold Linstrom and Rutherford B. Hayes, seven additional weeks were needed before coming to a conclusion. Harold Linstrom ended up winning the election by the narrowest margin in history." Mr. Felding stopped reading and turned to Gabby. "What else do you want to know?"

"Was he married?"

After momentarily searching for it, Mr. Felding found the page that mentioned the names of President Linstrom's family members. "His wife's name was Martha," he said. Then he looked at Gabby who was staring straight ahead at the wall and appeared to have an unknown expression on her face. It looked as though she was almost ready to say something, so Mr. Felding gave her some time to respond.

After a few seconds, a tear streamed down Gabrielle's cheek. Still looking at her, Mr. Felding asked out of concern, "What's wrong, Precious?"

"It's the name," said Gabby with teary eyes.

"The name of Martha?" asked Mr. Felding. Gabby gently gave a slight nod. "What about the name?"

"It feels like that name is in my heart."

Immediately dazed to some degree, Mr. Felding looked over towards the kitchen and saw Mrs. Felding who had been looking at them while standing at the edge of the living room right outside the kitchen ever since the tear fell down from Gabby's cheek.

Mr. and Mrs. Felding looked at each other while they both wondered why Gabby said what she said. A thought then came to Mrs. Felding. "Perhaps she knew someone who was close to her whose name was Martha," she said while another tear ran down Gabby's cheek.

Mr. Felding turned to Gabby and asked, "Did you once know someone named Martha?" Gabby shook her head.

"Quite often," said Mrs. Felding, "girls have a special place in their hearts for their mothers. Do you think Martha could be her mother's name and she just doesn't remember her?"

Mr. Felding immediately considered the idea to be very likely. "It's a strong possibility," he said. "Maybe we should get in touch with Officer Gunwell tomorrow to mention this to him, and then he can start searching for any lady named Martha to see if they can find Gabby's parents."

"That sounds like a good idea," Mrs. Felding said while walking over to the couch. She sat right next to Gabby, put her arm around her out of compassion, and said to her in a soft, gentle tone, "Cheer up, Sweetheart. There's nothing to be sad about. We might be able to help find your parents."

In the afternoon of the following day while Mr. Felding was away from home, Gabrielle thought about what might happen if her parents were found, which created more questions. After stepping out of her bedroom, she found Mrs. Felding sitting in the living room again, but she wasn't crocheting. This time, she was reading the library book that Mr. Felding had left at home. Gabrielle walked over to the couch again and sat down. "Mom," she said.

"Yes, Dear. What's up?" said Mrs. Felding while placing the book down onto her lap and looking over at Gabby.

"If someone finds my parents, what if I have to live far away? Will I ever get to see Molly or Sophie again?"

"Well, first of all," answered Mrs. Felding, "we don't know if your parents are going to be found, but I think it's worth a try. And if someone ends up finding them and they live far away, then we can hope they will bring you to this area to visit every once in a while." Mrs. Felding picked up the library book from her lap. Changing the subject while looking for the page, she said, "I was reading this book about

President Linstrom this morning. Would you like to know what I found?" she asked while raising her head from the book to look at Gabby who then nodded her head. Mrs. Felding found the page. "This book says he lived right here in River City for fifteen years prior to his presidency."

"Really?" said Gabby. "Can we go see his house?"

"I don't know where it was built, and that was over 150 years ago. I'm sure it's torn down by now."

"Does the book have the address of his house where he lived? Maybe we could go to the place where it was at."

"No, Sweetheart. There's no address in this book. But I found something else in here." Mrs. Felding turned a few pages. When she found the right page, she said to Gabby, "It mentions President Linstrom's children. He didn't have any sons, but he had four daughters. The names of his daughters from oldest to youngest were Abigail, Gabrielle, Sabrina, and Tabitha."

"Hey, one of them has *my* name!" said Gabby.

"Yeah, I wonder if your biological parents might have named you after her . . . that is, if they ever researched or somehow learned about President Linstrom's family."

"When were the girls born?"

"I don't know," said Mrs. Felding. "I tried looking for that, but there's nowhere in the book that mentions it. However, I went online this morning and found out that President Linstrom died on November 11, 1929 at the age of ninety-one. I also found out he was buried at Arlington National Cemetery in Arlington, Virginia. He's one of three presidents buried there. The other two are William Howard Taft and John F. Kennedy."

"Hmm," voiced Gabby. "What else did you find out?"

"That's everything so far. I couldn't find any answers to any of your other questions online, and as for this book that's quite thick, it will take a long time to read through all of it."

Forty-five minutes after the usual time of day when Mr. Felding had returned home on previous days, he finally walked into the house. "Something smells good," he said aloud.

Mrs. Felding heard him from the kitchen and came into the living room. "It's the food in the oven that you smell, and dinner will be ready in thirty minutes." Knowing that Mr. Felding had come home later than his normal time of arrival, she asked, "I assume you went to the police station?"

Mr. Felding nodded his head. "I told Officer Gunwell what happened, and he said he would get a search party together to start looking for anyone named Martha. He also said he'll check the records of deceased people during the past five years just in case a tragedy might have happened."

During dinnertime, Mr. Felding said, "You'll never guess what I found out about President Linstrom today."

"What did you find out?" asked Gabby.

"I was talking with some of the workers at the furniture store about our conversations regarding President Linstrom, and one of the employees said he majored in history and had done extensive research on President Linstrom. He said it was President Linstrom who started the Equality Party that he was registered in when he ran for president, but the Equality Party only lasted for four years. It quickly died out right after his presidential term. Then the employee told me about one of the promises that President Linstrom made. He had promised the entire country that everyone would have an equal amount of money, and he didn't think it was fair that some people were too rich while other people were too poor. So after he was elected, he signed an executive order to enforce everyone to have an equal amount of money."

"Then why was he the worst president if he made sure that nobody was poor?" Gabby asked.

"I'll explain that," said Mr. Felding. "From what I was told, there were small businesses that didn't need a lot of money to survive. When they got more than they needed, they didn't know what to do with it, so they started spending it until the spending got so out of control that their debts drove them out of business. And there were also big businesses that needed more money to survive, but they didn't have enough to stay in business after they were forced to give some of their earnings to the small businesses. And as for the citizens who didn't own a business, they eventually couldn't afford anything after the very few businesses that remained had to raise their prices so high to make up for the skyrocketed taxes that the government had to charge to keep *themselves* from going bankrupt. And that's how the first of the two Great Depressions started."

With most of Gabrielle's questions now answered, there was still one question that stood out to her that nobody had the answer to: Why did the names of Harold and Martha Linstrom feel familiar? Wondering how she would ever find the answer, Gabrielle had no idea that Mr. and Mrs. Felding were both wondering the same thing as to why those names felt familiar to her.

# 6

# THE UNKNOWN SOUND

It was the morning of Friday, the 25th day of October. Gabrielle was excited about the upcoming sleepover for later that evening. Earlier that week, Molly had come up with the idea of having Gabby come and stay for a night. Mrs. Robinson called Mrs. Felding to mention the idea. The two moms gave their permission, made arrangements, and jointly scheduled which night to do it.

Being Gabby's first sleepover and not knowing how it would be, she spent most of the day getting ready for it. She double-checked and triple-checked everything that she gathered together to make sure she wouldn't forget anything—her pillow, her favorite blanket, her teddy bear, a few other toys, three board games, a stack of paper, a pile of coloring books, a large amount of crayons, a few snacks, a pair of pajamas, her toothbrush and toothpaste, and a few other things.

When the time was approaching to go to the Robinsons' house, Mrs. Felding went to find Gabby to ask if she was ready. She entered Gabby's bedroom, and the first thing she noticed was an enormous collection of everything, and it was all accumulated together in a jumbled mess on her bed. Gabby stood at the foot of her bed and smiled. "I'm ready to go!" she said.

"Ready to go *where*? On a two-week vacation? Gabby, it's only going to be for one night. The Robinsons have games and toys to play with," said Mrs. Felding, taking a closer look at the accumulation, "and you don't need that much paper or that many coloring books." Then she stepped closer to Gabby's bed. "Here, let me help you go through this to pick out only the things you'll need."

Thirty minutes after three, Gabrielle and her mom started heading three houses down the street to the Robinsons' house. Mrs. Felding carried the pillow under her right arm, a loaded backpack on one shoulder, and a blanket draped over the backpack. Gabby carried her teddy bear and a sack of snacks.

While walking the short distance down the street, Mrs. Felding stayed on the right-hand side of the sidewalk to keep Gabby away from the road. Partway there while looking at Gabby to her left and seeing what she was carrying, Mrs. Felding got an idea. "Now that we've talked a lot about presidents, did you know that teddy bears were named after one of the presidents?"

"Really? Who?"

"His name was Theodore Roosevelt. The name of Teddy is short for Theodore."

"Why was a stuffed bear named after him?" asked Gabby.

"Along with being the president, he was also a hunter. While he was serving as the president, he went on a bear-hunting trip with some other hunters. He wasn't having any luck at finding any bears, so another hunter found one, tied it to a tree, and then brought President Roosevelt to it to let him be the one to shoot it, but he didn't think it was a good idea to shoot a bear that was all tied up. Later, when the owner of a candy shop who also made stuffed animals heard about the hunting trip, he made a stuffed bear, and then he got permission from President Roosevelt to name it Teddy's Bear. Years later, it was called a teddy bear."

"Huh," said Gabby in a tone of interest. "Did you once vote for him when he ran for president?" she asked, assuming that at Mrs. Felding's old age, she must have lived through the presidential terms of several presidents.

"Oh, no. He served *way* before my time! He was the 26th president. I was born when Richard Nixon was the president, and he was the 37th one."

Only a few feet away from arriving at the door, Gabby and Mrs. Felding had no chance to ring the doorbell. The front door opened in advance, and there stood Molly, excited as could be.

After Gabrielle was dropped off, Mrs. Felding walked back home.

At four o'clock, Mr. Felding returned back from work. The house seemed emptier than usual. "Is Gabby over at the Robinsons' house?" he asked.

Mrs. Felding nodded her head. "I got back just a few minutes ago from taking her over there." Then she briefly paused before changing the subject. "I wonder how Officer Gunwell is coming along with the search."

"He told me he'd call us as soon as he has any success," said Mr. Felding. "And I was thinking about that at work today. What if Gabby's biological mom's name is not Martha?"

"Then why was that name emotionally familiar to her? She wouldn't have cried for no reason."

"Well, here's what I was thinking. What if the name of Martha goes back more than one generation?"

"Then how are we supposed to ever find out who Martha is? We don't know how many generations ago, and we don't even know Gabby's last name."

"The name of Linstrom sounded familiar to her, didn't it?" asked Mr. Felding.

"I'm sure it did. Otherwise, she wouldn't have been so curious to know about President Linstrom without even knowing his first name at the time when she first heard about him from Sophie."

"Yeah," agreed Mr. Felding. "Perhaps President and Martha Linstrom are her ancestors. And maybe she felt emotional because she somehow has some sort of ancestral tie to them in her heart."

"But to see whether they *are* her ancestors in order to know for sure, how are we going to trace their ancestral lineage? We still don't know Gabby's last name, and we don't know if the lineage would be through her dad or her mom if we ever even find out who her dad and mom are," Mrs. Felding said.

"Instead of starting with Gabby and going back to President Linstrom, maybe we can search the ancestral records that go from President Linstrom to his descendants, and then see if we can find Gabby somewhere down one of the family lines."

Later that night when it was Molly's bedtime, Mrs. Robinson laid out some cushions onto the floor in Molly's bedroom for Gabby to sleep on. After that, she put bed sheets on them, making it look like a real bed. Gabby carried her blanket and pillow into the bedroom and placed them onto the bed of cushions.

When it was time to go to sleep, Molly and Gabby both climbed into their beds, and Mrs. Robinson turned out the lights on her way out. "Goodnight, Gabby," Molly quietly said.

"Goodnight, Molly," said Gabby in a whisper. The two girls closed their eyes.

A minute later, Gabby suddenly opened her eyes, still lying in the dark. "What did you say?" she asked quietly.

Not quite asleep yet, Molly heard what Gabby asked. "I didn't say anything."

"But I thought I heard something. What was that noise?"

"I didn't hear any noise," replied Molly. "But if you heard something, then maybe you heard my mom talking to my dad on the phone."

"Where's your dad?" Gabby asked.

"He's on a long business trip. He goes on a lot of business trips. When he comes home, he stays for only two or three days before he has to go on another trip."

"Oh, okay. Goodnight," said Gabby.

"Goodnight," said Molly.

The next morning at eleven o'clock, Gabrielle opened the front door to the Feldings' house. She stepped inside and shouted, "Mom! Molly's here! She's ready for her lesson!" while Molly followed her inside.

Mrs. Felding came out from the hallway. "Hi, girls!" she said just before walking past the girls towards the front door. "How was the sleepover?" she asked Mrs. Robinson at the doorway.

Mrs. Robinson replied, "The two girls had a good time together, and Gabby was no trouble at all." Then she handed the backpack, the blanket, and the pillow over to Mrs. Felding. "But there's just one thing," she added. "All morning, she kept hearing a noise. She kept asking us what the noise was, but we didn't hear anything other than the noises that we were making as well as barking dogs and traffic. We asked her what the noise sounded like, and she said she didn't know. She said it was too quiet to tell what it was."

"It could have been anything," said Mrs. Felding. "Maybe a twig, a bird, or a squirrel on the roof." Mrs. Robinson nodded her head in agreement. "But thanks for taking care of Gabby and for letting me know how it all went."

Once again, Gabby stood beside the piano throughout Molly's entire piano lesson.

After Molly went back home, Gabrielle sat on the piano bench. From what she had spent many hours practicing in addition to what she had learned from Molly's and Sophie's piano lessons as well as her own, she practiced until it was time for Sophie to arrive, not including the time that she spent eating lunch.

Throughout Sophie's piano lesson, Gabrielle stood beside the piano, trying to learn as much as she could, although a more complicated lesson was harder to understand.

After forty-five minutes, Sophie stood up from the piano bench to start heading back home. "We'll see you next week," Mrs. Felding said while Sophie started walking towards the front door.

"What was that?" Gabby asked in alarm.

"What was what?" asked Mrs. Felding.

"I heard something," said Gabby.

"I didn't hear anything . . . not anything out of the ordinary," said Mrs. Felding.

Without reaching for the doorknob, Sophie stopped at the doorway and turned around. "I didn't either," she said while turning to face Gabby. "What did you hear?"

"I don't know," said Gabby, sounding somewhat scared.

"What did it sound like?" Sophie asked.

"I don't know. It was too quiet to tell what it was."

Mrs. Felding turned to Sophie. "Gabby was at Molly's house this morning, and they said she was hearing quiet things all morning."

Sophie turned back to Gabby. "There are lots of quiet noises. Maybe you heard my footsteps on the floor," she said, referring to the few footsteps from the piano to the front door on the carpeted floor.

"No, that's not it. It was something else." Gabby paused for two seconds before she suddenly grew an expression of fright. "I heard it again! What was that noise?"

Mrs. Felding and Sophie looked at each other with expressions of uncertainty. Then Mrs. Felding turned to look at Gabby. "We don't know what you're hearing, Sweetheart."

"It *could* be a slight ringing in your ears," Sophie suggested.

"No, it wasn't a ringing sound," said Gabby.

"Well, no matter what it was," said Sophie, "at least it wasn't a monster. Just be glad there's no such thing as monsters! And I need to go home now. I'll see you next week."

Later that night after Gabrielle was put to bed, Mr. and Mrs. Felding sat on the couch. Before watching their late shows on television, they talked about the day. "How was your day at work?" asked Mrs. Felding.

"It was crazy," answered Mr. Felding. "This morning, an unsatisfied customer returned a brand new washing machine that he bought yesterday. He said it was making some loud noises. This afternoon, we all heard a loud crash on the street right in front of the store, so I ran out the front doors with two other employees to see what happened, and the noise turned out to be an old vehicle with a very loud muffler."

"And speaking about noises," said Mrs. Felding, "at least you knew where those noises came from. This morning, Mrs. Robinson told me that Gabby was hearing noises that they couldn't hear. This afternoon right after Sophie's piano lesson, Gabby acted scared about a noise that she heard. Both Sophie and I couldn't hear whatever she was hearing, and she heard it twice. We asked her what it sounded like, and she said it was too quiet to tell what it was."

"Huh . . ." Mr. Felding voiced out of interest. "It's interesting that she couldn't see or hear Officer Gunwell, some workers at foster-care agencies, some foster-care couples, and some cars that everyone else could see and hear, and now she's the one who's hearing something that nobody else can hear."

"How are we ever going to find out what's causing this?" asked Mrs. Felding. "I remember you once said she was just pretending everyone was invisible as well as ignoring most of the cars, but how can she be pretending to hear a noise when she seemed scared about it?"

"I would say that, in addition to not knowing how she knew about a horse and buggy, why she didn't know what a car was, who bought her an old-fashioned dress, where she learned the first steps of how to play the piano, who taught her how to play *Graces*, where she came from, what her full name is, and who her parents are, this is probably something else that we'll eventually find out. I don't know when or how we'll find the answers to anything about her that nobody knows, but let me tell you . . ." said Mr. Felding, "River City is getting crazier!"

# 7

# THE BIG SEARCH

It was the morning of Tuesday, the 29th day of October. While getting ready to go to school, it came to Molly's attention that Halloween was only two days away, and she didn't have a costume to wear. "Mom," she said, "what should I be for Halloween?"

"You can be whatever you'd like to be," her mom answered.

"But I don't know what I want to be, and my costume from last year doesn't fit me anymore."

"Well, how am I supposed to know what you're going to be if *you* don't know? Do you really need to dress up every year? Maybe you could skip this year and not wear any costume."

"But my class at school is going on a little parade on Halloween, and my classmates will all be dressed up. I don't want to be the only one in my class without a costume!"

"Then maybe we can go shopping for a costume after school today," said Mrs. Robinson.

When Molly returned home from school in the afternoon, she found her mom to mention the idea she had thought about earlier that day at school. "Hey, Mom, can I call Gabby to see what she'll be wearing for Halloween? Maybe I can be whatever she's going to be."

"Sure," said her mom while reaching for her cell phone that was within arm's reach. She grabbed it and dialed Mrs. Felding's number. "Here, it's ringing," she said, handing the phone to Molly who took ahold of it.

Meanwhile, Mrs. Felding was in her bedroom at the computer, working on genealogical research to try to trace a family line from

President Linstrom down to Gabby when she heard her phone ringing in the living room. She quickly left her bedroom, entered the living room, picked up her phone, and answered it. "Hello."

"Is Gabby there?" a five-year-old voice asked.

Mrs. Felding recognized the voice of who was calling. "Yes, Molly, she's here. Would you like me to get her for you?"

"Yeah."

"Okay. Hold on." Mrs. Felding lowered her phone. "Gabby!" she hollered. "Phone for you!"

Gabby came into the living room and got the phone from her mom. She put it up to her ear while Mrs. Felding headed back to her bedroom to continue the research. "Hello."

"Hi, Gabby! This is Molly."

"Hi, Molly!" said Gabby, excited that Molly was calling her on the phone. "Do you want to come over to my house to play?"

"Not right now," said Molly. "I wanted to ask you if you have a costume to wear for Halloween."

"Halloween?" uttered Gabby in a sour, unpleasant tone.

"What's wrong with Halloween?" Molly asked.

"I don't like it."

"Why don't you like it?"

"It's the day when the bad guys come and throw rotten vegetables at houses. And they also might take the hinges off the gate to your fence. They do lots of bad things and make a mess of the town."

"Huh? They do?" asked Molly. "I never saw anyone do that."

"You never did?" asked Gabby. "You never saw any rotten vegetables on the outside of your house or saw the gate to your fence taken off?"

"No, I never did. All I know is that my class at school is doing a fun parade with everyone dressed up, but I don't have a costume."

"How do you get a costume?" asked Gabby. "Does someone have to make one?"

"No. We buy one from the store. My mom is taking me to the store soon to get a costume, but I don't know what I want to be."

"Maybe you can see what the store has, and then you can get the one you like the best," Gabby suggested.

Thinking about being dressed in a costume, Molly got an idea. "Hey, if we both wear a costume, then we can go trick-or-treating together!"

"Trick-or-treating? What's that?" Gabby asked in a state of wonder.

"You don't know what trick-or-treating is? It's when you knock

71

on the doors to a lot of houses, and you get lots of candy!"

"Candy?" repeated Gabby, growing a big taste for the idea. "But I don't have a costume."

"Maybe you can come with us to get one at the store," said Molly.

Not wanting to pass up a chance to be with Molly, Gabby wasn't about to decline the offer. "Yeah! But let me ask my mom."

"Okay," said Molly.

Gabby lowered the phone and hollered for her mom who soon came back into the living room. "What is it, Sweetheart?" asked Mrs. Felding.

"Can we go with Molly to get a Halloween costume at the store? She said they're leaving soon, and I want to go with her to do trick . . ." said Gabby, pausing because she couldn't remember what Molly called it. "Trick or . . ."

"Trick-or-treating?"

"Yeah. Can we go?"

"Alright. Let me get ready, and then we'll follow Mrs. Robinson to the store."

Mrs. Felding went to get ready, and Gabby resumed talking to Molly. "My mom said we can follow you there, so wait for us!"

Minutes later, two cars headed off to the store.

After finding the aisles with costumes, Molly, Gabby, and their moms started looking at each costume to see what the options were. An elegant princess costume immediately caught Molly's eye. "Can I be a princess?" she asked her mom.

Mrs. Robinson looked at the price. "That's too expensive. Let's look for ones that are more affordable."

"Will you get me this pirate costume?" Gabby asked Mrs. Felding.

"Arrrgh!" said Mrs. Felding in a piratelike voice. She took a look at the price. "Not if ye don't want to walk the plank!" Changing back to her regular voice, she told Gabby, "This is the same price as the princess costume. Let's keep looking."

Following several unsuccessful persuasions from the two girls, the moms eventually found ones in their price range that each of the girls accepted.

Nighttime came. Right after Gabby was put to bed, Mrs. Felding heard her phone ringing from the living room. *Who could be calling this late?* she wondered while she walked into the living room to where her phone was located. She picked it up and answered it. "Hello."

"Hi, Mrs. Felding. This is Mrs. Robinson. The reason why I'm calling is because I wanted to tell you what Molly told me about what Gabby told her. You really have a strange daughter!"

"Uh . . . well, she's a bit peculiar . . . but what did she tell Molly?" Mrs. Felding asked while she sat down on the couch beside Mr. Felding.

"After we got back from shopping for costumes, Molly told me about her idea for trick-or-treating, and she was surprised that Gabby didn't even know what that was."

"Well, she's only four years old. She probably couldn't remember from when she was three."

"Oh, you haven't heard the best of it! According to what Molly heard from Gabby on the phone, Gabby thought Halloween was the day when people throw rotten vegetables at houses and take hinges off gates to fences. Now, where did she get these crazy ideas?"

"I have no idea," said Mrs. Felding. "I don't know if she just made that up from her imagination, if she heard that from someone, or if she dreamed about it and thought it was real."

"Just so you know, Molly sounded a little scared when she told me because she didn't know if what Gabby told her was true or not, so you might want to have a talk with that daughter of yours," said Mrs. Robinson in a stern tone of concernment.

"Yes, I will right after she wakes up in the morning. Is there anything else I should know about?"

"Not that Molly told me."

"Okay. Thanks for calling to let me know."

After the phone call, Mr. Felding asked, "What was that all about?"

"Mrs. Robinson told me what Gabby told Molly who later told *her*. It seems that Gabby had a crazy idea that crazy people go around throwing rotten vegetables at houses on Halloween as well as taking off the hinges to the gates of fences."

"I wonder where she got that idea," said Mr. Felding.

"I don't know, but it somewhat scared Molly after she wasn't sure whether it was true or not, and I know Gabby wouldn't intentionally scare her best friend."

"With that in mind, we know she didn't make up the story," Mr. Felding concluded.

"But did she hear it from someone else, or did she dream about it in a dream that seemed real?" Mrs. Felding wondered aloud.

At that point, Mr. Felding seemed to be deep in thought. "I'm wondering . . ." he said slowly.

Mrs. Felding waited for him to continue. "Wondering what?"

she asked.

"Do you remember the day when we brought Gabby home from the police station?" Mrs. Felding nodded her head. "Officer Gunwell mentioned some historic things that she knew about—an outhouse, candles and lanterns—in addition to knowing about a horse and buggy, the heating of food with fire . . ."

"Are you saying this could be another piece of history that she knows?"

"There's only one way to find out," said Mr. Felding, motioning down to Mrs. Felding's cell phone.

Mrs. Felding used her phone to search through the Internet. After a few minutes of searching different websites with no luck in finding anything about rotten vegetables being thrown, she wondered where Gabby had gotten the idea. "I can't find any websites that tell about what Gabby told Molly," she told Mr. Felding.

"Maybe you could try typing something different in the search," Mr. Felding said.

Instead of searching for the history of Halloween, Mrs. Felding searched for the throwing of rotten vegetables, and she soon found a website that mentioned it. "Here it is," she said. Then she read part of the article. "In the mid to late 19th century, Halloween was not like it is today. People wore costumes not just for fun, but to ward off ghosts. Pranksters reserved that day to pull off their pranks. They tipped over outhouses whether or not someone was inside. They also threw rotten vegetables at houses, soaped windows, unhinged fence gates, coated chapel seats with molasses, and several other pranks. Over the years, homeowners became more and more unhappy until they eventually started giving out free candy to the pranksters to keep them out of Halloween mischief. In 1921, Halloween was finally declared an official holiday." Mrs. Felding then lowered her phone and looked over to Mr. Felding.

"Now we know she didn't dream about it," Mr. Felding said.

"She must have heard it from someone. Even if there was a chance she could have seen it in a book or gotten online from the phone or the computer, she doesn't know how to read. And I'll have to call Mrs. Robinson tomorrow morning to tell her the history about this just so she doesn't think Gabby is too crazy."

In the morning of Halloween, Gabrielle entered the kitchen while breakfast was being cooked. Standing at the oven range, Mrs. Felding turned her head towards the entryway and saw Gabby all dressed up in her Halloween costume. "Well, good morning, you pretty cowgirl!" she said in a cheerful tone. Once again, just like she had done the first time

she was dressed into an outfit that was worn by the Felding daughters, Gabby positioned herself into a few different poses for showing off what she was wearing. "Would you like to help me with breakfast by setting the table?" Gabrielle smiled and nodded while starting to walk over to the corner of the countertop where the breakfast dishes were placed, and she soon had the table all set.

Right after the last dish of food was placed onto the table, Mr. Felding walked into the kitchen. One of the first things that drew his attention was seeing Gabby in her costume. "Happy Halloween, Precious!" he told her as soon as she looked over at him to see him coming.

Gabby smiled. "Happy Halloween, Daddy!"

"It looks like you're ready to ride horses!" Mr. Felding told her.

"No. I'm ready to go trick-or-treating . . . not ride horses! Silly Daddy!"

Later that evening at seven o'clock, Mrs. Felding and Gabrielle arrived at the door to the Robinsons' house under the dark sky, having walked there by the light of the moon and the streetlights. Gabrielle rang the doorbell, and Molly, being dressed up as a ladybug, soon opened the door and invited them inside.

Gabrielle noticed three unfamiliar faces of kids dressed in Halloween costumes in the living room. She turned to Molly and asked, "Who are they?"

"These are my friends from school," replied Molly. "They're in my kindergarten class. I invited them to come, and I have three more friends who are coming." Pointing out one at a time, she mentioned their names. "This is Celeste Samuelson, Scarlett Stevenson, and April Erickson." And facing her school friends, she introduced her neighbor. "Hey, everyone, this is my friend, Gabby."

"Hi," all three of them said to Gabby.

A few seconds later, Mrs. Carlson arrived with her son, Mason. The doorbell sounded, Molly answered the door and invited Mason inside, and then came Mrs. Davidson to drop off her daughter, Elsa.

Molly closed the door, and she introduced Mason and Elsa to Gabby.

A minute later, Mrs. Herbertson came to drop off her son, Ezra.

Molly introduced Gabby and Ezra to each other, and everyone was soon ready to go.

Mrs. Felding and Mrs. Robinson walked down the sidewalk with all eight kids, going from house to house, each of them carrying a Halloween bucket for getting candy. Residents at several houses were surprised at how many kids there were in just this one group of trick-ortreaters, but luckily, there was plenty of candy for each of the kids.

At each house, Gabrielle insisted on being the last one of the kids to get candy. Whenever there was a variety of candy to choose from, she wanted the other kids to choose first. Knowing she would be getting her share of candy no matter who was first and who was last, it made her feel happy just to see smiles on the faces of the other kids after they got what they wanted.

At eight o'clock, everyone returned back to the Robinsons' house. Within the next few minutes, the moms of each of Molly's six school friends came to pick them up.

Mrs. Felding and Gabrielle returned back home. Sitting in the living room, seeing them step into the house, Mr. Felding asked, "How did it go?"

Giving no chance for Mrs. Felding to say anything, Gabrielle immediately answered. "I made six new friends!"

"Six friends in just one evening?" asked Mr. Felding.

Mrs. Felding explained, "They were all Molly's friends from school. She invited them to come, so we ended up taking eight kids with us."

Gabrielle walked over to Mr. Felding and held out her Halloween bucket. "See how much candy I got?" she exclaimed out of excitement.

Mr. Felding took a peek into the bucket. "Wow! Looks like enough to feed an army! But don't eat it all in one day. Otherwise, you'll need to go see the doctor if you get sick from too much candy, and then you'll need to go see the dentist after the sugar ruins your teeth," he said. Still talking to Gabby, he changed the subject. "Did you hear any quiet noises today like you were hearing last Saturday?" Gabby thought for a second, and she shook her head. "Well, whatever you were hearing, at least it wasn't a ghost, or I'm sure you would have heard it again today if it was."

In the middle of the following Wednesday, the 6th day of November, knowing the next day would be Thursday, Gabrielle had another question to ask. This time, she found Mrs. Felding in the master bedroom in front of the computer, working more on genealogical research in a wholehearted attempt to find Gabby's biological parents. "Mom," she said right after entering the bedroom.

Yes, Sweetheart," said Mrs. Felding.

Gabby's attention was immediately diverted over to the computer screen. "What are you doing?" she asked while walking closer to the computer. Then she stopped beside Mrs. Felding who continued to research.

"I'm looking through names of people to see if I can find your parents."

"But how can you find them if you don't know what their names are?"

"It's called genealogy. Your dad and I figured you might have ancestral ties to President and Mrs. Linstrom. That means you might be related to them somehow," said Mrs. Felding. Looking at the computer screen, she added, "So I'm seeing if I can trace a family line from them to you, and if I can find a girl down one of the family lines with your name who was born close to 2015, then we can assume that's you, and we'll know who your parents are," she explained. Then she turned to face Gabby. "Did you come in here just to see what I was doing?"

"No. I wanted to ask you when Thanksgiving will be. Is it tomorrow, or is it the last Thursday of the month?"

"Thanksgiving is always on the fourth Thursday of November, but that's not always the last Thursday of the month."

"But I thought it was either on the first Thursday or the last Thursday. Who changed it?"

"This is how it's always been. Where did you get the idea that Thanksgiving comes on any other Thursday of the month?"

"I don't know. But the first and last Thursdays are the only Thanksgiving days that I can remember."

"What do you mean *remember*? They've *always* been on the fourth Thursday of the month." Mrs. Felding paused while she thought about other times when Gabby had come up with crazy ideas. "Is this another piece of history that you somehow know about?" Gabby shrugged her shoulders. Then Mrs. Felding turned back to the computer and started searching for websites about the history of Thanksgiving.

Gabrielle left the bedroom in search of better entertainment. Mrs. Felding continued searching on the computer until she came across a few websites that answered the question as to why Gabby thought Thanksgiving fell on any other day besides the fourth Thursday of November.

After Gabrielle was put to bed that night, Mr. and Mrs. Felding found themselves back on the couch in the living room. Curious to know why not much was said at dinnertime, Mr. Felding mentioned, "You hardly said anything about the day. Did nothing happen today?"

"I didn't want Gabby to start losing hope about her parents being found," said Mrs. Felding, explaining why she didn't talk much about the day at dinnertime. "I finished going through all the family lines from Abigail, and nobody who was born within the past few years has the name of Gabrielle."

"Well, there are still three more daughters of President Linstrom to search from. There might be a good chance that Gabby is a descendant of the second daughter named Gabrielle."

"Yeah, there are still plenty of family lines to search through, but I don't think Gabby should know the results until we find her parents. Otherwise, it could crush her hopes, and it could make her feel very devastated."

Mr. Felding nodded his head in agreement. "Did anything else happen today?"

"Oh, you better believe it!" said Mrs. Felding while nodding her head. "The mystery of Gabby strikes again!"

"What now?" Mr. Felding asked.

"Gabby asked me when Thanksgiving will be, and I told her. Then she told me that the first and last Thursdays of November were the only Thanksgiving days that she could remember."

Mr. Felding expressed a look of wonder on his face. "Where did she come up with that idea?"

"I don't know. But then I looked it up online, and I found out Thanksgiving wasn't proclaimed a national, annual holiday until October 3, 1863. In years before that, it was celebrated, but each state chose their own day to celebrate it, anywhere from October to January. After President Lincoln declared it a national holiday, he invited everyone in the country to observe the last Thursday of November as the day to celebrate it. In 1865, President Johnson moved Thanksgiving to the first Thursday of November, and that's the only year that Thanksgiving was on the first Thursday ever since 1863. It was then moved back to the last Thursday of the month until President Grant moved it to the third Thursday in 1869, which was the only year between then and now that it was held on the third Thursday, but Gabby didn't mention anything about remembering Thanksgiving being on the third Thursday."

Another look of wonder was shown on the face of Mr. Felding. "Another mystery to add to the collection? How many more mysteries about Gabby could there be? Maybe we should just stop trying to figure her out and just assume that she must have been raised by someone at an unknown place at some point in time."

"But we shouldn't stop trying to find her parents. And just in case she's not a descendant of President Linstrom, I hope Officer Gunwell can eventually have success in his search."

The following day on the 7th of November while Mr. Felding was away at work, Mrs. Felding and Gabrielle headed to separate rooms after eating lunch. Mrs. Felding went to the master bedroom to resume the ancestral search on the computer while Gabrielle went to her own bedroom to play with toys.

During the next few minutes while playing with her toys, Gabrielle's hair kept getting in front of her face too much to keep up the level of entertainment, which caused a degree of annoyance that gradually increased boredom to the point that it wasn't fun anymore, and she wondered what else to do. Knowing that her mom was doing boring things on the computer again, she started feeling mischievous like a regular four-year-old. She walked towards her bedroom doorway, exited her bedroom, crossed the hallway, entered the bathroom, and began searching for anything that could entertain her. With nothing fun in sight at that instant, her curiosity led her to search additional places. She opened the top drawer of the vanity, took a peek inside, and found some haircutting supplies including a pair of scissors. Immediately, she remembered seeing both her mom and Mrs. Robinson using scissors at different times, and it only took a second to know what to do next.

After Mrs. Felding spent the afternoon at the computer, Mr. Felding returned home from work. Mrs. Felding heard the front door being opened and closed, so she left the computer and soon walked into the living room. "Welcome home, Honey!" she said.

Mr. Felding gave a half smile. Then he glanced around the living room. "Where's Gabby?" he asked.

"She's in her bedroom. She's been playing with her toys all afternoon ever since we finished lunch," said Mrs. Felding. For a brief moment, she and Mr. Felding quietly listened for any sounds, but they couldn't hear anything. "I *thought* that's where she was." Wanting to find out, Mrs. Felding hollered, "Hey, Gabby! Where are you?"

A few seconds later, Gabrielle entered the living room from the hallway. Immediately, both parents noticed a drastic change in her looks. "What in Heaven's name happened to you?" asked Mr. Felding while looking at Gabby, stunned at the sight of her new length of hair. He turned to Mrs. Felding and asked, "Did you cut her hair?"

Looking at Mr. Felding, Mrs. Felding replied, "No, I didn't." Then she turned to Gabby. "What have you been doing?" she asked, sounding disappointed.

Taking another brief look at Gabby, Mr. Felding quickly spoke up, giving no time for Gabby to have any hurt feelings. "I think she looks kinda cute," he said. "She definitely looks quite different than before, but if her bangs were trimmed more evenly, I think we could get used to it."

On the following Monday, the 11th day of November, Gabrielle sat in the living room while she colored pictures of unicorns in one of her coloring books. After having asked her mom several times throughout the early morning about what time it was, she had entered the living room with her coloring book and crayons about fifteen minutes before eleven o'clock, knowing that the mail always came around eleven. That day, she was determined to be the one to check the mail although she knew none of the mail was ever addressed to her. She colored while she constantly listened closely for the postal truck to stop at the mailbox.

A good length of time passed, and Gabrielle finished coloring five pictures. As much as she colored, she figured the mail had to have come already, but she hadn't heard the postal truck. She didn't know what time it was, and she assumed her mom was in the master bedroom where she had been spending a lot of time during the past several days.

Gabrielle entered the master bedroom and found Mrs. Felding at the computer again. "Hey, Mom," she said.

"What do you want, Sweetie?" Mrs. Felding asked softly while continuing to search on the computer.

"What time is it?"

Mrs. Felding looked over at a nearby clock. "It's a few minutes after eleven. Why do you keep asking what time it is?"

"A few minutes after eleven? Can you come outside with me to the mailbox? I want to check the mail," Gabby said, making it a point to abide by Mrs. Felding's wishes to not go outside alone anymore.

Mrs. Felding turned to face Gabby. "The mail won't be coming today, Sweetheart. It's a holiday."

"A holiday? Today?" Gabby said in a tone of bewilderment. "I never heard of a holiday on the 11th of November."

"It's Veterans Day today."

"What's Veterans Day?" asked Gabby.

"It's the day when we commemorate the veterans who fought in wars."

"Like the Civil War?"

"No. That war was way before Veterans Day started. This holiday marked the end of the First World War."

"First? Was there more than one world war?"

"There were *two* world wars."

"World War? I didn't even know there was *one*! Was the first one right after the Civil War?" asked Gabby.

"No. It was several years later."

"How many years later?"

"Hmm . . . I don't know. Would you like me to find out?" asked Mrs. Felding. Gabby nodded her head. Then Mrs. Felding turned back to the computer and looked for some websites about the history of Veterans Day as well as the dates of the different wars.

After a few seconds, Mrs. Felding found a website that listed the earlier wars. "It says the Civil War started on April 12, 1861 and ended on April 9, 1865." Soon, she stumbled upon another website with plenty of information about Veterans Day, and she read some of it to Gabby. "Veterans Day started out as Armistice Day on November 11, 1919 in recognition of the end of World War I on November 11, 1918, although the war was not officially ended until the Treaty of Versailles was signed on June 28, 1919, which was exactly five years after the assassination of Austrian archduke Franz Ferdinand on June 28, 1914 that started World War I a month later on July 28, 1914. After World War II that lasted from September 1, 1939 to September 2, 1945 and the Korean War that lasted from June 25, 1950 to July 27, 1953, President Dwight D. Eisenhower officially changed the name of Armistice Day to Veteran's Day on June 1, 1954 to include those wars in honoring the veterans who served." Mrs. Felding turned to face Gabby. "So that's how Veterans Day got started. And to answer your question," she said, turning back to the computer to look at the dates one more time, "it looks like the First World War started a little more than forty-nine years after the Civil War ended." Gabby grew a look of confusion on her face. Looking at her, Mrs. Felding asked, "What's wrong?" At that point, knowing the mysteries of Gabby that contained no answers, Mrs. Felding was about to hear the biggest mystery of them all.

"Somebody once told me the Civil War started a few years ago," said Gabby, "and I don't know much about time. How did so many wars happen in only a few years? And with so many wars, is that how the cemetery got so big?"

"What?" asked Mrs. Felding, not knowing what to say. "I don't suppose you know who told you about the Civil War . . . do you?" Gabby shook her head. "Uh . . ." Mrs. Felding voiced. Then she took a few seconds to try to think of any possible explanation. "Maybe someone told you about the Civil War a few months ago, and maybe it just seems like it happened a few years ago because of when you were told. And as for the cemetery, there might be a few veterans who were buried there after getting old, but I don't think anyone who died in any war is buried there."

"Then how did the cemetery get so big?"

"Like I told you before, it must be another cemetery that you're thinking about."

For the remainder of the day, Gabrielle wondered why she never heard of Veterans Day, and how something that almost seemed like yesterday could be so long ago.

After the usual, nightly routine, Mr. and Mrs. Felding sat on the couch as usual, getting ready to watch their usual shows on television. Mr. Felding then asked his usual question. "Did anything happen today while I was at work?"

Mrs. Felding replied, "I worked more on the ancestral research. I'm almost finished going through the family lines of Sabrina, but I haven't had any luck yet."

"Wait," said Mr. Felding. "Sabrina? I thought you were going from the oldest to the youngest. What about Gabrielle?"

"I couldn't find any family lines under Gabrielle. I couldn't even find a spouse. She must have never gotten married."

"Did you find out what day Gabrielle was born and what day she died?"

"She was born on May 9, 1865, but I couldn't find a death date. She either ended up missing and was never found, or the people who put the genealogy website together forgot to put in that information."

"Hmm . . . What else happened today?" Mr. Felding asked.

Wondering how much to say, Mrs. Felding let out an exasperated sigh. "Well, I guess you could say that another Gabby mystery can be added."

"What happened *this* time?"

"She didn't know today was a holiday, and I found out she never heard of Veterans Day."

"A lot of kids her age haven't heard of Veterans Day. What's so mysterious about that?" Mr. Felding asked.

Mrs. Felding continued. "She also never heard of World War I or World War II. However, she mentioned the Civil War. What other kid would know about the Civil War without even hearing about either of the two world wars?"

"That's easy. Kids hear different things, and they remember a lot of it. She must have heard someone talk about the Civil War—maybe from Sophie—and she never heard anyone talk about the world wars." Mr. Felding paused for a brief moment. Then he looked into the eyes of Mrs. Felding. "You still haven't told me what this additional mystery is."

"I thought you gave up on trying to figure her out."

"Yeah, but it would still be nice to know what all these mysteries are."

"Well, if I tell you about *this* one, then you'd *really* want to give up on trying to figure her out!"

"Huh? Is it really that perplexing?" asked Mr. Felding.

Mrs. Felding nodded her head in confidence. "Just trust me on this. By the way, she didn't know who told her about the Civil War, so it wasn't Sophie."

On the following Sunday, the 17th day of November, Gabrielle sat between Mr. and Mrs. Felding at church. Mrs. Felding listened to some of what the preacher said, but most of her attention was focused on the thoughts of still having no success at finding Gabby down any family line of descendants of President Linstrom. She was almost finished searching through the descendants of Tabitha, and the hope that remained in the heart of Mrs. Felding was becoming very slim.

After arriving back home from church a few minutes after noon, the Felding family had lunch.

Afterwards, Mr. Felding spoke to Gabrielle while they walked into the living room. "Hey, Gabby, did you listen to what the preacher said?"

"Uh-huh," said Gabby while nodding her head. "He talked about love."

"Do you remember what he said about love?" Mr. Felding asked while Mrs. Felding headed to the master bedroom to finish her ancestral search on the computer after she had finished quickly clearing the dirty dishes from the table.

"Yeah. He said we should love our neighbor, which means everyone. We should help them when they need help, and treat them how we want to be treated."

"Do you remember what else he said?"

"He said we should especially love our family members because God put us together in groups of families."

"Ooh, it sounds like you paid attention to everything he said."

"Yeah," said Gabby. "Mom told me I can be smarter if I keep asking questions, but if we don't pay attention to what people say, then we can't be smarter."

"You're right, Precious. We can't learn if we don't listen."

Gabby gave a smile and started heading to her bedroom. She took a few steps, and then she all of a sudden stopped. She quickly turned her head to the right and to the left. "What was that?" she asked in a slight tone of panic.

"What was what?" Mr. Felding asked.

"I heard a noise."

"A noise? What did it sound like?"

Gabby turned around to face Mr. Felding. "I don't know," she said. "It was too quiet."

"Well, your mom is at the computer. Maybe you heard her typing on the keyboard, clicking the mouse, moving her chair . . ."

"No. It wasn't that. It was something else," interrupted Gabby, still somewhat frightened.

"Was it the same noise you heard when you had a sleepover with Molly?"

Gabby nodded her head. "Uh-huh." Suddenly, she felt more frightened. "I heard it again!"

"I didn't hear anything," said Mr. Felding. "If it's only a noise, then don't worry about it. Quiet noises can't hurt anyone."

Gabrielle quickly calmed down. "Okay," she said before she turned back around and continued on her way to her bedroom where most of her entertainment was located.

For the remainder of the afternoon, the house was quiet. Mrs. Felding continued to work on the ancestral research, Mr. Felding stayed in the living room while reading a newspaper, and Gabby played with her toys in her bedroom. Before the time of dinner preparation, Gabrielle heard the quiet noise three more times, but she always kept in mind what Mr. Felding said about noises not hurting anyone.

Later, Gabrielle started hearing louder noises that were coming from the kitchen. She went to the kitchen to see what was happening, and there she found Mrs. Felding who was getting some pans, bowls, and ingredients out for making dinner. Gabrielle stayed in the kitchen to help, and Mrs. Felding gave instructions to her, one at a time, of what to do.

While Mrs. Felding was adding ingredients together into one bowl, Gabrielle was mixing other ingredients together in another bowl. "What did you say, Mom?" asked Gabrielle.

"When?"

"What did you say just now?"

"I didn't say anything."

"But I heard

someone say something," said Gabby.

"Maybe your dad said something, or maybe he has the television turned on."

Gabby placed the stirring spoon onto the countertop, stepped down off the stepstool, went to the kitchen entryway that faced the living room, and took a look. Undoubtedly, the television was off, and it appeared that Mr. Felding's attention was deep into the newspaper. Not wanting to disturb him, Gabby went back to the stepstool to resume. "No, it wasn't Dad who said something, and the television isn't on. Are you sure you didn't say something?" she asked Mrs. Felding.

"Yes, I'm sure. Maybe you heard someone outside talking loud enough for you to hear their voice."

"Maybe," said Gabrielle, considering what Mrs. Felding said. However, she didn't know the voice she heard was the same quiet and suspicious sound that she had been hearing.

At Gabrielle's bedtime, Mrs. Felding tucked her into bed. "Goodnight, Sweetheart," said Mrs. Felding. She leaned over and gave Gabby a kiss on her forehead. "I'll see you tomorrow."

In the living room, Mrs. Felding sat down on the couch. Also sitting on the couch, Mr. Felding asked, "How much more is there to go on the ancestral search?"

"I finished today," said Mrs. Felding. "I only found one Gabrielle in the descendants of Tabitha who was born in a more recent generation, but she was born in 1998."

"Then we still have yet to find out why the names of Harold and Martha Linstrom sounded so familiar to Gabby."

"I wonder if Officer Gunwell had any success."

"He said he'd call us as soon as he has any success, but he hasn't called us yet," said Mr. Felding. "Maybe I'll go talk to him at the police station sometime in the next few days if he doesn't call before then."

"That sounds like a good idea. And I don't know why there are so many mysteries about Gabby. Maybe there was something to it when Officer Gunwell warned us about her."

"Or maybe we just need to be patient and wait for the mysteries to be solved. And talking about mysteries, it was earlier this afternoon when she was scared of a quiet noise she heard. She said it was the same noise when she had the sleepover with Molly."

"Oh, really? It was about three weeks ago when she last heard that sound. I wonder why she's hearing it again. And talking about sounds, it was while Gabby was helping me prepare dinner today when she thought I said something to her at a time when neither one of us were saying anything. I ended up telling her it might have been someone outside who was being noisy."

"It still remains a mystery as to what she thinks she's hearing," said Mr. Felding. "I wonder what the next mystery is going to be."

# 8
# TIME VS. TIME

On Saturday, the 23rd day of November, just like every Saturday, Gabrielle was once again excited for Molly to come. With toys to keep her occupied, she stayed in the living room to be close to the front door for when the doorbell would be heard.

Twenty minutes after ten, she heard a voice. "She's here!" Gabby hollered. Feeling excited, she quickly stood up and ran to the door while Mrs. Felding rushed from her bedroom into the living room to see what was happening.

Gabby opened the door. "What are you doing, Gabby?" asked Mrs. Felding, knowing what time it was. Gabby looked outside from the doorway. "What's outside?"

Seeing nobody outside at the doorway, Gabby looked to the driveway, turned to face down the sidewalk in one direction, and then looked down the sidewalk in the opposite direction. Not seeing anyone in sight, she stepped away from the doorway and closed the door from inside. "I thought I heard someone talking outside, and I thought it was Molly coming."

"We still have forty minutes until she comes," Mrs. Felding said. "You must have heard someone else outside."

"But there's nobody outside anywhere," said Gabby.

"Then you must have heard another noise that sounded like someone talking."

"No, it wasn't another noise. I heard a voice."

"What did the voice say?" asked Mrs. Felding.

"I don't know. It was too quiet."

"Well, don't worry about it. Just play some more with your toys until Molly comes." Then Mrs. Felding headed back to her bedroom to continue making the crocheted doll that she had been working on.

Forty minutes later, the doorbell was heard. "She's here!" Gabby shouted again while dashing the short distance to the door. Three seconds later, she opened the door. "Hi, Molly!"

"Hi, Gabby!"

At that time, Mrs. Felding showed up at the doorway. "Come in, Molly," she said.

For the next thirty minutes, Mrs. Felding taught Molly another piano lesson while Gabby stood beside the piano, watched, and listened.

Afterwards, Mrs. Robinson arrived. In just a short time, she and Molly started heading back home.

Gabby shut the door from inside after she and Molly said their goodbyes, and Mrs. Felding started heading back to the master bedroom. Suddenly, Gabby heard her name. "What, Mom?" she asked aloud.

Mrs. Felding immediately stopped. Standing at the end of the hallway just barely outside the living room, she turned around to face Gabby. "Yes, Sweetheart, what is it?"

"I thought you wanted me. Didn't you say my name?"

"No, I didn't," answered Mrs. Felding. Then she turned back around and resumed heading to the master bedroom.

Gabby grew excited. "Maybe it was Molly!" Quickly, she opened the door again, looked outside, and saw Molly and her mom walking off the driveway onto the sidewalk along the road. "Molly!" she said loudly.

Molly and Mrs. Robinson both stopped and turned around. "What?" asked Molly in a volume that was loud enough to be heard.

"Did you say my name just now?"

"No. I'm just walking back home."

"Okay. Bye!"

"Bye!" said Molly.

Once again, Gabby shut the door, and she wondered who said her name. If it wasn't Molly or Mrs. Felding, then who else could it have been? *There's no such thing as ghosts,* she thought, *so it couldn't have been a ghost.* She also eliminated the possibility of thinking she was just hearing things. Without a doubt, she was certain she heard her name. However, the voice she heard was a very soft, faint voice that was almost like a whisper with no vocal sound, so it was impossible to determine who said it.

Suddenly, the recollection of exactly what the voice said was drawn to her thoughts, and she realized she had heard the voice calling her by the name of Gabrielle. She knew that everyone called her Gabby, and she didn't know anyone who ever called her Gabrielle. Coming to the conclusion that it was impossible to know who said her name, she decided not to worry while she remembered what Mr. Felding said. *If quiet noises can't hurt anyone, then quiet voices can't hurt anyone either,* she thought.

Throughout Sophie's piano lesson, Gabrielle stood beside the piano, watching and listening as much as she could. Once again, Sophie didn't mind having an audience.

After the forty-five minute lesson, Sophie was curious to know how much Gabby had learned by observing so much. She turned to Gabby. "Hey, Gabby, since you've been watching my lessons for several Saturdays, you know how *I* play. Could you play something for me on the piano so I can hear how *you* play?" she asked while she and Mrs. Felding stood up from the piano bench.

Gabby sat down at the piano. After having practiced for fifteen minutes every day for several weeks, she played her recently mastered version of "Twinkle, Twinkle, Little Star," using both hands. Then she played "Row, Row, Row Your Boat" with no mistakes.

Sophie was impressed. At the end of the song, she complimented Gabby while she applauded. "Nice!" she exclaimed.

"Hey, Gabby," said Mrs. Felding. "How about play the other song for her that you've been working on."

After hearing Mrs. Felding's suggestion, Gabby was a bit hesitant to play it. She wasn't anywhere close to mastering it, and she didn't want Sophie to be unimpressed. Not wanting Mrs. Felding to feel rejected by declining her suggestion, she slowly raised her fingers above the keys. Uncertain about whether she should lower her fingers down onto the keys, she debated within herself about what she should do. With a hesitant expression, she turned to look at Sophie. "You can do it," encouraged Sophie. Gabby then placed her fingers onto the keys and began to play a simplified version of "Ode to Joy."

After a few seconds into the song, she suddenly stopped and turned to face Sophie. "Huh?" she asked.

"Keep going . . . unless you don't remember any more of it," said Sophie.

"But I *was* playing it. You said my name just to tell me to keep going?"

"I didn't say your name," Sophie said.

Gabby quickly turned to face Mrs. Felding. "I didn't say your name either. Go ahead and play some more," said Mrs. Felding, motioning to the piano keys.

"But someone said my name," said Gabby.

Sophie and Mrs. Felding looked at each other, and Sophie shrugged her shoulders. Speaking to Sophie, Mrs. Felding mentioned, "Earlier today, she thought she heard me say her name."

"Maybe it was that quiet noise she heard again," said Sophie.

"No, it wasn't that quiet noise," said Mrs. Felding, not knowing that Sophie was unknowingly correct. "She said it was a voice."

Sophie faced Gabby. "Now you're hearing voices instead of noises? But I didn't hear a voice."

"That's because it was too quiet," said Gabby.

"If it was really that quiet," said Sophie, "then how did you hear it over the volume of the piano?"

"I don't know," said Gabby. "I just did."

"Hmm," voiced Sophie. "Well, no matter what you heard, what was the title of the last song you were playing?"

"It's called 'Ode to Joy,'" Gabby said.

"Ode to Joy?" repeated Sophie. "That title doesn't sound familiar. Is it a new song?"

"Oh, no," said Mrs. Felding. "It was first written as a poem in 1785, and Beethoven later composed it into a symphony in 1824."

"Whoa, it's that old?" said Sophie, looking at Mrs. Felding. "Why didn't you want to teach Gabby a newer song?"

Mrs. Felding replied, "Gabby's actually the one who wanted to learn this one. After she completed 'Row, Row, Row Your Boat,' I asked her what she wanted to learn next. I read the titles of several beginner piano songs to her that were all newer than this one, and she said she never heard of any of them. She wanted to play one that sounded familiar to her, and she's the one who mentioned Beethoven."

Sophie turned to Gabby. "You knew about Beethoven? Nobody your age has ever heard of Beethoven!"

"*I* did," said Gabby. "Someone once told me about him."

"Who?" asked Sophie.

Gabby shrugged her shoulders. "I don't know," she said.

"Well, if you know about Beethoven," said Sophie, "I've been learning about other composers—more recent than Beethoven—in my music class at school. Have you heard of George Gershwin?" Gabby shook her head. "He composed several songs including 'Rhapsody In Blue' and 'I Got Rhythm.' Do those sound familiar?" Again, Gabby shook her head. "Okay. Have you heard of Scott Joplin?"

"No," Gabby said.

"He composed the famous song called 'The Entertainer.' Does that one sound familiar?" asked Sophie.

"No," said Gabby while shaking her head.

"No?" repeated Sophie who would have been more surprised if Gabby was any older than four. "Well, how about Sergei Rachmaninoff? Have you heard of him?"

Gabby expressed a facial look of unfamiliarity. "Who?"

"Hmm," voiced Sophie. "It doesn't sound like you've heard of him either."

"Are they still alive?" Gabby asked.

"No, they aren't. They were all born more than one hundred years ago," answered Sophie.

Gabby was confused. "More than one hundred years? Then why did you say they were more recent than Beethoven? He was born less than one hundred years ago."

"Uh . . . no, Gabby," said Mrs. Felding. "He was born in 1770. That was 249 years ago."

"But someone told me he was born less than one hundred years ago."

"Maybe they were talking about someone else," said Mrs. Felding.

Sophie turned to Gabby again. "Have you heard of *any* composers besides Beethoven?"

"Uh-huh," said Gabby while nodding her head. "Mozart, Chopin, and . . . the new guy."

"The new guy?" asked Sophie. "You actually heard about a recent composer? Do you remember his name?"

Gabby took a moment to try to remember his name. *Mozart, Chopin, and . . .* she thought, silently going over the names again in her head. "I think it was a long name that's hard to say." Trying to remember the name and how to pronounce it, she decided to give it one more shot. "Oh, now I remember. His name is Tchaikovsky. I haven't heard any of his songs yet, but I heard he's very good!"

"Tchaikovsky?" repeated Mrs. Felding. "Sweetheart, there's only one composer named Tchaikovsky that I'm aware of, and just because you haven't heard any of his songs doesn't mean he's a recent composer."

"But isn't he still alive?" asked Gabby.

"Heavens, no!" said Mrs. Felding. "He lived a long time ago."

"Before Beethoven?"

"No, not that long ago. I'm not sure exactly when. Let me find out." Mrs. Felding grabbed her phone to find a website about Tchaikovsky. She searched for a few seconds, and she found the answer. "He was born in 1840, and he died in 1893."

"Yeah, that *was* a long time ago!" said Sophie. "He died five years before George Gershwin was even born!"

*But I thought he was still alive. How could it be that long ago?* Gabrielle wondered. "If he really lived a long time ago, then what songs did he write?" she asked.

"I don't know," said Sophie. "We haven't gotten that far back in my music class yet. The oldest composer who we're learning about so far is Scott Joplin, and he was born in 1868."

"I know some of the songs by Tchaikovsky," said Mrs. Felding. "He composed '1812 Overture' and 'Violin Concerto.' Have you heard of those?" she asked Gabby who then shook her head. "And another popular one he did is called 'The Nutcracker.' Does that one sound familiar?"

"The Nutcracker?" repeated Gabby. "It sounds familiar," she said, taking a few seconds to try to think of why it sounded familiar, "but I don't think I ever heard a song with that name. Someone once read a book to me that was called *The Nutcracker and the Mouse King*."

Mrs. Felding couldn't recall ever hearing about a book by that title before. "I never heard of that book," she said.

"Do you remember who read it to you?" Sophie asked Gabby.

"I can't remember," said Gabby.

"Well, I need to go back home," Sophie said while she started walking to the front door. I'll see you again next Saturday."

While Gabrielle was in bed that night, Mr. and Mrs. Felding sat on the couch in the living room. "Another interesting day?" Mr. Felding assumed.

Mrs. Felding nodded her head. "Like always."

"What happened *this* time?"

"You'll never believe it! Today, she said she heard a quiet voice, but nobody else could hear it. Apparently, the voice called her by name, and she heard it more than once. She thought it was either me, Molly, or Sophie who said her name, but none of us mentioned her name at the time she heard the voice. But that's not all. Right after Sophie's piano lesson, Sophie wanted to hear how Gabby was coming along at what she's been learning on the piano. After Gabby played part of 'Ode to Joy,' the three of us started talking about classic composers. Along with Beethoven, Gabby had also heard of Mozart and Chopin, but here's where it gets interesting. She thought Tchaikovsky was the new guy, and she never heard of any composers who were born after him. She never heard of any songs that were composed by Tchaikovsky, but 'The Nutcracker' sounded familiar to her only because someone once read a book to her that was called *The Nutcracker and the Mouse King*.

Afterwards, I looked up the title of that book online, and I found a website that said it was published in 1816, and that's also the book that inspired Tchaikovsky to compose 'The Nutcracker.' I didn't even know such a book existed, so how did she know about a book that was written so long ago?"

"It's not how *she* knew about it," said Mr. Felding. "It's whoever read her the book. But I wouldn't consider the age of the book as a mystery. The Bible was written many centuries ago, and it's not out of print, so whether the other book is out of print or not, it could have been an old book that was handed down through generations."

"That's a possibility, but what gets me wondering is how she knows about everything that's very old, and nothing that's any newer. She even told me she wants to play 'Moonlight Sonata' when she gets a little older, and I never told her about that song. It's another one that Beethoven composed," said Mrs. Felding.

"Today at work, I was also wondering how she knows so much about history," said Mr. Felding. "I've been trying to find out how she didn't know about anything new when we found her, and who told her about everything that happened or existed a long time ago. I'm still trying to find out how she knew about a horse and buggy and didn't know what a car was. And while I was at work, I realized we haven't taken Gabby to the furniture store yet, so maybe you could take her on Monday since I work most of the day, and then we'll find out if someone told her about the antique styles of furniture compared to the newer styles now days."

"That sounds like a good idea, so I'll plan on doing that. But for now, let's watch our shows before it gets too late."

The following Monday on the 25th day of November, Mrs. Felding talked with Gabrielle about the plans of going to the furniture store just to look around. After eating lunch and getting ready, Mrs. Felding helped Gabrielle get buckled onto the booster seat in the car before they headed off to the furniture store.

Soon after they entered the store and started looking at the numerous selections of various types of furniture and appliances, Gabrielle noticed her dad at a distance in another section of the store. She pointed to him while saying, "There's Dad!" and started walking towards him.

Mrs. Felding looked in the direction to where Gabrielle was pointing. Quickly, she got Gabby's attention. "No, Gabby! Stay here." Gabby immediately stopped and turned around to face Mrs. Felding. "It looks like your dad is with another customer. If he's helping the customer with a sale, then we don't want to interrupt. Let's just look around the store and wait until he's done."

While walking through the different sections of the store, Gabrielle was puzzled once again. Although the furniture was a similar style to what Mr. and Mrs. Felding had in their house, she often turned her head in different directions to look everywhere in trying to find the styles that she was most familiar with.

Eventually, Mrs. Felding and Gabrielle arrived at the location where the couches were stationed. Mrs. Felding sat down on a couch that looked relatively comfortable while Gabrielle walked around the couch area, appearing like she was looking for something.

After noticing that Gabby was not interested in sitting down, Mrs. Felding continued to watch her for a moment while she seemed to be acting suspicious. "What's wrong, Sweetie? Are you looking for something? You should come feel how comfortable these couches are!"

Gabby briefly continued to face different directions in a hopeless search. Then she turned to face Mrs. Felding. "Where are the other couches?" she asked.

"The couches are all right here. What couches are you trying to find?" said Mrs. Felding while standing up and starting to walk over to Gabby.

"The ones that have wood around them. And some of them had a lot of buttons on the back part."

Continuing to walk the short distance to Gabby, Mrs. Felding reached into her purse and pulled out her cell phone. Previously assuming that Gabby would bring up this topic, she had gotten prepared. She turned on the phone, and shown on the screen were photos of antique couches she had found online earlier that day. When she arrived at Gabby's side, she held out the phone to show her. "Are you talking about couches like these?" Mrs. Felding asked.

Looking at the photos on the phone, Gabrielle grew another expression of familiarity on her face. "Yeah, like those," she said. "Where are these couches? Are they at another furniture store?"

"As a matter of fact," said Mrs. Felding, "they are, but I don't know where those furniture stores are. I found these photos online from websites that don't have a street address," she explained while she put her phone away, "so maybe these antique couches are only sold online."

"What does *antique* mean?" Gabby asked.

"Antique means it was made a very long time ago."

"Are those couches old?" asked Gabby, pointing to Mrs. Felding's purse where the phone had been placed.

"Lots of them are actually new from wherever antique styles are made, but it's the style that's old."

Later that night, Gabrielle sat in the living room in her pajamas while watching cartoons on television, having already brushed her teeth. Although the cartoons were no entertainment for adults, Mr. and Mrs. Felding sat in the living room with Gabby. Mr. Felding kept his attention on what he was reading in the newspaper, and Mrs. Felding kept her attention on doing her puzzle book while constantly staying aware of the time.

When the clock reached Gabrielle's bedtime, Mrs. Felding immediately spoke without hesitation. "Time for bed, Gabby."

"Okay," Gabby said while taking ahold of the remote. She pointed it towards the television and pushed the red button to turn it off. Although she wanted to watch more cartoons that she had been enjoying, she had an even greater desire to follow Molly's example of obeying her parents, knowing that obedience in the home generally ends up with better results than the contrary.

Mrs. Felding set her puzzle book down, stood up, went with Gabby to her bedroom, and tucked her into bed. Once again, she leaned over and gave Gabby a kiss on her forehead. "Goodnight, Gabby," said Mrs. Felding.

"Goodnight," said Gabrielle. "I love you, Mom."

Mrs. Felding smiled. "I love you too, Princess."

A few minutes later, sitting on the couch beside Mrs. Felding, Mr. Felding spoke quietly as to not wake or disturb Gabrielle. "I went to the police station during my lunch break today."

"Did Officer Gunwell say anything about finding Gabby's parents," said Mrs. Felding while Mr. Felding shook his head, "or anything that might lead up to it?"

"No. He said his search crew found several ladies named Martha in both the living and the deceased, but none of them were any possibility of being related to Gabby in any way. He also said this was the most impossible search he had ever done in his twenty-six years as a police officer."

"So let me get this straight," said Mrs. Felding. "The names of Harold and Martha Linstrom sounded and felt familiar to Gabby, but there are no direct, ancestral lines between them, and we know the name of her mother is not Martha?"

As complicated and ridiculous as it seemed, Mr. Felding could not deny what his wife had just said. He nodded while he said, "It sounds like you hit the nail on the head."

Wanting to figure it out by making sense of anything, Mrs. Felding started asking, "But why . . ."

Hearing his wife speak in a tone of great confusion at the beginning of a question that was followed by a pause because of not quite knowing what to ask, Mr. Felding discontinued her question. "Don't try to figure anything out. This is Gabby we're talking about. Trying to figure out anything about her is like trying to balance a vertical toothpick on top of another vertical one. She's with us, we're a family, and that's all we can figure out."

# 9

# BACK IN THE DAYS

Throughout the remaining days before Thanksgiving, Gabrielle constantly continued to hear the quiet voice whisper her name. At one point, Mrs. Felding wished she had a Halloween costume to wear just to ward off ghosts after being tired of hearing Gabby ask who said her name. As time went on, the voice kept calling out to Gabby more and more often, but she was always the only one who could hear it. Mr. Felding even wondered whether Gabby was just pretending to hear voices just like the day they found her when she pretended Officer Gunwell was invisible.

On the night before Thanksgiving, Mrs. Felding tucked Gabby into bed. "Mom," Gabby said quietly.

"What is it, Sweetheart?" responded Mrs. Felding in a low volume.

"How are we going to find out who keeps saying my name?"

"Gabby, we've been through this several times, and your dad thinks you're just pretending to hear voices."

"No, I'm not pretending," said Gabby while shaking her head, facing upward while resting on her pillow. "I know I could hear someone saying my name."

"Well, let's stop talking about it and get to sleep. Let's try to have a good holiday tomorrow by not saying anything about it. Alright?" said Mrs. Felding in a gentle tone.

"Alright," agreed Gabby. "I love you, Mom."

"I love you too, Sweetheart. Goodnight." Mrs. Felding leaned over, gave Gabby a kiss on her forehead, and started heading away. She turned out the bedroom light on her way to the living room.

Later that night while everyone was asleep, a louder voice sounded. It was the same voice, but it wasn't a whisper anymore. This time, a vocal sound was heard. "Gabrielle," the voice called out.

Gabrielle immediately awoke, and the sound of the voice instantly caught hold of her memory. "Ma!" she said aloud right after opening her eyes. "Ma, where are you?" she asked in the dark. But there was no response.

After waiting a few seconds for an answer to her question, Gabby let out a big yawn. Having heard the voice, she knew that her mother must have been somewhere near. Feeling quite sleepy with heavy eyelids, she decided to wait until morning to find her mother, so she closed her eyes and went back to sleep.

The morning of Thanksgiving Day arrived. Gabrielle awoke to the smell of breakfast being cooked. She got out of bed, got dressed for the day into one of the outfits that was worn by one of the Felding daughters, and then started heading to the kitchen.

Halfway to the kitchen from her bedroom, Gabrielle heard her name from the same voice, loud and clear. She stopped and turned around to look behind her, but there was no sight of her mother. "Where are you, Ma?" she said quietly as to not let Mrs. Felding hear, remembering the agreement she had made to not say anything about hearing voices for helping everyone to have a good holiday.

A moment later, Mrs. Felding caught the sight of Gabby at the kitchen entryway. "Good morning, Sweetheart."

"Good morning, Mom," said Gabby while entering the kitchen.

"I thought I heard you say something a few seconds ago. Were you talking to someone?"

Not wanting to break her agreement, Gabby quickly tried thinking of something to say besides mentioning a voice that nobody else seemed to hear. "I was talking to myself," she said. Wanting to remain honest, and knowing that nobody else could hear the voice that she could hear, she knew her answer to Mrs. Felding's question was an honest answer in the point of view of everyone who couldn't hear the voice.

"Well, breakfast is almost ready, and your dad should be here in just a minute," said Mrs. Felding while carrying the dishes to the table, knowing that most kids at Gabby's age have quite the imagination, and not wondering why Gabby was talking to herself.

After everyone was finished eating breakfast of pancakes and scrambled eggs, they went into the living room to watch the Thanksgiving Day parade on television just as Mr. Felding had suggested during breakfast time. "Is anyone else coming to spend Thanksgiving with us?" asked Gabby.

"No, Sweetheart," answered Mrs. Felding. "Our four kids are all married, and it's the in-laws' turn for Thanksgiving this year."

They all sat down, and Mr. Felding grabbed the remote to turn on the television. "Then what are we going to do today if nobody else is coming?" Gabby asked.

Mrs. Felding replied, "After the parade, your dad and I will start preparing the Thanksgiving dinner. He has the day off work, so we'll all be home throughout the day."

"Dinner?" expressed Gabby. "What about lunch? What if I get hungry?"

Mr. Felding then replied, "Traditionally, it's called Thanksgiving dinner, but it will be ready at about two o'clock for a late lunch. It's one of the biggest meals of the year, and it's not good to eat too much when it's too late in the day, so we'll have to eat enough to last for the rest of the day."

While watching the parade, Gabrielle was struck with amazement. She had never seen so many people in one crowd before, nor had she ever seen balloons the size of a building. While being amazed throughout the entire broadcast of the parade, she also heard her name a few more times, but Mr. and Mrs. Felding didn't seem to hear it. However, the more she heard the voice of her mother, the more that things were brought back to her memory.

After the parade, Gabrielle went into the kitchen with Mr. and Mrs. Felding to help prepare the food. The adults worked mostly around the oven and the stovetop while Gabby helped gather ingredients as well as stir mixtures of ingredients together.

Just as Gabby expected, she continued to hear her name. But where was her mother? And how could Gabby hear a voice from someone who was nowhere to be seen? Occasionally, Gabby turned her head to look around the room to see if her mother was in sight, but she didn't dare say a single word about it.

Sitting at the table, eating their Thanksgiving feast, Gabby was silent. She wanted to tell Mr. and Mrs. Felding the things she remembered, but they all related to hearing her mother's voice. Still determined to keep her agreement she had made with Mrs. Felding the night before, she didn't know if saying anything that related to hearing a voice would ruin anyone's holiday.

Realizing the silence from Gabby, Mr. Felding assumed it was because she couldn't think of anything to say. With everyone feasting upon their Thanksgiving meal, he turned to her and asked, "How do you like it, Gabby? Does it taste good?"

Gabby turned to Mr. Felding, gave a half smile, and said, "It tastes . . ." Suddenly, she heard her name from her mother's voice once again, which brought back another memory. She looked away from Mr. Felding, and it appeared that she was staring off into space.

Mr. Felding waited a few seconds for Gabby to think of the word to describe how the food tasted. Eventually, he realized the blank look on Gabby's face wasn't because she was trying to think of a word. "What's wrong, Precious?"

"I remember something."

"What do you remember?" asked Mrs. Felding.

Gabby spent three or four seconds to think about what had just now come to her memory, and then she said, "I know where I live."

Mr. and Mrs. Felding looked at each other in response to Gabby's reply, and then Mrs. Felding turned back to Gabby. "You remember where your house is?"

"Yeah. It's close to where you found me."

"Uh," voiced Mr. Felding, "we found you about six months ago. How long have you known this?"

"I just now remembered," said Gabby.

"But, Sweetheart, the field where we found you has nothing besides trees, and there are no houses anywhere along that road," said Mrs. Felding.

"No," said Gabby while shaking her head, "there *has* to be a house in the field because that's where I came from."

"Precious," said Mr. Felding, "just because you came from the field doesn't mean there was a house there."

"No," corrected Gabby, "I was talking about the house where I came from . . . not the field."

"But there are no houses anywhere around there," said Mrs. Felding.

"Yes, there is," disagreed Gabby. "It's not far from where you found me."

"Well, how about we drive to the place after we finish eating," Mr. Felding said, "and we'll show you there aren't any houses." Gabby gave another half smile and nodded her head.

After they all finished their feast and cleared off the table, they grabbed their coats, left the house, got into the car, and drove to the field, which was located two miles away. While driving to the field, Gabby paid close attention to the directions in how to get there.

Mr. Felding parked the car on the side of the road—the side by the outskirts of the field where Gabby was at when they first saw her. Then they got out of the car. When they were all standing close to the car on the passenger side, Mr. Felding told Gabby, "Okay. Take us to where you think the house is at, and we'll follow you."

Gabby started heading away from the road into the forest of trees, and her foster parents followed. "It's not far from the tree stump," she said. However, there was no tree stump in sight.

After walking for a minute, Mrs. Felding had a thought. Speaking loud enough for Gabby to hear above the sound of footsteps, she mentioned, "What if we find your house? Will your parents be there? And how would you know your parents if you can't remember their names?"

"My ma's name is Martha, and my pa's name is Harold," said Gabby in a tone of confidence while continuing the journey.

Mr. and Mrs. Felding looked at each other with a look of astonishment, and Mr. Felding shrugged his shoulders. Quietly, he said, "I suppose it's possible for the names of both parents to be the same as President and Mrs. Linstrom."

In a low volume, Mrs. Felding added, "And who refers to their parents by the names of ma and pa anymore?"

Gabby started walking slower. Looking to the right and to the left, it appeared as though she was lost. "Why are we slowing down?" Mr. Felding asked. "Are you lost?"

Gabby stopped. She slowly continued to turn her head in different directions. "I'm not lost," she said. "But these trees weren't here before."

"Which trees?" asked Mrs. Felding.

"Almost all of them. There were only a few trees when I was here before." Gabby paused while she turned her head once again to see so many enormous trees that were nowhere in her memory before the day when Mr. and Mrs. Felding found her. "And the road where we parked was a dirt road that wasn't paved. I remember there were trees on the other side of the road, and there were no buildings." Then she turned back to the direction where she had been walking, and she slowly continued.

Mr. and Mrs. Felding looked at each other once again, both feeling somewhat perplexed. "She *does* have quite the imagination," whispered Mrs. Felding.

"She has to be pretending again," said Mr. Felding in the same volume. "But are we ever going to find out why?"

Suddenly, Gabby shouted for joy. "There's the tree stump!" she exclaimed while she pointed to it. She ran over to it in the distance of a few yards. She sat down on the stump that stood about eighteen inches above the ground with the top of it that sloped down at an angle. And speaking loud enough for Mr. and Mrs. Felding to hear through the short distance while they continued to walk to the same location, Gabby said to them, "This used to be my favorite tree stump. I used to sit here a lot."

When the adults reached the tree stump, Mr. Felding said to Gabby, "You said your house was not far from the tree stump. Now that you found the stump, where's the house?"

"It's on the other side of the little pond," replied Gabby.

Mr. and Mrs. Felding looked around in all directions, and there was no pond in sight. "How far away is the pond?" asked Mr. Felding.

Gabby pointed in the direction. "It's right over there."

The two foster parents took one more look. "There's no pond over there," Mrs. Felding said.

Gabby stood up from the stump. She looked in the direction where she remembered the pond was located. With no pond to be seen, she started wondering whether she was lost. Wondering if she had found a different tree stump, she examined it and, sure enough, it was the same stump with part of a thick root that stuck out of the ground about two inches at the very base of the stump. Making sure she wasn't confused with directions, she took one more look at where the thick root pointed, which always faced the pond. To satisfy her curiosity, she headed away from the stump in search of the pond, and the parents followed.

After walking slowly for another two minutes, she finally came to the conclusion there was not only no pond, but there was also no house. Again, she stopped. Feeling and sounding worried, she said, "What happened? Where is it? Where's the house? It was right here!" Then, speaking much louder, she shouted, "Ma! Pa! Where are you?"

Suddenly, she heard the voice of her father calling out her name, sounding as though he was only a few feet away. "Gabrielle!"

Gabby turned to look in all directions, but her pa wasn't anywhere in sight. *Was that another voice that Mom and Dad can't hear?* she thought. She briefly looked over to Mr. and Mrs. Felding who both had unknown looks on their faces, but neither one of them was responding to her father's voice that she had clearly heard. *They probably didn't hear him, so I better not ruin their holiday.*

"Sweetheart," said Mrs. Felding in a gentle tone, "there's nothing around here. This is what we tried to tell you before we left home. It doesn't look like there was ever a pond or a house around here."

"But there *was*. They were right here. I remember."

"Whether there was or wasn't, we certainly can't do anything about it now," said Mr. Felding. "Let's go home and enjoy the rest of our holiday."

That night, Mrs. Felding tucked Gabby into bed. "We've had quite a day today, so we need to get to sleep quickly." She leaned over and gave Gabby another kiss on her forehead just like she had been doing every night for several weeks. "Goodnight, Gabby."

"Mom," said Gabby, "is it okay if I tell you other things I remember?"

"Only if it doesn't lead to looking for something that doesn't exist. Is there something else you can remember?"

"Uh-huh. I remember my sisters."

"You do? Do you remember having any brothers?"

"I don't have any brothers. I only have three sisters."

"And do you remember their names?" asked Mrs. Felding.

"My older sister is Abigail, and my younger sisters are Sabrina and Tabitha."

Immediately startled at what she had just heard, Mrs. Felding quickly assumed that Gabby must have somehow been pretending, or that it must have been a huge coincidence. She then gave Gabby a half smile. "Well, let's go to sleep now. I love you."

"I love you too, Mom."

Mrs. Felding walked to the doorway, turned out the light, closed the bedroom door on her way out, walked through the hallway, entered the living room, and sat down on the couch beside her husband.

Mr. Felding noticed a startled look on her face. "What's wrong?" he asked.

"I think this one tops them all. Earlier today, Gabby told us the names of her parents . . ."

"And she must have been pretending," interrupted Mr. Felding, "because Officer Gunwell already did a search for anyone named Martha, and we know the conclusion of that."

"But it's not just the names of her parents. Just one or two minutes ago, she told me the names of her three sisters—Abigail, Sabrina, and Tabitha."

"She's definitely pretending. Maybe she wants to pretend to have sisters, and she must like the names of President Linstrom's daughters." Mr. Felding paused for a moment. "And she can't be the same Gabrielle who was President Linstrom's daughter. Traveling through time only happens in movies and books. It doesn't ever happen in real life."

"When will we find out the reasons for anything about her?" asked Mrs. Felding.

"I don't know, but I think we'll need to have a good talk with her tomorrow about being honest. It's one thing to pretend, but when it leads to searching for something that was never there, then one's imagination could get out of control."

Meanwhile, Gabrielle couldn't get to sleep. She kept hearing the voices of both her mother and her father calling out her name. She hadn't seen them in over six months, and her desire to see them again was constantly increasing. She also wondered how everything could change so much in the time of only six months—how the cemetery could get so big, how hundreds of buildings were built, how numerous cars were made, where the horses and buggies went, how drastic the style of clothing had changed, how the school went from one room to multiple rooms, how so many things were invented, what happened to her house and the little pond, and many more thoughts that kept her awake for much of the night.

The next morning just minutes before the break of dawn, Gabrielle awoke to the sound of her mother calling out her name once again. Lying in the dark, not knowing what time it was, her overwhelming desire to see her parents and her sisters kept her awake. She hadn't gotten much sleep, but the amount of sleep she got was enough to wonder how she was ever going to see her family again. She

 sat up in bed, faced the window that let in a touch of moonlight, and she thought back to the day when she first saw Mr. and Mrs. Felding. *Before I walked along the road,* she thought, *I remember I stood up from sitting on the tree stump, and I felt lost because nothing looked familiar. Then I walked to the road to try to find someone to help me, and that's when I first saw Mom and Dad. But how did I get to the tree stump? Where was I at before I sat down on it?*

After a few minutes of wondering where she came from before the point of finding herself on the stump six months ago, she decided it was hopeless. No matter how hard she tried, she couldn't remember how she got there. A tear streamed down her cheek while she figured she might never see her family again. But how could she hear their voices?

At the break of dawn with the smallest ounce of sunlight in the sky, Gabrielle's curiosity started leading her to different thoughts. *If I go back to the tree stump, will it help me remember where I came from? But how am I going to get there? I don't think Mom or Dad would want to take me back there again. And if I go by myself, then Mom will get mad at me.*

Gabrielle was placed into a difficult situation. The only way to find out where she came from and how she was ever going to see her family again would be to disobey her foster mom. And getting someone else such as Mrs. Robinson to take her there was just as unlikely as getting her foster parents to take her. But how would they believe her reasoning for going back to the tree stump any more than they believed she was hearing voices?

One more time, Gabrielle heard her mother's voice calling out her name. Wanting so desperately to see her again, she concluded that the only way to see her mother was to find out where she came from, and there was only one possible place to do that. However, the only way to get to the place was to be disobedient, but Gabby was still determined to be like Molly.

Another tear ran down Gabrielle's cheek as she looked out the window at the sky that was getting an ever slight touch brighter. There was just no way to return back to the stump and remain honest. Then another thought came. *If I go alone,* she thought, *and if it helps me remember where I came from, then maybe Mom will understand why I went all by myself.*

Finally, Gabrielle stood up. Still a little too dark, she found her way over to her bedroom door, and she turned on the light. Although the time was only 5:42 in the morning, she got dressed for the day into another outfit that was worn by the Felding daughters. She put on her shoes, grabbed her coat and her teddy bear, returned to her bedroom door, turned out the light, quietly opened the door, and silently headed to the front door without making the slightest sound.

When she arrived at the door, she slowly put on her coat. Then she left and closed the door behind her as quiet as can be. She took a few steps to begin her long journey before she stopped and turned around to face the house. Looking at the house, she thought to herself, *I'll come back later today after I find out where I came from, how I got here, and where my family is.* However, she had no idea how the day would turn out. She turned back around and headed on her way.

Walking down the sidewalk past the Robinsons' house, everything was quiet and peaceful. According to what she saw, there were no cars on the street. The daylight in the sky had noticeably increased, and it was light enough to see everything, especially with the added light that was still coming from the streetlights. Constantly, she paid attention to which roads to take while always remembering how to get to the destination from what she observed the previous day.

Close to seven o'clock after walking the two-mile distance, Gabrielle safely arrived onto the field of trees, which was about the same time Mrs. Felding woke up.

Three minutes later, Gabrielle found the stump and walked over to it. She sat down on it and tried to remember what happened over six months ago. She held on to her teddy bear and waited for the memory to come back.

Gradually, she found herself struggling to grab on to a memory that seemed to be lost forever. How did she get separated from her family, and what happened before sitting on the stump on the day when the world drastically changed? As long as it would take to remember, Gabrielle decided she wasn't going to leave until she had answers to her questions. After all, if she were to return home with no logical reason as to why she disobeyed, then it wouldn't be a pretty sight.

Every minute that passed, Gabrielle tried harder and harder at her attempt to remember. Her desire to see her family was also increasing more and more with time.

Thirty minutes after seven, she started feeling hungry. She had not yet eaten breakfast, and the memory that she endeavored to find had also not come back. With nothing to eat, her only option for filling her stomach was to walk two miles back home. Unknowingly, there was also a grocery store located half a mile away in the opposite direction, but with no money, she wouldn't have been able to purchase anything if she had known where to go. Nevertheless, she was still committed to not leaving the tree stump until her questions were answered.

Ten minutes later with still no hope of remembering how she got to the tree stump in the month of May, she pondered the sound of her mother's voice. Then she thought about the times she spent with her family before she was somehow detached from them. She missed the times when she played games with Abigail and Sabrina. She missed the times when she helped take care of her baby sister, Tabitha. She missed the hugs and kisses from her mother, and she missed the times that were spent with her father including helping to milk the cows. With so many memories she missed so much, she wished she could live those memories once again. She wished so hard that all other wants seemed trivial.

Suddenly, she remembered who she is. *I'm Gabrielle Anne Linstrom,* she thought. Then she looked all around her at the vast amount of trees, and most of them started fading away.

After a few seconds, the trees that were fading away were all gone, and the land was widespread. It was back to how it looked before she had forgotten on that day in May, and she was also back to the year of 1869, which was something she wouldn't know until later. She turned her head, and she saw the small pond. And looking farther away in the same direction, she noticed a familiar house that stood a ways off at a distance. Everything was now restored to her memory including what happened on the day when everything changed and memories were forgotten.

With joy that filled her heart to the fullest extent, she quickly grew a big smile, stood up from the tree stump, and ran the distance past the pond all the way to the house.

A few feet away from reaching the front door, Gabrielle heard familiar voices coming from inside. Even though anyone in this situation would normally feel excited to see loved ones who haven't been seen for a long time, she started feeling nervous. What would she say? How would she explain her drastic change of life during the previous six months? Who could possibly explain the trees fading away as well as the house that came back after it didn't exist? No matter what she would need to try to explain, Gabrielle knew she couldn't stay outside forever, so she started inching her way to the door and slowly started to open it.

Standing by the stove in the kitchen, working on cooking breakfast, Mrs. Linstrom turned her head to see who was coming as soon as the door started to open. *What on earth is happening? Who forgot to latch the door?* she started thinking to herself. Then the door opened a little more, and a four-year-old face came into view. "Gabrielle?" asked Mrs. Linstrom. "Is that you?"

Gabrielle looked in the direction where her mother's voice was coming from. For the first time in over six months, they were finally reunited. Gabrielle gave a big smile. "Ma!" she said in a joyful tone. Suddenly, she dropped her teddy bear, and the two of them ran to each other in the short distance, met halfway, and gave each other the biggest possible hug.

Tears of joy ran down Mrs. Linstrom's cheeks. "Where *were* you? We've been looking all over for you!"

"I was staying in a house with . . ."

Right at that moment, Mr. Linstrom walked into the room while asking his wife, "Whom are you talking to?" Immediately, he noticed the four-year-old girl who then turned to face him, but it took him a second to realize who was standing there. "Is that Gabrielle?"

"Pa!" she said, giving another big smile. Without hesitation, she ran over to him and gave him a big hug.

"I almost didn't recognize you with your haircut," said Mr. Linstrom to his daughter, "and it looks like you've grown an inch or two."

"Who cut your hair?" Ma asked Gabrielle right when Abigail walked into the kitchen after entering the house through the back door, carrying a basket of eggs.

"The eggs are all gathered," said Abigail, immediately seeing a young girl in a strange outfit from behind. "What in the world?" she expressed right before placing the basket gently onto the table.

Gabrielle turned around and recognized her older sister. "Abigail!"

"Gabrielle! You came back?" The two sisters hurried toward each other and gave each other a hug. Then Abigail took a step back and briefly examined what Gabrielle was wearing. "What in the world are you wearing? You should know that girls don't wear trousers!"

109

Up until that point, Ma and Pa were both too overjoyed in seeing Gabrielle to notice her outfit. "Your sister's right," said Pa. "Go change into something more appropriate."

"But I don't have anything. Remember? The dresses I had six months ago were all getting too small, and I'm even bigger now than I was."

"What about the dress you were wearing when you left us last May?" Ma asked. "That one had a little bit of room to grow into it, so it should fit you by now. Where is it?"

Gabrielle replied, "I left it at the other house."

"What other house?" asked Pa.

"The house where I was staying when I was gone."

"For being gone this long, and seeing you're still alive," said Ma, "someone must have fed you and took care of you. Whom did you stay with?"

"And where's their house?" asked Pa.

"I stayed with the Feldings, and they live two miles away," Gabrielle answered.

"Felding?" asked Ma. "The name doesn't sound familiar. Do you know their first names?"

"Yes," said Gabrielle. "Their names are George and Linda."

"Hmm," voiced Ma. "I haven't heard about them. How long have they lived there?"

"I don't know," said Gabrielle, "but I stayed with them ever since the officers let me out of the police station."

Ma and Pa looked at each other with facial expressions of extreme disappointment and concern, knowing that Gabrielle just confessed she spent time with the police. Pa took a few steps toward Gabrielle, and then he stopped. He put his hands on his hips and spoke firmly to her. "Now, young lady, why did you leave us?"

"I didn't leave you," said Gabrielle in a tone of innocence. "All I did was sit on the tree stump and, a minute later, I saw hundreds of trees around me. Then I got lost."

"Gabrielle," said Ma, "you wouldn't have gotten lost if you didn't go wandering off into the woods."

"But I didn't wander off. When I saw hundreds of trees, it was when I was still sitting on the tree stump."

Knowing how widespread the land looked from the stump, Ma and Pa looked at each other once again, and they were both speechless at that point. "We'll talk more about this after breakfast," Ma said.

With the front door still opened, Pa walked towards it to close it. Standing within reach of the door, he looked down and saw a stuffed

110

bear lying on the floor. He bent down, picked it up, and closed the door. "Where did this toy bear come from?" he asked.

Gabrielle turned to look at Pa. "That's mine. The officers at the police station gave it to me."

Ma turned to face Abigail. "Could you go wake up Sabrina for me? It's time for breakfast."

"Okay," said Abigail in a willing manner while starting to head to the back area of the house where Sabrina and Tabitha both slept.

Ma turned to Gabrielle and said, "Gabrielle, you used to be so good at setting the table. If you remember how, could you set the table for me while I get these pans ready?"

While Ma turned to face the stovetop, Gabrielle replied, "That's what I did a lot at the other house. They even called me an expert at it!" Then, feeling too warm with the heat from the fire in the fireplace, she took her coat off without thinking, and she placed it onto the back of one of the chairs by the table.

Ma turned her head back towards Gabrielle and was immediately stunned by the sight of bare arms. She rushed to the master bedroom, grabbed an extra shawl, and hurried back where she quickly put the shawl around Gabrielle who was standing by the hutch. While helping her daughter dress more modestly, she explained, "We don't dress like that. What you put on is not proper." Gabrielle looked at her ma with an expression of knowing she would need to unlearn what she had learned the past six months. "Now, go ahead and set the table." Gabrielle then took the plates and other needed dishes out of the kitchen hutch, carried them to the table, and set the table even better than she had done in that house before.

Meanwhile, Mrs. Felding was finished cooking breakfast when Mr. Felding walked into the kitchen. "It smells delicious as usual. Where's Gabby?" he asked.

"She's probably still sleeping," said Mrs. Felding. "She must have gotten worn out from all the walking in the field of trees yesterday. I'll go wake her up."

When Mrs. Felding approached the bedroom doorway, she noticed the door wasn't closed. She continued towards the bedroom and looked inside, only to find an empty bed. "Gabby?" she said while she stepped into the bedroom. "Are you in here?" With no response, she stepped back into the hallway. "Gabby!" she said louder. Then she checked the living room, but still no sight of her.

Mrs. Felding entered the kitchen. "Gabby's gone again. She's nowhere in the house," she told her husband, sounding a bit worried.

"Again?" said Mr. Felding. "Did she not listen when we told her to not leave by herself?" For a second, he recollected some thoughts. "The first time she left by herself, she went to the Robinsons' house. After that, she went to meet up with Sophie on the way to school."

"Well, she's not with Sophie, and there's no school today," said Mrs. Felding. "Even if today was a school day, Sophie wouldn't let Gabby be too far away from home without one of us. And if she's at the Robinsons' house, I'm sure Mrs. Robinson would have called us by now."

"Unless she snuck out just a minute ago and hasn't reached their house yet," added Mr. Felding. "Knowing Gabby, she must be in the neighborhood somewhere, but we can't skip breakfast and start looking for her now. Today's the biggest sales day of the year, and I can't be late for work. I'm sure we'll find her just like we did before."

# 10
## NEW DISCOVERIES

All besides Tabitha who was still asleep, the Linstrom family sat around the table while eating breakfast. Pa couldn't bear the thoughts of the immodesty in Gabrielle's outfit—pink jeans, a light blue t-shirt, and shoes that were very unique. Although her shoes did not bother him, he couldn't wait until after breakfast to bring up the subject. With the two parents sitting at each end of the table, he looked across the table at his wife and said, "How will we go into town to get Gabrielle's dress? She needs to come with us to show us where the Feldings live, but we can't have her seen out in public like this."

Having heard the dilemma, Abigail suddenly got an idea. "Since I have two extra dresses, she could wear one of mine," she kindly suggested.

Ma turned to Abigail. "But your dresses are much too big for her. They'll look too baggy, and the hem will go too far below her knees for her to run anywhere."

"I won't mind," said Gabrielle.

"I think that's our only option," said Pa. Then he turned to face Abigail. "Abigail, go help your sister change into one of your dresses after breakfast. Afterwards, you can ride with us into town, and we'll drop you off at the school on our way to pick up Gabrielle's dress."

At that moment, nine-month-old Tabitha started crying. "Sounds like Tabitha's awake," said Ma as she excused herself from the table.

Gabrielle turned to see where Ma was going. "That's not where your bed is," she told Pa. "Does Tabitha sleep with me and Sabrina now?"

"We moved your bed up to the loft. You sleep with Abigail now."

Gabrielle looked towards the loft. "But there aren't any stairs."

"When you were gone,' Pa explained, "we didn't know if you were ever coming back until a few weeks ago when we started hearing your voice. I don't know how we couldn't see you, but we figured you'd eventually show up, so we moved your bed up to the loft because Tabitha didn't need us close to her at nights anymore, and because we figured you're old enough and big enough to climb the ladder."

"But why can't we have stairs like everybody else?" asked Gabrielle.

The answer was obvious to Abigail. "There's no space," she said, glancing over to the ladder and then back to Gabrielle. "Just look where the ladder is. If stairs were there, they'd have to be in front of the door, and then we'd have to use the back door all the time."

"And even if we had space for stairs," Pa told Gabrielle," we can't afford to build them. It's going to be at least three weeks before we can afford to buy you another dress. And that's why we need to go into town to get the one you left." Then he looked at the breakfast plates in front of Abigail and Gabrielle, and they were both empty. "If you two are finished, why don't you take Sabrina over to your ma , go up to the loft for Gabrielle to change, and I'll go out and hitch up the team." He stood up at the table, walked a little closer to the front door, stopped, and turned to face his daughters again. "And we need to get started soon. We have a long drive ahead of us. With two miles to travel, it will take about half an hour to get there, and another half an hour back."

"But, Pa," said Gabrielle, "instead of riding the wagon, why don't we just use a car? That way, we'll get there a lot sooner."

"Use *what*?" asked Pa.

"A car," said Gabrielle. "It has a motor, and it goes a lot faster than horses."

"Oh, you must mean a passenger car. But if you're talking about a train, the railroad doesn't go through town, and we can't afford tickets right now," Pa said. At that point, Gabrielle was speechless, knowing that Pa had never seen a car before, and probably wouldn't know how to drive one. "Go on and change, and I'll go get the wagon ready." Then he headed outside while seven-year-old Abigail helped two-year-old Sabrina down from the chair.

The three girls found their mother taking care of Tabitha in the back part of the house, although it was not technically a bedroom due to the house being so small with a lack of rooms. "Stay here, Sabrina," said Abigail before she and Gabrielle turned around and started heading to the loft.

"Oh, Abigail," said Ma, quickly getting Abigail's attention. The two girls immediately stopped and turned around to face Ma. "There's something I just now remembered. One of your two extra dresses is your Sunday dress you wore yesterday, and we only wear our Sunday dresses on Sundays. Be sure to give Gabrielle the other dress."

"Okay," agreed Abigail. "Come on, Gabrielle."

"Wait a minute," Gabrielle said. Facing Abigail, she asked, "Why did you wear your Sunday dress yesterday when today is Friday?" Giving no time for Abigail to respond, she quickly faced Ma and asked, "Do we wear our Sunday dresses on holidays?"

"Today isn't Friday," said Abigail. "It's Monday!"

"And we only wear our Sunday dresses on holidays if there's a special occasion, but not on every holiday," said Ma.

"But today can't be Monday," said Gabrielle. "Thanksgiving was yesterday, and I thought it was always on a Thursday."

"No," corrected Ma, "yesterday was Sunday. It was just yesterday when we asked the preacher at church to pray that you would come back to us, and it only took a day for the prayer to be answered. And as for Thanksgiving, it *is* always on a Thursday, but President Grant moved it to the third Thursday this year, so it fell on the 18th, which was almost two weeks ago."

"But it was yesterday when I ate a big turkey meal, and Mrs. Felding said Thanksgiving was always on the fourth Thursday of the month."

"Why did the Feldings make you wait until yesterday to celebrate Thanksgiving?" Abigail asked. Gabrielle shrugged her shoulders, confused about which day of the week it really was, and wondering whether her foster parents were telling her the truth or if they were misleading her about the day of Thanksgiving.

"It was only six years ago when Thanksgiving officially became a national holiday, and it's mostly been on the fourth Thursday except the year when you were born when President Johnson moved it to the first Thursday, three years ago when the last Thursday fell on the fifth Thursday of the month, and this year on the third Thursday, so I don't think Mrs. Felding knew what she was talking about," said Ma. "But let's not worry about it now. Go get changed, or Abigail will be late for school." Without delay, Gabrielle followed Abigail up to the loft.

After changing into a dress along with an extra pair of bloomers and an extra pinafore, Gabrielle didn't have any shoes or boots that were the modern-day style for those days, so she put back on the shoes along with the socks that she had brought from the future.

When all the womenfolk were ready and all bundled up, they headed to the front door. Ma carried Tabitha and carefully walked beside Sabrina. "Don't forget the eggs," she said. Abigail grabbed the basket of eggs. They soon left the house and met up with Pa at the wagon. Pa helped the three oldest girls into the back of the covered wagon before walking along the right side of the wagon to the front. In a gentle manner, he took Tabitha from Mrs. Linstrom who then climbed up onto the front seat. Pa carefully handed Tabitha up to Mrs. Linstrom before climbing up onto the front seat from the other side of the wagon. In just a short time, they were heading on their way down the long lane.

When they reached the end of the lane, Pa steered the horses in making a right-hand turn onto the street. Although Gabrielle wasn't needed for directions yet, she constantly looked outside from the front of the wagon to learn her way around the city. While making the right-hand turn, everything looked completely different again. There were no buildings along the street, there were no cars, and the street itself was not paved anymore. "Where are the buildings?" Gabrielle asked in a state of wonder. "Did someone tear them all down?"

There aren't any buildings yet," said Ma. "We're not in town yet."

"Where are the cars?" Gabrielle asked. "And why isn't this street paved anymore like it was this morning? Who turned it back into a dirt road, and how did they do it so fast?"

Ma and Pa looked at each other with blank looks on their faces. "We don't know what you're talking about," said Ma.

"But isn't this Cherry Street?" asked Gabrielle.

"No. We're on Maple Street," replied Pa.

"Maple Street?" repeated Gabrielle. "Mrs. Felding said it was almost one hundred years ago when the name of Maple Street was changed to Cherry Street."

Ma and Pa briefly thought about what Gabrielle had just said. "The name of this street has *always* been Maple Street," Pa mentioned.

"Either Mrs. Felding didn't know what she was talking about again, or she must have been referring to a different street in another town or city," Ma said.

In response to that, Pa turned to Ma and asked, "What do you mean *again*?"

Ma explained to Pa everything Gabrielle had told her about Thanksgiving.

While looking at where they were going, Gabrielle kept an eye out for another road to the left, and she knew it wasn't far down the street.

A few minutes later, not having seen a road that veered off to the left, Gabrielle was placed into a state of wonder again. Wondering if she missed it, she asked her parents, "Did we pass another road yet?"

"Not yet," said Ma.

"But there's a road up here to the left that's down the street a ways that we'll be taking," Pa said.

*It wasn't this far,* Gabrielle thought. *Where's the road?*

Half a mile down the street from the end of their lane, they came to the road on the left-hand side that Pa had mentioned. Pa steered the horses to the left, and now they were on the road that led into town.

Up to that point, Gabrielle hadn't seen one single building. The land on both sides of the street was widespread with a few trees that were spaced out. Everything looked familiar to her from what she remembered before she first met Mr. and Mrs. Felding, but nothing looked the same as it did during the past six months. How everything was built so fast and torn down so fast was beyond Gabrielle's imagination. However, what was more perplexing to her than how was why. Why would an entire city be torn down within six months after being built?

Along the road, they came up to some buildings including several houses and a blacksmith's shop before arriving at the mercantile that was half a mile from the turn off Maple Street. Not far from the mercantile was the school. "Here we are at the mercantile," said Pa while he parked the wagon in front of the building. He climbed down from the front seat, walked to the back of the wagon, helped Abigail down, and took ahold of the basket of eggs to sell to the mercantile. Abigail walked the remaining distance to the school while Pa took the eggs inside. Ma and the three youngest girls waited in the wagon.

Gabrielle looked at the mercantile and noticed some words attached to the front of the building above the doors. "Ma," she said.

"Yes?" asked Ma in a gentle tone.

"What does that say up there?" Gabrielle asked while pointing to the words.

Ma turned to Gabrielle to see what she was pointing at, and then she faced the mercantile. "It says River Town Mercantile."

"Why does it say River Town? Don't we live in River City? And how can there be over twelve thousand people in the city when there aren't many houses?"

Ma gave a slight chuckle. "What? I don't know where you're getting these crazy ideas! The population of River Town is a little over four hundred. How did you come up with the name of River City with that many people?"

"That's how many people Mrs. Felding told me."

"Either Mrs. Felding never knows what she's talking about, or perhaps she was referring to the population of the county."

"But everybody was calling this place River City, and even Molly said it was."

" Molly? Who's Molly?"

"She's my best friend who lives three houses away from Dad and Mom . . . I mean Mr. and Mrs. Felding."

"Dad and Mom?" Ma repeated. "Were you away from us for so long that you considered them as your parents?"

"They said they were my foster parents."

"Why would they say that without trying to come find us first?" asked Ma, feeling somewhat brokenhearted that another couple in town had taken her daughter.

"But they *did* try to find you. Not long ago, Mr. Felding told me Officer Gunwell did a big search for you, but he couldn't find you."

"Who's Officer Gunwell? Is he a county officer? The only officers in town are Sheriff Badger and his deputy."

"Sheriff Badger is back in town?" said Gabrielle. "The other officers didn't know who he was."

"He never left town, so why do you say he's back? And why do you say *other officers*? The only other officer is the deputy."

"No, there were about nine or ten officers."

"Then you must be talking about the county officers, but the county office is ten miles out of town. That's at least two hours away. Who drove you that far?"

"I didn't go to the county office. I went to the police station in town, and it wasn't far away. It only took five minutes to ride from the police station to the Feldings' house."

"Then their house is close to the Sheriff's office?"

"No. Their house is farther from the office than it is from their house to our house, so it's probably three miles away from the office."

"Three miles in five minutes? Gabrielle," said Ma, "horses that pull wagons, buggies, carriages, or stagecoaches can't go *that* fast."

"But I didn't ride anything that was pulled by horses. I rode in a car."

*A car?* Ma thought to herself. "The only cars to ride that I know about are passenger cars, but the railroad doesn't go through town . . . especially anywhere near the sheriff's office. Where do you come up with these silly ideas?"

It was at that time when Pa came out of the mercantile with an empty basket. He walked to the back of the wagon, handed the basket to

Sabrina, returned to the front of the wagon, and climbed back onto the front seat. "Okay, Gabrielle," he said, "now to get your dress. You need to tell me how to get to the Feldings' house."

"There was a road that turned off Maple Street, but it's not this road. It was closer to where we live," Gabrielle said.

"But we didn't pass any roads," said Pa. "Was it down the street on the other side of our lane?"

"No. It was on this side."

"Well, let's go check it out." Pa turned the wagon around and started driving the half-mile distance back to Maple Street. "Did anything happen while I was in the mercantile?" he asked his wife.

"Oh, you should have been here!" exclaimed Ma. "Gabrielle thought this town was called River City with over twelve thousand people living here. Apparently, everyone was calling it River City including her best friend named Molly who lives three houses away from the Feldings who called themselves Gabrielle's foster parents after an officer named Officer Gunwell tried searching for us in this small town, but couldn't find us. And now there's a police station that's three miles away from where the Feldings live, and it only takes five minutes to go from one place to the other because of something that's not on a railroad track or pulled by a horse."

As ridiculous as it all sounded, Pa burst out laughing. Speaking louder towards the back of the wagon, he told Gabrielle, "You need to stop these silly birthday wishes!" And still having a few chuckles to let out, he added, "It sounds like wishing to go into the future has expanded your imagination far and wide!"

Ma gave a small chuckle and a slight nod in agreement to Pa's last comment. However, Gabrielle wasn't laughing. She knew what she had seen, she knew where she had been, she knew what she had lived through, and she knew of the people whom she had met. But what happened to it all, and where did everything go?

When they reached Maple Street, Pa veered the horses to the right to head back where they came from. Throughout the entire distance from that point to their lane, they watched for another road that connected to Maple Street on either side.

Unsuccessful at finding any other road by the time they got to their lane, Gabrielle wasn't sure what to think. Not only were the paved roads turned into dirt roads, but other roads also didn't exist anymore. She thought back to the previous day. When she was with her foster parents, the little pond and her house did not exist, and she couldn't see her family anywhere. And now that she was back with her biological family, some roads and buildings didn't exist. But was it possible she wouldn't be able to see Molly, Sophie, or the Feldings anywhere?

Pa parked the wagon on the side of the street close to their lane. "You still haven't showed us how to get to the Feldings' house, and we didn't see any other roads. How did you go the two miles from their house to our house? Did someone give you a ride, or did you walk?"

"I walked, but nothing looks the same as it did earlier this morning. A road that was between their house and our house is not there anymore."

"Well, I have an idea," said Pa. He steered the horses to the left and started heading down the lane to their house. "If you walked, then there might have been something we couldn't see from the wagon. So after we get back home, I'll go with you when you're ready, and we'll walk to the Feldings' house."

A while after arriving back home, Gabrielle was ready to leave again. "I'm ready to go," she told Pa.

"Before we leave, we need to bring the other outfit you were wearing so we can give it back to the Feldings," Pa said.

"But they gave it to me," said Gabrielle, gloomily speaking and feeling sad about giving back what had been given to her.

"You should know it's not proper attire for girls to be wearing trousers. Now, go up to the loft and bring down the outfit."

Immediately, Gabrielle headed to the ladder. Above the desire to keep her belongings, she was still determined to be like Molly. And wanting to see Molly again, she climbed up to the loft, grabbed the outfit, and carried it down the ladder. Then they headed on their way.

Past the end of the lane after turning to the right onto Maple Street, Gabrielle started to think about the trees that faded away, and she wondered if other things had also faded away. Nothing looked the same as it did just hours ago. "Pa," she said. "If trees can fade away, can roads and buildings fade away too?"

Pa wasn't sure what she was trying to ask. "Everything can fade off into the distance if we're going away from it. Is that what you mean?"

Gabrielle shook her head. "No, that's not what I mean. When I was on the tree stump this morning, I started to see through the hundreds of trees around me."

"First of all," said Pa, "there aren't hundreds of trees around the stump. Secondly, anyone can see through a forest if they can find space between the trees."

"No, I'm not talking about seeing between trees. I'm talking about seeing through each tree when they start to disappear. Can roads and buildings disappear too?"

"I don't know what you're trying to say. If you're talking about fading away like magic . . . no, it's not possible."

"Then why did everything look so different earlier this morning?"

"What looked different?"

"Everything! Hundreds of trees were around the stump, the house and the pond were not there, this road was paved, lots of buildings were around here, and cars were going on this street . . . but they weren't trains."

Pa briefly thought about it. "It sounds like someone's been telling you some crazy stories. I bet it was the Feldings who don't seem to know what they're talking about and can't even dress appropriately. But if it was just this morning when you walked back home from their house, then just show me the way so we can get your dress and get on to other things."

In Gabrielle's point of view, it didn't seem like the conversation about things fading away was going to lead anywhere, so she decided to remain obedient and do what her pa told her to do by at least attempting to find the Feldings' house. With no roads to take as well as no landmarks, the only things she had to go by were distance and direction. She knew which direction the currently nonexistent road headed, so all she needed to do was try to remember how far she walked from the road to the field of trees.

When she came to the approximate distance to the best of her memory, she stopped. Standing there, she turned around to see how far they had walked from the end of their lane that was still seen a ways down the street at a distance. Although there was no lane earlier that morning, she did her best to visualize what she had seen at the time of walking to the field of trees. "This looks like it's close," she said.

"Close to what?" asked Pa. "Why are we standing here?"

"I think this is where I turned from the other road."

"What other road? There aren't any other roads here."

"There used to be," said Gabrielle in a tone of full confidence. Then she turned in the direction where the other road used to lead to, and she started heading across the field.

Pa started to follow. "Where are you going? There's nothing built down in this direction." Gabrielle continued to walk forward. "The only thing you'll find if you keep walking this way might be an Indian teepee . . . and we don't know how friendly the Indians will be," said Pa, trying to get Gabrielle to turn around.

After almost an hour of walking from their house, Gabrielle was convinced that something was wrong. Nothing that was in existence earlier that morning was seen anywhere. The entire time of walking was all on widespread land with not one single road. "Like I tried to tell you," said Pa, "there's nothing here."

"But I *know* there was," said Gabrielle. "Where did everything go?"

"There was never anything here. Did you forget where the Feldings live, or are you trying to keep that immodest outfit by not leading me to their house?"

"No, I'm not," Gabrielle said in total sincerity. "This area around here is where they lived. Honest, Pa!"

Standing there, Pa looked around in all directions. Nothing was in sight besides land and a few trees. "This is where they lived? And Thanksgiving was yesterday?" Briefly, he looked around again. Then, looking at Gabrielle, he said, "Gabrielle, you've always been an honest girl, and you've always been obedient just like Abigail. Your ma and I have been trying to teach you basic values such as modesty and integrity, and it seems like you're straying away from these principles. Where have we gone wrong?"

"But I *am* being honest, Pa! I'm trying to find their house, but it's not here anymore," Gabrielle voiced with a slight sound of sadness. She was almost in tears. However, it wasn't what Pa said that almost brought her to tears. It was wondering where Molly, Sophie, and her foster parents all went, and wondering if she would ever see them again.

Seeing the sad expression on Gabrielle's face and looking deeply into her tearful eyes, Pa changed the subject. "Well, let's just go back home. We'll figure out something another time. We have a long journey ahead of us with a whole hour of walking to do."

An hour later, Pa and Gabrielle arrived back home. As soon as Gabrielle stepped into the house, Ma saw her still holding the outfit that she was supposed to take back to where it came from. "What happened?" Ma asked. "I assume you didn't find the house?"

Pa stepped through the doorway right behind Gabrielle. "That's right," he replied.

Looking at Gabrielle and not believing she couldn't find the house, Ma said to her, "You used to be very good with directions. No matter where you went, you always found your way back. So if you were at the Feldings' house just this morning, then why couldn't you find it?" she asked while shaking her head in a manner of disappointment. Feeling utterly bewildered about not knowing where anything went, Gabrielle was at a loss for words, so she shrugged her shoulders, which caused Ma to feel upset. "Gabrielle Anne Linstrom, I want an answer from you!" Ma said somewhat scornfully in a raised voice.

"It wasn't there," answered Gabrielle in a state of sorrow. Hearing Ma's harsh words in addition to wondering where people whom she cared about had gone, she suddenly broke into tears, quickly placed the outfit onto the table, ran over to the ladder, and climbed up to the loft.

Pa walked over to Ma and stood beside her. Not knowing the main reason why Gabrielle was crying, he quietly explained to Ma what had happened as well as what Gabrielle had told him. "I didn't believe what she was telling me, but then I saw a familiar look in her eyes, and it was the same look she had before these past few months when she was telling the truth."

"The truth?" said Ma in a tone of unbelief. "If anyone can find their way back to anywhere they've been, *she* can. And houses don't just disappear!"

"Yes, I know," said Pa, "but I also remember that look in her eyes. Somehow, she's telling the truth. I don't know how it could be true, but somehow or other, it is. So let's not be too harsh on her. After all, we haven't seen her for six months, and today's the first day that she's back with us."

"Alright," Ma calmly agreed. Then she turned to look at the table. She walked over to it, picked up the pink jeans and the t-shirt, and quietly said, "But until we find out where the Feldings live, I'm putting this outfit away." With no regard as to what the outfit meant to anyone else, she walked away from the table into the master bedroom where she put the clothes away in a place that would be very hard to find. *She's NOT wearing these again!* she thought. *I just hope we can afford another dress for her before desperate times come for Abigail. And Mr. Stevens better not change his mind about buying the cow!*

Thirty minutes after two, Abigail returned home from school. By that time, Gabrielle had stopped crying and was down from the loft. She saw Abigail step through the doorway into the house. "I'm back from school," Abigail said for everyone in the house to hear.

"Did you see Molly?" Gabrielle asked her.

"Uh . . . I don't know anyone named Molly," said Abigail.

"Maybe she's in a different class."

"What do you mean? The school is only one room, and that's where everyone meets."

"Everyone is meeting in one room again?" asked Gabrielle. "But Sophie said there are hundreds of kids who meet in lots of different rooms."

"Who's Sophie?" asked Abigail. "And if she said there are hundreds of kids, then she must have been to a big city that she was talking about."

"No, she was talking about the school right here in River City."

"Did you say River City?" Abigail asked. "We live in River *Town,* and there's not even that many people living in the town for there to be hundreds of kids around here."

As confused as she was, Gabrielle thought for a moment. "Are you sure there's nobody named Molly at school? She's five, and the grade she's in is kindergarten."

"Huh? Kinder *what?*"

"Kindergarten," Gabrielle said again.

Abigail thought for a second. "Kindergarten? It sounds familiar, but I can't remember where I heard . . . oh, now I remember! A few weeks ago, Ms. Roberts told everyone at school that another class called kindergarten is starting in some schools. In this country, it was started thirteen years ago by someone who spoke German. Then the first kindergarten in the English language started nine years ago in Boston, but we don't have any kindergarten around here. It's only grades one through eight."

"It only goes through eight? But Sophie said she's in the ninth grade."

"You still haven't told me who Sophie is," said Abigail.

"She's another friend from school. And who is Ms. Roberts?"

"She's the school teacher, but nobody at school is in the ninth grade."

"Are you sure?" Gabrielle asked.

"Yes, I'm sure," said Abigail. In a state of curiosity, she quickly glanced around the room to see if anyone else was there. "Where's Ma?"

"She's feeding the chickens behind the house."

"Where's Pa?"

"He's feeding the cows."

"Where's Sabrina?"

"She's helping Ma feed the chickens."

"Where's Tabitha?"

"She's taking a nap, so Ma wanted me to stay inside in case Tabitha wakes up," answered Gabrielle. "Who drove you home from school?"

"I walked home."

"You walked a mile by yourself?"

Abigail thought it was a silly question. "Of course I did. I always do unless Ma and Pa are in town when school gets out. Why do you ask?"

"Because Mrs. Felding said we live in a wicked world with bad things happening, and she said it could be dangerous for children to walk far distances without a trusted adult."

"What?" asked Abigail, having never heard such a thing. "Did she say that today? And why are you still wearing my dress? Didn't Pa drive you to the Feldings' house to get yours?"

"He tried, but the house wasn't there anymore."

"Not there anymore? What do you mean? Weren't you there just this morning? And if you walked two miles from there all by yourself, then why were you worried about me walking one mile from school all by myself?"

At that moment, Ma, Pa, and Sabrina walked into the house. Then Pa closed the door. Both parents noticed a startled look on Abigail's face. "What's wrong, Abigail?" asked Ma. "Did something bad happen at school today?"

Realizing why Ma was asking, Abigail quickly fixed her facial expression back to normal, shook her head, and said, "School was okay."

"Then what's wrong?" asked Pa.

Having no intention of tattling on her sister or ignoring Ma and Pa, Abigail quickly tried thinking about how to put it into words. Soon realizing she didn't know what to say, she looked over to Gabrielle who was still wearing her dress.

"Oh, you're wondering why Gabrielle isn't wearing her own dress?" Ma asked.

Giving no time for Abigail to respond, Pa assumed that was the reason for the facial expression, and he explained, "We tried looking for the Feldings' house to get her dress back, but we couldn't find where they live. Apparently, there's something else none of us knows, so we'll have to wait to find out."

Thinking about what was troubling her the most, Abigail somewhat expressed another facial look that Ma noticed. "What else is wrong?" Ma asked.

Wanting to resolve the matter, Abigail asked, "Is it safe to walk to school and back home by myself?" Gabrielle listened to the conversation.

"What a silly question!" said Ma. "Of course it is. That's what children of all ages have been doing for years."

"And there are no bears or mountain lions between here and there," Pa added.

Now having a peaceful assurance about the safety of walking alone, a random thought came to Abigail's memory. She turned to Gabrielle. "Hey, Gabrielle, do you want to play *Graces* like we used to?"

"Yeah!" said Gabrielle with a smile.

"Yeah?" Abigail wondered aloud. "What does that mean?"

"I think it means *yes*," said Pa. "I don't know where she comes up with these new words and ideas."

Abigail quickly climbed up to the loft, got the game of *Graces*, and brought it down the ladder. Then she and Gabrielle headed to the front door. "Gabrielle, don't run too fast in that dress," said Ma.

# 11
# ANOTHER HOPELESS SEARCH

Meanwhile, Mr. Felding returned home from work at four o'clock. As soon as he stepped into the house through the front doorway, not seeing Mrs. Felding in sight, he hollered, "I'm home! We had the best sales day all year! Thank goodness for Black Friday!" At that moment, Mrs. Felding walked into the living room with a worried look on her face. "What's wrong? You didn't find Gabby?"

Mrs. Felding shook her head. "First, I checked at the Robinsons' house. Then I called Mrs. Jackson, and she and Sophie both knew nothing of her whereabouts. Later, I drove to the field of trees. I spent two hours searching almost the entire field, but I couldn't find her anywhere even when I cried out her name several times. Do you think she might be permanently gone this time? What if we never see her again?"

Mr. Felding thought for a second. "Why did she leave if it wasn't to go see Molly or Sophie like before?" he asked.

"It's not because she doesn't love us anymore. Every night when I tuck her into bed, I always tell her I love her, and she always says the same back to me. But could she be upset at us for not believing her about the house and the pond in the field of trees?"

Mr. Felding shook his head. "I don't see why she would be upset when she didn't see a house or a pond either. Maybe she heard me last night saying we'll need to talk with her about being honest, and maybe she was afraid to talk with us about that."

Mrs. Felding thought for a second. "Yeah, you *could* be right about that. And if she was afraid, then maybe she ran away from home."

Looking towards the hallway where Gabby's bedroom was located, a thought came to Mrs. Felding, and she headed to Gabby's bedroom while adding, "And there might be a way to find out whether she ran away or not." Curious to know what she had in mind, Mr. Felding followed.

After entering the bedroom, Mrs. Felding began to search everywhere to see what was missing. "How would you know if she ran away or not?" Mr. Felding asked.

Mrs. Felding replied, "If she went to someone's house with plans on coming right back, then she would have left everything here."

"Unless she took something to play or do with a friend."

Mrs. Felding kept searching. She started looking in Gabby's closet. "Her coat isn't here."

"That proves she left the house," said Mr. Felding, "but it doesn't prove if she ran away or not. She might have gone to see someone, knowing she'd be back shortly."

"It looks like her old-style dress with the bonnet is still here, and I think she would have taken this if she had plans on never coming back." Mrs. Felding was starting to feel relieved about what the evidence was showing, but just to make sure, she kept searching through the bedroom.

Two minutes after searching frantically, Mrs. Felding discovered something. "Her teddy bear isn't here. Now, why would she take her teddy bear to someone else's house unless it was for a sleepover? She must have taken it for company, which means she must be alone." She then felt an immeasurable amount of worry along with a touch of sadness. "Oh, Honey, what if she gets lost and can't find her way back?"

Momentarily thinking about it, Mr. Felding started feeling worried as well. "I think we need to go to the police station and talk with Officer Gunwell. Maybe he can get a search party together."

"But how would anyone in the search party know who to look for? We have no photos of Gabby."

"Maybe we can at least find out what she's wearing by going through her outfits," Mr. Felding suggested.

Mrs. Felding searched through every outfit in the closet as well as the chest of drawers. Eventually, she came to the conclusion of what Gabby was most likely wearing. "The only things that aren't here are the pink jeans and the light blue t-shirt."

Without delay, now having a description to provide, Mr. and Mrs. Felding headed off to the police station.

From right inside the entrance doors at the station, they immediately saw Officer Gunwell sitting at the same desk, doing some paperwork. To waste no time, they hurried to the desk. "Officer

Gunwell!" Mrs. Felding blurted out in a restless tone while she and Mr. Felding were only a few feet away from reaching the desk.

A second later, Officer Gunwell looked up from his paperwork right when they arrived in front of his desk. "Oh, it's you two again!" he said in a cheerful manner. "Hey, I'm sorry I couldn't find your foster daughter's mom. Maybe her mom's name is something besides Martha. Have you looked into that? And is that why you're here? Do you have additional information about her biological parents?"

"No, we're not here regarding her parents," said Mr. Felding. "It's Gabby. She ran away, and we think she might be lost."

"What caused this? Do you know why she ran away?" asked Officer Gunwell.

"No," said Mr. Felding. "We've been raising her with lots of love and lots of care. But she *has* been shouting out for her parents lately."

"And she's been calling them Ma and Pa," added Mrs. Felding.

"That's interesting," said Officer Gunwell. "Hardly anyone now days calls their parents Ma and Pa anymore . . ."

"And so we have reason to suspect she might have gone searching for her parents," interrupted Mr. Felding.

"And evidence that says she might be alone," said Mrs. Felding. "I had a good talk with her about not wandering off by herself, and I don't know why she didn't listen."

"Well, let me get some information," said Officer Gunwell. He opened a desk drawer, reached in, and pulled out a missing-child report. "Do you have any kind of photo identification of her?"

"No, we don't," said Mrs. Felding.

"But we can give you a description," said Mr. Felding.

Ready to write it down on the report, Officer Gunwell asked, "Okay, what's the description?"

Mr. Felding described Gabrielle. "She's about four years old, about forty inches tall, and weighs about forty pounds. She has light brown hair and blue eyes. She's probably wearing pink jeans and a light blue t-shirt . . ."

"Unless she's outside in the cold, wearing her dark blue coat with tiny hearts on it over her t-shirt," interrupted Mrs. Felding.

Officer Gunwell took a few seconds to finish writing the description on the report. As soon as he was finished, he raised his head to face the Feldings. "And when did this happen?" he asked.

Mr. and Mrs. Felding turned to look at each other with blank looks on their faces. Then Mr. Felding turned to face the officer. "She was with us last night. She was gone before breakfast this morning, but we don't know what time she left."

"And I checked with her friends and their parents," added Mrs. Felding, "but they had no information. Also, we took her to the field of trees on Cherry Street yesterday because she said there was a house there. So I went back to the field today to see if she was there, but I couldn't find her."

"Umm," voiced Officer Gunwell, "she said there was a house there?"

"That's correct," replied Mrs. Felding.

Officer Gunwell continued. "Our city records contain addresses to about three or four houses that were located in that field, but the records show that the last of those houses was torn down about sixty years ago."

Mr. and Mrs. Felding looked at each other again, and both of them were not sure what to think. "How did she know there was a house there?" asked Mrs. Felding quietly. Mr. Felding shrugged his shoulders.

"With the information you've given me, I'll gather together a search team, and we'll do everything we can do to find her," said Officer Gunwell.

Twenty minutes till five, Pa headed towards the front door. Gabrielle noticed he was going somewhere. "Where are you going, Pa?"

"Out to the barn to milk the cows."

Immediately, Gabrielle remembered she enjoyed helping Pa with that in times past. "Can I come help?" she asked somewhat excitedly with a smile.

"Sure, if you'd like," said Pa.

Gabrielle grabbed her coat, put it on, and left the house with Pa who closed the door behind him.

While walking from the house to the barn, Pa looked at Gabrielle. "That's quite an interesting coat. I don't think I ever saw anything like it," he told her. "Did the Feldings give it to you?" Gabrielle nodded her head in response. Pa wasn't sure whether the Feldings even existed, or if Gabrielle had really gotten the coat from somewhere else and was using imaginary people to keep from saying where it really came from. However, he remembered the look he had seen in Gabrielle's eyes, which was enough to trust every word from his daughter regardless of how ridiculous she would sound. "Have you been keeping up on the practice of milking cows these past few months?" he asked. Gabrielle shook her head. "Didn't the Feldings have any cows?"

"No," said Gabrielle.

"Then someone must have delivered milk cans to them," said Pa, hoping that finding out who delivers milk cans to residents in town would be a way to find out where the Feldings live.

"Milk cans?" Gabrielle vocally wondered while she briefly tried to remember what a milk can is, but was unsuccessful. "What's a milk can?"

"It's what milk gets delivered in. You've seen milk cans at the Robinsons' house when you were taking piano lessons . . . and we need to get you going on piano lessons again."

"Robinson? Hey, that's Molly's last name!"

"Your friend who lives three houses away from the Feldings?" Gabrielle nodded her head. "Then maybe we could ask Mr. and Mrs. Robinson if they're related to anyone named Molly, and maybe we can find out from them where Molly lives," said Pa, hoping this idea could lead to where the Feldings live, unlike the idea about milk cans. "And if the Feldings don't have any cows or milk cans, then how do they get any milk? Do they get it from a nearby neighbor?"

"No," said Gabrielle. "They get milk from the grocery store."

"What's a grocery store?" asked Pa. "If you're talking about the mercantile, they don't sell milk there."

"I'm not talking about the mercantile. I'm talking about the grocery store in town that sells lots of food."

Going along with Gabrielle's creative imagination, knowing there was no such store in town, Pa said, "I wonder how much they charge for milk."

"Last time Mrs. Felding took me there, milk was about three dollars for a gallon."

"Three dollars for only one gallon? It must have been golden milk that came from a golden cow! At that price, it would only take ten gallons of milk to equal the value of a cow." Curious to know more about the imaginary store, Pa went on to ask, "And what else did the Feldings buy at the grocery store?"

At that moment, Pa and Gabrielle entered into the barn. "Everything," said Gabrielle. "That's where they buy all their food. And I really like the Pop-Tarts! Can we go get some?"

Immediately, Pa was left to wonder. "If there was any such thing, then we could. But I never heard of that before."

"But Mrs. Felding said they were invented fifty-five years ago."

"If they've been around for that long, then they certainly haven't reached this town yet. I've been to every store in town, and there's nothing that's called Pop-Tart," Pa said right before he grabbed the stool and the bucket to get ready for milking.

"Yes, there is!" disagreed Gabrielle. "The Feldings buy them all the time, and I've eaten plenty of them!"

"Okay," said Pa, "let's make a compromise. If you show me where the Feldings live, then I'll ask them where they got the Pop-Tarts."

Gabrielle was left with no response. Not only did the Feldings seem to have disappeared with no trace of where they went, but now she was also saddened there would be no more Pop-Tarts. At that point, the only thing she could do was look forward to the day when she would find out why the world drastically changed again like it did six months ago. But how was she ever going to find out?

Forty-five minutes later, Pa and Gabrielle returned to the house after milking the two cows. It was almost too dark to see, so Pa lit the lantern. Gabrielle observed what he was doing, and she wondered why he was still using a lantern. "Pa," she said, "why can't we just use a light bulb?"

"Because they're too expensive. They only last a few hours, and we can't afford to keep buying them all the time. Even if we could, the mercantile doesn't sell them. We'd have to travel to a big city like Nashville or Knoxville. And if we found a light bulb, then it wouldn't work by itself. In order for it to work, we'd also have to buy a battery to connect it to, but we're definitely not that rich."

With the rest of the family listening, Abigail asked, "What's a light bulb?"

Pa explained, "It's an electric thing that gives off light. After Benjamin Franklin discovered electricity more than one hundred years ago, the first electric light was invented about sixty-seven years ago by Humphry Davy who also invented an electric battery, but the light didn't last long. The first constant light that stayed on wasn't invented until about thirty-four years ago when light bulbs were being improved, and the inventors are still working on trying to make improvements."

Once again, Gabrielle was confused. How did every light bulb during the past six months last a long time, how were they so affordable, how did they work with just the flip of a switch instead of being connected to a battery, why were the inventors still trying to improve the light bulb, how did Pa not know anything about long-lasting bulbs that were used in town during the past six months, and where were the houses and other buildings that had so many light bulbs in them?

When it was time for bed, having already put Sabrina and Tabitha to bed, Ma climbed up to the loft with Abigail and Gabrielle, leaving the lantern on the table that was not far from the bottom of the ladder, which gave enough light for how small the house was. The two sisters each climbed into their own bed. Abigail was the first one into bed, so Ma tucked her in, leaned over, and gave her a goodnight kiss on her forehead. "Goodnight, Abigail."

"Goodnight, Ma," said Abigail.

Ma then moved over to Gabrielle's bed and started tucking her in. "And for you, young lady, it's been a while since I've done this," she said in a gentle tone.

Again, Gabrielle was at a loss for words, but in a different way. Thinking about how much she had missed being tucked in by her ma, the only thing she could do in response was give a big smile.

After Ma tucked her in, she looked into Gabrielle's eyes and immediately realized how much she had missed her daughter. "I'm glad you're back here at home," she said. Gabrielle was still at a loss for words, so she gave another big smile. And realizing how much she had also missed seeing her daughter's smile, a tear streamed down Ma's cheek. "I'm sorry about sounding upset earlier today. Your pa later explained everything to me." From then on, Ma always kept in mind how honest Gabrielle had always been in the past, and she refrained from ever assuming there was any change in her honesty.

With a smile still on her face, Gabrielle sat up as she pushed off the blankets, and she gave her ma a big hug. "I love you, Ma!" she said.

Ma returned the hug. "I love you too." Then Gabrielle returned her head to the pillow, and Ma tucked her in again.

"Ma," said Gabrielle, "I wish you could meet Molly. I hope I can see her again sometime."

"Yes, I wish I could meet her too . . . and the Feldings. I talked with your pa, and we're going to start trying to find out why everything appears to be the opposite of what you've been telling us all day."

"But I was telling the truth."

"Yes, I know," said Ma with a gentle voice. "That's why we're going to find out, and maybe it will lead us to where Molly lives." Gabrielle liked that idea, and she smiled again. To finish putting her to bed, Ma leaned over and gave her a kiss on her forehead. "Goodnight."

"Goodnight, Ma."

The following day on Tuesday, the 30th day of November, Ma was busy cooking breakfast. Pa had gotten up at the break of dawn to milk the cows. As soon as Abigail and Gabrielle were both awake, dressed for the day, and down from the loft, breakfast was getting close to being ready. Ma turned to Gabrielle and said, "Gabrielle, could you go wake up Sabrina for me?"

Gladly, Gabrielle nodded her head with the response, "Yes, Ma," and she immediately started heading towards the back part of the house.

She stood beside Sabrina's bed. "Wake up, Sabrina!" But as sleepy as she was, Sabrina's eyes stayed closed. "It's time to get up!" said Gabrielle while gently shaking her younger sister. But that didn't work either. She then took the top part of the blanket and pulled it up to cover Sabrina's head. A second later, she quickly pulled the blanket back down while saying, "Peekaboo!" Next, she repeated the process by pulling the blanket up. "Where's Sabrina?" She waited a second, quickly pulled the blanket off, and exclaimed, "Peekaboo!" Sabrina opened her eyes and started to smile. Afterwards, Gabrielle repeated once more by pulling the blanket up over her sister's head. "Where's Sabrina? I can't see her anywhere! Where did she go?" Lickety-split, she pulled off the blanket. "Peekaboo!"

After breakfast, Abigail left the house and went off to school. Pa needed to clean the barn, so he spent some time doing that along with hitching up the horses to the wagon.

When Pa came back into the house, he asked Gabrielle if she was ready to leave. Earlier during breakfast time, they had talked about the plans of taking her to the sheriff's office to try to resolve some mysteries.

As soon as Gabrielle was ready, she and Pa left the house while Ma stayed home with Sabrina and Tabitha. There was no need for everyone to go along.

Pa lifted Gabrielle up to the front seat of the wagon. He then climbed up, and they soon started down the lane.

On their way, Gabrielle looked all around the area at the dirt road and the wide, open fields while she listened to the sound of horse hooves on the ground as well as the turning wheels of the wagon. Not only did everything look different than it used to, but everything also sounded different.

Eventually, another memory of the previous six months came to her thoughts. While looking at the road and fields, she recalled the sights and sounds that she had seen and heard above her. It was immediately brought to her attention that she couldn't hear anything coming from a much higher altitude anymore, so she raised her head to look up at the sky, and it only took a few seconds to draw Pa's attention to where she was looking. He wondered what she was looking at. "What do you see up there?" he asked. "Clouds? Birds? Blue sky?"

"No," answered Gabrielle. "I'm looking for airplanes and helicopters, but I don't see any."

Immediately, Pa was stumped. But for the sake of not making light of Gabrielle's imagination, he decided to play along. He looked upwards and glanced around through the sky, pretending to look for whatever Gabrielle was trying to find. "I don't see any either," he said.

Gabrielle turned to face her pa. "Pa," she said. "When were airplanes and helicopters invented?"

Again, Pa was stumped. This time, he couldn't play along by making up an answer because he didn't even know that airplanes or helicopters were an invention, and he always remained truthful for being a good example of honesty to his four daughters. "I didn't know they were invented. I thought you were just pretending and creating new words."

"No, I'm not pretending. When I was with Mr. and Mrs. Felding, I saw lots of them flying over River City . . . I mean River Town. Didn't you see them too?"

"See what? The only inventions that were ever in the sky that I know about are hot air balloons, gliders, and ornithopters."

"What's an ornithopter?" asked Gabrielle.

"Well, first I'd like to know what a helicopter is," Pa said.

Several minutes later, Pa and Gabrielle arrived at the sheriff's office. They climbed down from the wagon and made their way to the office door.

Inside, Sheriff Badger was sitting behind his desk. He looked towards the door as soon as it started opening, and he soon recognized Pa. Being that the town was so small, the sheriff knew everyone in town. "Howdy, Mr. Linstrom. What can I do for you today?" Right away, Sheriff Badger saw a little girl coming in behind Mr. Linstrom. "And who's this you have here?" Before Pa could say a word, Sheriff Badger recognized her, although she was slightly taller with shorter hair. "Could this be Gabrielle?" Gabrielle looked at the sheriff whom she recognized, and she nodded her head. Sheriff Badger turned back to face Mr. Linstrom. "Where did you find her?" he asked.

With a question in mind, Gabrielle turned to look upwards at Pa. "How did he know I was gone?" she asked.

Pa looked at Gabrielle. "I told him soon after you disappeared, and he searched everywhere for you."

"And you've been my only case of lost children that I haven't been able to find," Sheriff Badger added. "Where have you been this whole time?"

"I was staying with the Feldings in town," said Gabrielle.

Sheriff Badger grew an expression of wonder on his face, and he turned to Pa. "With *whom*?"

"According to Gabrielle," said Pa, "there's a couple in town by the names of George and Linda Felding, and they live three houses away from a little girl named Molly Robinson."

"Robinson?" repeated Sheriff Badger. "Any relation to Frank and Edna Robinson?"

"I don't know," said Pa. "We'll have to find out as soon as we resume Gabrielle's piano lessons."

"Well, I thought I knew everyone in town," said the sheriff, "but I've never heard the name of Felding." Facing Gabrielle, he asked, "Are you sure they live in town?" Gabrielle nodded her head.

"After she came back to us," Pa said, "she referred to River Town as River City."

"That's what the Feldings, Molly, and everyone else was calling it, and even the workers at the grocery store," Gabrielle said.

"The workers at *what*?" asked the sheriff.

"She said there's a grocery store in town that apparently sells a gallon of milk for the same price as a barrel of flour, and they also sell something called Pop-Tart. She said the streets were filled with cars that weren't part of a train, there were lots of buildings everywhere, airplanes and holy . . ."

"Helicopters," corrected Gabrielle.

"Yes. Airplanes and helicopters in the sky—not a type of bird, but some kind of invention," continued Pa, "everyone dressed immodestly in something called a t-shirt, and a huge school with several rooms inside."

Sheriff Badger stood up from his seat. "Well, I know one thing that's for sure," he said. "That's definitely not a description of River Town. I know this town inside and out, and I've never seen foreign objects flying in the sky. If you're talking about buildings everywhere along with a huge school, then you must be thinking about a big city, but I can guarantee there's no city in the state of Tennessee by the name of River City." The sheriff paused for a second. "Did you come all this way just to tell me about a place that doesn't exist?"

"I know it sounds crazy," said Pa, "and I didn't believe it at first, but I think everything Gabrielle told me is somehow true."

"Only in a fairy tale," Sheriff Badger said with confidence. "That's definitely not this town."

"But if it's somehow true without knowing how it could all be true," Pa told the sheriff, "I wanted to ask if you could help us by searching for anyone with the name of Felding."

Sheriff Badger looked at Pa and started to wonder if he had gone crazy. Then the sheriff turned to look at Gabrielle who looked back at him. Almost in an instant, something seemed to touch his heart when he noticed an innocent sparkle in her eye with a face that was far beyond precious. Somehow, he saw an unusual glow in her that was

136

indescribable, which he had never seen in any other child. At that point, it was impossible to refuse to help the Linstroms in their search. He looked back at Pa and replied, "You've been good citizens of this town, so anything you want me to do, I'll help you in any way that I can."

# 12
# A DECEMBER TO REMEMBER

The next day on Wednesday, the 1st day of December, Pa drove Gabrielle to the Robinsons' house after making plans to resume piano lessons. Frank and Edna Robinson were a much older couple, but Edna was still able to teach piano lessons. She had been teaching for almost fifty years, and she was the only piano teacher in town. The Robinsons lived on Maple Street not too far from River Town Cemetery in the opposite direction from the end of the Linstroms' lane than where the mercantile, the school, and much of the rest of the town was located.

After traveling the distance of a little less than half a mile, Pa and Gabrielle arrived at the Robinsons' house, climbed down from the wagon, walked to the front door, and knocked.

A few seconds later, Mrs. Robinson opened the door. Immediately, she noticed Pa and a little girl, but the short-haired girl did not look familiar. Mrs. Robinson spoke in recognition of whom she knew. "Hi, Mr. Linstrom and . . ." She assumed the girl was one of Mr. Linstrom's daughters. Using the process of elimination, the girl was not Abigail or Sabrina, and definitely not Tabitha. Having no clue who else the girl could be besides a Linstrom girl, Mrs. Robinson remembered having Gabrielle as one of her students. "Is this Gabrielle?"

"Yes, ma'am," said Gabrielle while nodding her head.

"I didn't recognize you with your shorter hair," said Mrs. Robinson.

"She cut it herself," said Pa. "She did it before she came back to us, and I almost didn't recognize her either."

Mrs. Robinson took a closer look at Gabrielle's haircut. "I've never seen a four-year-old who can cut her own hair so straight!" she said before stepping back into the house. "Please come in!"

Pa and Gabrielle entered the house. Mrs. Robinson closed the door behind them. Then Pa continued, "Apparently, she was staying with someone in town during the last six months with the last name of Felding, and she said it was Mrs. Felding who trimmed her hair."

"Felding?" asked Mrs. Robinson. "The name doesn't sound familiar. Are they new in town?"

"That's what we've been trying to find out. Gabrielle said she stayed with them during the last six months, but we haven't found them, and we asked Sheriff Badger to help search for them."

"They live three houses away from Molly," said Gabrielle.

Mrs. Robinson looked at Gabrielle. "And who's Molly?"

"She's my best friend, but we don't know where she is."

"Her name is Molly Robinson," Pa said. "Do you have any family members or know anyone by that name?"

"Hmmm . . . Molly," Mrs. Robinson said quietly to herself while she tried to think if the name sounded familiar. However, the name didn't ring a bell. "I don't know anyone named Molly, but it sure sounds like a pretty name!" Then she looked at Gabrielle again. "Are you ready for more piano lessons?"

"That's what we came here for," said Pa while Gabrielle nodded her head. "We wanted to schedule a day and time to do it."

"Well, instead of standing here," said Mrs. Robinson in the process of moving to a nearby chair, "let's take a seat. Make yourself at home," she told Pa and Gabrielle while motioning to a couch that was located close to them.

They all sat down, and Gabrielle soon noticed the style of the couch with a wood frame and lots of buttons on the cushions of the backrest. "How did you get an old style couch?" she asked.

Mrs. Robinson was confused. "What do you mean? It's the same couch we had when you were here for piano lessons before. We got it two years ago when it was brand new, and couches like this are still at furniture stores."

"But not the furniture store in town," said Gabrielle.

"In town?" asked Pa, looking at her. "There are no furniture stores in town."

"I got my couch from over in the city about fifteen miles away," said Mrs. Robinson.

"But the furniture store here in town is where Mr. Felding works. I was there about a week ago, and they had lots of couches. None of them had wood around them," explained Gabrielle, then turning to face the back part of the couch that she was leaning back against, "and none of them had this many buttons."

Pa looked at Mrs. Robinson who had a confused look on her face. "It sounds like something else we'll have to find out," he said after hearing the innocence in Gabrielle's voice. "It might not sound true right now, but there must be something nobody knows, and we're trying to find out what it is."

"Okay," said Mrs. Robinson, still confused and starting to wonder what was happening in the minds of younger generations.

Pa spoke to Mrs. Robinson. "And getting back to piano lessons," he said, turning to face Gabrielle in making sure she wouldn't stay on the topic of couches, and then turning back to Mrs. Robinson, "what days and times do you have available?"

"I can do Saturdays at noon just like we were doing before Gabrielle went missing," suggested Mrs. Robinson.

"That should work for us," said Pa.

"Saturday?" said Gabrielle. "That's the same day Mrs. Felding teaches piano lessons to Molly and Sophie!"

Mrs. Robinson looked confused again about what in the world Gabrielle was talking about, not knowing anything about another piano teacher in town. Pa noticed her expression. "I don't know what she's talking about either, but we're trying to figure it out," he said.

After Pa and Gabrielle left the Robinsons' home that day, Mrs. Robinson pulled out her diary. Anytime there was something that was said or something that happened that she wanted to remember, she always wrote it down. And this was definitely a day she wanted to remember.

The following Saturday on the 4th day of December, it wasn't long before noon when Pa went outside to hitch the team of horses to the wagon.

Fifteen minutes before noon, Gabrielle came outside and was dressed in her coat. She was all bundled up for the cold weather and ready to go. She walked towards the barn where the horses and wagon were stationed. Pa helped her up onto the seat before he climbed up, and they started the ten-minute drive to the Robinsons' house.

After they arrived close to noon, Mrs. Robinson let them inside. Pa sat on the couch to wait throughout the lesson for taking Gabrielle back home, and Gabrielle sat on the piano bench. Mrs. Robinson sat on a wooden chair in front of the piano next to Gabrielle.

As soon as they were situated, Mrs. Robinson began. "Let's start from where we left off. As I recall, we were working on 'Twinkle, Twinkle, Little Star.' Let's place your fingers on . . ."

"I already know how to play it," interrupted Gabrielle. "Mrs. Felding taught me."

Mrs. Robinson and Pa looked at each other with a look of wonder. They wondered how Gabrielle could possibly learn something from someone who didn't exist. Still wondering, Mrs. Robinson turned back to Gabrielle. Wanting to know if what was spoken was true, she said, "Let's hear how far you've come. Can you play it for me?"

Gabrielle played the entire song with no mistakes. As soon as she finished, Mrs. Robinson started to believe that what Gabrielle said about Mrs. Felding must have somehow been true, but Pa wasn't sure what to think. "And I can play 'Row, Row, Row Your Boat' that Mrs. Felding taught me," said Gabrielle. Then she began to play it.

After Gabrielle got started, Mrs. Robinson stood up, walked over to the couch, and sat next to Pa. "I thought I was the only piano teacher in town," she said.

"That's what I thought too," said Pa. "I was starting to wonder if she learned these songs from you before she came back to us."

Mrs. Robinson shook her head. "Not from me," she said. "I heard of 'Row, Row, Row Your Boat' before, but I never heard it played to this tune. If she didn't make this up all by herself, then she must have another teacher who has a copy of music I've never seen . . . unless the other teacher is the one who came up with this tune."

When Gabrielle came to the end of the song, she overheard the two adults talking. Unaware of what they were talking about, she continued on the piano, playing what she knew of "Ode to Joy."

"I thought I was going to teach a beginner piano lesson today," said Mrs. Robinson, "but it sounds like someone else already did that." Suddenly, her attention was drawn back to the piano. Feeling startled, she asked, "And where did she learn 'Ode to Joy' from?" Pa was also startled, and he had no response.

Not having reached perfection, Gabrielle made several mistakes, but continued to play what she knew until she stopped partly through the song. She hadn't yet learned the remainder of it. Mrs. Robinson stood up and walked back to the piano. "It sounds like Mrs. Felding did a good job of teaching you," she told Gabrielle. At that moment, she found a teaching opportunity she couldn't pass up. She sat back down on the wooden chair. "Let's start from where you left off." Then she began to teach Gabrielle the rest of "Ode to Joy."

For the remainder of the thirty minutes, Pa wondered how it could be possible that Gabrielle was taught by someone who couldn't be found anywhere in town, and was unknown to everyone besides her. At this point, all he could do was hope Sheriff Badger would be successful at solving the mysterious mystery.

Pa and Gabrielle arrived back home. As soon as they stepped into the house, Ma faced Pa and asked, "How did it go? Did Gabrielle make any improvements?"

"More than that," replied Pa.

"What do you mean?"

"She already had 'Twinkle, Twinkle, Little Star' perfected as well as another version of 'Row, Row, Row Your Boat' that we never heard before. In addition, she played part of 'Ode to Joy' that she already knew."

*Already knew?* thought Ma. *It must have been the past six months that Gabrielle had gotten that far in her piano lessons, and Mrs. Robinson is the only piano teacher in town.* "Oh, really? Did Mrs. Robinson . . ."

Pa interrupted while shaking his head. "No, she didn't."

Ma turned to Gabrielle. "Then how did you get so far in your lessons? Did someone else in town teach you?"

"I learned from Mrs. Felding," said Gabrielle. "She's Molly's and Sophie's piano teacher, and she taught me too."

Ma and Pa looked at each other with expressions of great bewilderment. Ma was starting to wonder whether Gabrielle had been referring to Mrs. Robinson by the name of Mrs. Felding, but after knowing it wasn't Mrs. Robinson who taught her, there was definitely something that someone needed to find out.

Almost two weeks later on Friday, the 17th day of December, Abigail left the house after breakfast and started walking to school. It was the last day of school before the Christmas break.

Walking down the lane, she saw a man driving a wagon behind another team of horses, heading in the opposite direction towards the house. Halfway down the lane, they started crossing paths. "Whoa," the man said to his horses while pulling on the reins and coming to a stop. Abigail also stopped walking and faced the man. "Is this the way to the Linstrom house?" the man asked.

"Yes, it is," replied Abigail.

"I understand Mr. Linstrom has a cow for sale."

"Yes, he does. He's my pa. You must be Mr. Stevens."

"The man gave a nod. "That's correct," he said.

"My name's Abigail. I'm heading off to school. My pa will be happy you came."

"It was a pleasure meeting you," said Mr. Stevens.

"Same here," said Abigail. Then they both continued on their way.

A moment later, still sitting at the breakfast table, Pa heard the sound of a horse along with the sound of wagon wheels approaching the house. "That must be Mr. Stevens," he said to Ma and the girls while he stood up and made his way to the front door.

Outside, Pa walked to the barn where he soon met Mr. Stevens who parked his wagon beside Pa's wagon before climbing down. "You must be Mr. Stevens," said Pa while reaching out his hand. Both gentlemen greeted each other with a handshake.

"I understand you have a cow for sale, and it sounds like I found the right place. I met your daughter down the lane, and she introduced herself. You sure do have a sweet girl."

"Thanks," said Pa. "And I have three younger ones in the house." Then he started walking to the barn. "The cow is in here." Mr. Stevens followed while carrying a length of rope.

In the barn were Mr. Linstrom's two horses, two young calves, and two dairy cows. When they came to the cows, Pa showed Mr. Stevens the one that was for sale, which was the youngest and the better of the two. "Here she is," Pa said.

Mr. Stevens took a look at the cow. "Looks like a fine cow," he said. "Young and strong."

"She's over two years," said Pa. "She gave birth to one of the calves about six months ago."

"And how is she with milk?" asked Mr. Stevens.

"She's been giving some quality milk, and I doubt you'll find better milk anywhere else."

"I understand your price is twenty-five dollars?"

"Yes, sir," said Pa.

Mr. Stevens took one more look at the cow for sale, and it wasn't hard to make a final decision on the sale. "Okay, I'll take her," he said while Gabrielle entered the barn to see what was happening. Mr. Stevens reached into his pocket and pulled out the exact amount of payment, handed it to Pa, and turned towards the barn doorway where he noticed a younger girl. "This must be one of your daughters."

"This is Gabrielle," said Pa.

"What are you doing with Betsy?" Gabrielle asked Pa.

"I'm selling her to Mr. Stevens. And then we'll have enough money to buy you another dress," Pa said while Mr. Stevens leashed the cow with the rope.

As soon as the rope was tied, Pa slowly walked towards the barn doorway with Mr. Stevens who started leading the cow outside. Gabrielle stepped out of the way.

When the two men reached the doorway, Mr. Stevens looked at

143

Gabrielle who was looking at the cow and watching its departure. Through his eyes, he noticed something about her countenance that gave him the belief that there was something precious and special about her.

After Mr. Stevens came to his wagon, he started tying the other end of the rope to the back of it for leading the cow to his house. When the rope was tied, he looked over again at Gabrielle, and something seemed to touch his heart. There was something about her glowing countenance that seemed to shine with Heaven's light. Remembering what Mr. Linstrom had told his daughter in the barn, and seeing the young girl wearing a dress that was a bit too big for her size, he needed to find an excuse for doing what he felt strongly inspired to do. He turned to briefly face his newly purchased cow once more. Next, he walked over to Pa while reaching again into his pocket and pulling out five more dollars. "She's such a fine cow. I think she's worth more than what you asked for, and I wouldn't feel right without giving you this," he said while handing the extra money to Pa who was unaware of the real reason for the extra payment.

The following day on the 18th of December, the Linstrom family got all bundled up for the cold weather, left the house soon after breakfast, and climbed onto the wagon for going into town to get what was needed the most—a dress for Gabrielle.

After entering the mercantile, both Ma and Abigail helped Gabrielle look through the dresses to choose which ones to purchase. Because Pa had received more money than expected, he had enough for three dresses—one Sunday dress, and two everyday dresses. There wasn't enough space in the clothing section for everyone to look through the dresses, so Pa took the two youngest girls and browsed through other sections of the mercantile.

Trying to find dresses with the best fabric patterns, they also needed to find the right size that would fit Gabrielle. While searching, the wife of the storeowner, Mrs. Walters, noticed three womenfolk and went to see if they needed help. When she approached them, she spoke in a friendly, businesslike tone, "Welcome to River Town Mercantile! We have a large range of dresses of all sizes. Which one of you are you shopping for?"

Abigail pointed to Gabrielle. "For her," she said.

"Well, you've come to the right place!" said Mrs. Walters with a smile. "What type of dress are you looking for?"

"We're looking for one Sunday dress," said Ma, "and we also need two other dresses for every day."

Mrs. Walters took one more look at Gabrielle. "That's quite an interesting coat! I've never seen one like it before." Then she faced

Mrs. Linstrom and asked, "What store did you find it at?"

Ma replied, "I didn't find it anywhere. Gabrielle got it from someone, but it's a long story we're trying to figure out."

Before long, the family left the mercantile with three new dresses for Gabrielle along with three matching bonnets, an extra pinafore, two extra pairs of bloomers and stockings, and an extra pair of laced boots like the ones that seemed to have disappeared.

Standing by the wagon, an idea came to Pa. Looking across the street, he said, "While we're here, let's see how Sheriff Badger is coming along on his search." The family placed the clothing into the wagon, and they walked with Pa across the street to the sheriff's office.

Sabrina and Gabrielle were the first ones to enter after Pa helped open the door. Gabrielle wanted to make sure Sabrina knew where they were. "This is the sheriff's office." And seeing Sheriff Badger behind his desk, she mentioned to her younger sister, "And this is Sheriff Badger."

As soon as Sheriff Badger saw the entire Linstrom family, he knew why they had come. He faced Ma and Pa. "I've searched all over town, and there's nobody by the name of Felding," he said.

"How about a nearby town or city?" asked Ma.

"I've checked in all surrounding towns and cities, and there are no records anywhere that contain the name of Felding. The nearest Feldings I could locate are living in Missouri over six hundred miles away."

Suddenly, Gabrielle felt devastated, having heard what Sheriff Badger said, which made her start to believe she might not get to see Mr. and Mrs. Felding ever again. "Why did they move to Missouri?"

Sheriff Badger looked at Gabrielle who had an expression of grief with sadness in her eyes that were looking back at him. Immediately, he recalled the sweet, adorable face he had seen almost three weeks previous to that day, which still seemed to have an angelic glow, yet the sparkle that had been in her eyes was now hidden behind the sadness, and he wished there was something he could do to brighten her day. "I'm sorry, Sweetie, but I did my best. There's nobody who goes by the names you told me, but I don't think they moved to Missouri. The Feldings who live there are not George and Linda." Then the sheriff turned to Pa. "Did you meet with Edna Robinson to ask if she knew anyone named Molly?"

"Yes, I did," said Pa. "I've been driving Gabrielle to her house for piano lessons, and she said she didn't know anyone named Molly."

"Then the only possible conclusion is that those people don't exist, and it's all a fairytale," said Sheriff Badger.

145

Ma shook her head. "No," she said to the sheriff with certainty. "Gabrielle learned some additional songs on the piano when she was lost during the last few months, and it wasn't Mrs. Robinson who taught her. Gabrielle said she took piano lessons from Mrs. Felding. Are you sure there's nobody by that name?"

"Wait a minute!" exclaimed Sheriff Badger. "How can a four-year-old girl take piano lessons from someone else when Edna Robinson is the only piano teacher in town?"

"That's what *we're* trying to figure out," said Pa.

"Well, let me search again, and right at the moment that I find anything, I'll drive over to your place to let you know," said the sheriff.

Having heard what Sheriff Badger said, knowing that all hope was not gone in finding her foster parents and her best friend, it returned hope into Gabrielle's heart, which brought back the sparkle in her eyes. The sheriff faced her once more, catching sight of the restored sparkle, and it was confirmed to him once again in his heart that there was something precious about her, yet there were no words to describe what it was.

When the Linstrom family arrived back home, still in the wagon, the time was getting close to noon. Pa needed to take Gabrielle to the Robinsons' house for another piano lesson, so Ma took Abigail, Sabrina, and Tabitha into the house while Pa and Gabrielle stayed in the wagon and soon headed down the lane again.

At the Robinsons' house, Pa sat on the couch just like before. Sitting at the piano, Mrs. Robinson had different plans for the piano lesson that day. "When learning the piano," she said to Gabrielle, "it's not just learning how to play with your fingers, but it's also important to learn about who composed these songs. Do you remember from a few months ago when I told you who composed 'Ode to Joy'?"

"Beethoven," answered Gabrielle.

"Correct," said Mrs. Robinson. "You have a good memory!"

"And he's an ancient composer who was born 249 years ago," Gabrielle continued.

"No," corrected Mrs. Robinson while shaking her head. "He was born in 1770, and that was ninety-nine years ago. Where did you get the idea he was born 249 years ago?"

"That's what Mrs. Felding told me."

"Are you sure she was talking about Beethoven? Maybe she was talking about someone else."

"I thought she was talking about Beethoven," said Gabrielle. "And she said Tchaikovsky lived a long time ago."

"Tchaikovsky?" repeated Mrs. Robinson. She shook her head

once again. "He was born only twenty-nine years ago. Maybe Mrs. Felding thinks twenty-nine years is a long time."

"But Sophie said he died five years before George Gershwin was born."

"Who's Sophie?" asked Mrs. Robinson.

Listening to the mysterious conversation, Pa spoke in reply. "She's one of Mrs. Felding's students."

"And who is George Gershwin?" Mrs. Robinson asked. Pa shrugged his shoulders.

"He's an ancient composer," replied Gabrielle.

"And you said he lived *after* Tchaikovsky?" asked Mrs. Robinson.

Gabrielle nodded her head. "And so did Scott Joplin."

"Scott Joplin? I never heard that name before."

"He was another composer," said Gabrielle.

"Two composers who lived after Tchaikovsky?" Mrs. Robinson asked. Gabrielle nodded her head. "One of Tchaikovsky's first compositions called 'The Storm' was composed only five years ago, and he's been composing music every year ever since then. His first published symphony was only three years ago, so how can someone be born five years after a death that never happened? You might want to have a talk with Mrs. Felding as soon as you find her. It sounds like she has some false information that needs to be corrected before she teaches these ideas to any other student."

Eventually, Mrs. Robinson gave up on trying to teach anything about composers. It seemed that whatever she tried to teach, Gabrielle already knew. And anything that only Gabrielle knew was known to Mrs. Robinson as false information.

Later that afternoon, Pa explained to Ma what was said at the Robinsons' house, but it was no big surprise to either of them. Ever since Gabrielle's return after months of being lost, there was hardly anything that was normal about her. It was always one mystery after another, and both Ma and Pa wondered how much a few months of time could possibly change one girl. But the biggest problem for them was how to change Gabrielle back to the girl she used to be in the days when she wasn't always coming up with crazy ideas.

In the afternoon of the following Monday on the 20th day of December, Pa, Abigail, and Gabrielle bundled up warmly for the cold weather, and they headed out the door while Ma stayed home with Sabrina and Tabitha. Abigail carried the basket of eggs she had gathered earlier that day.

When they came to the covered wagon, Abigail gently placed the basket of eggs into the wagon, and the two girls stood there while Pa momentarily stepped into the barn to grab the axe that he took with him. Then they all climbed into the wagon and set off to find a Christmas tree to take home with them. It was the first day off school for the Christmas break.

Planning to drop off the eggs at the mercantile, it was conveniently on their way to a different field that had many sizes of evergreen trees to choose from. Halfway to the mercantile, they noticed a few snowflakes falling. "It's snowing!" said Gabrielle.

Pa started feeling worried about the weather, hoping it wouldn't get much worse for ruining their plans of getting a tree. "Let's hope it doesn't start coming down too heavy," he said.

By the time they arrived at the mercantile, the snowfall had somewhat increased. Now it was more than just a few snowflakes. As soon as they were parked, Pa hopped down from the driver's seat and hurried to the back where he lifted each of the girls down from the wagon. Abigail took the basket of eggs and carried it with her carefully while they all quickly walked to the entrance door of the mercantile.

Just when the door started to open, Mr. and Mrs. Walters looked to see who was coming. Not only were Pa, Abigail, and Gabrielle coming inside in a manner of wasting no time to close the door, but they also brought in a cold draft that was soon felt throughout the store. "It looks like it's picking up out there," said Mrs. Walters while looking outside through the window.

"What can we do for you?" asked Mr. Walters.

"We brought more eggs," said Abigail while taking them to the counter where Mr. and Mrs. Walters were standing.

Carefully, she handed them the basket. Pa and Gabrielle stood right behind her. Mrs. Walters briefly looked at the eggs to make sure they weren't cracked. "As usual, they look good, so we'll credit this to your account," she said while she carefully took the eggs out of the basket.

"What else can we do for you?" asked Mr. Walters.

"Nothing else," said Pa. "We need to get going in case it gets any worse out there." Then he and the girls turned around after Abigail grabbed the empty basket, and they started walking to the door.

"Let's hope the weather will stay calm for your travel back home," said Mr. Walters. "The Farmer's Almanac predicts a big snow storm sometime this winter."

Halfway to the door, Gabrielle stopped and turned around to face Mr. Walters. "We're getting a Christmas tree!" she said with a smile.

"Come along, Gabrielle," said Pa right after turning around to face her. "We need to hurry in case a storm comes."

"Well, good luck out there," said Mrs. Walters. "And safe travels!"

"We'll be wishing you the best!" hollered Mr. Walters while the Linstroms were stepping out of the mercantile.

After Pa and the girls were on the wagon, they continued a mile down the road past the school.

Twenty minutes later, they arrived at the field that had loads of evergreen trees including different types of fir trees, pine trees, and spruce trees. Pa parked the wagon beside the road. He helped each of the girls down onto the ground, and he grabbed his axe. By that time, a constant, small breeze had started, the snow was falling twice as much as when they were at the mercantile, and the temperature had dropped by eight degrees during the past hour. "Let's not waste any time in choosing a tree," said Pa. Quickly, they walked onto the field and started searching.

A minute later, an impressive-looking tree caught Gabrielle's eye. "Let's get that one!" she said, pointing to the tree that stood a few yards away. Then they all walked closer to it.

After Abigail examined the size of it, she shook her head. "It's too big. We don't have a place in the house to put it."

Pa briefly examined the size as well. "Your sister's right," he said to Gabrielle. "The only place for a tree is right by the front window, and this tree isn't going to fit there. Let's choose a smaller one." At that moment, a stronger gust of wind fleetingly blew across the field. "I hope we can make it home if this is the snow storm that Mr. Walters was talking about from the almanac."

"Pa," said Gabrielle. "Don't you know how much it's going to snow today?"

"No, I don't. But we can't take any chances. We need to get home as soon as we can," answered Pa.

"But you would know if it's going to stop snowing later today if we had a television or a radio."

"If we had *what*?" Pa asked. Immediately, he assumed Gabrielle's outrageous imagination was at it again. "Oh, never mind! Let's just find a tree."

Almost instantly, Abigail spotted a smaller tree at a distance and pointed to it. "How about that one over there?"

"Let's go take a look," said Pa.

When they reached the tree, there was no doubt that it was the perfect one. Having found a Balsam Fir that was skinny enough to fit almost anywhere, Pa got to work on starting to chop it down, and within a few minutes, the two girls were helping Pa carry it to the wagon.

On their way back home while passing the school and the mercantile, the snowfall had increased substantially, and the wind was blowing more than twice as hard. The temperature had dropped another few degrees, and everyone's noses and cheeks were starting to feel numb. Pa had to be careful at steering the horses in case they were to get spooked by the storm at any moment. At the same time, his thoughts were drawn to the conversation in the field of evergreen trees regarding the amount of space in the house. He thought ahead to the future when his four daughters would be more grown up, and how there wouldn't be enough space for everyone to sleep. He knew there was not enough room to put two larger beds where Sabrina and Tabitha slept, and there was no space in the loft to put any extra beds. He was definitely not rich enough to buy a bigger house, he didn't have enough money to build an extra room on to the house, and no amount of eggs taken to the mercantile would be enough to solve the problem. Wondering what to do when that time would come was something that kept his thoughts busy for the next several minutes.

Meanwhile, from inside the house, Ma could hear the wind blowing outside. The clouds that filled the sky had gotten considerably darker, large snowflakes were falling in great abundance, and Pa and the girls had not yet returned home. She stood by the front window and looked outside. The daylight was still making it light enough to see everything, but it appeared to be getting darker practically by the minute. *I hope they're okay,* Ma thought to herself, constantly having a prayer in her heart that they would return home in safety. Then she went back to her bed where Sabrina and Tabitha were at, and she held both of the girls to comfort them from the sounds of the storm.

Several minutes later, the wagon came to a stop in front of the barn. "We need to get the tree inside before it gets any worse," Pa hollered to the girls at the back of the wagon over the sound of the wind, "and then I need to unhitch the team and take the canvas off the wagon before the wind gets too strong. So let's hurry!" With no time to lose, he jumped down from the wagon, rushed to the back, and lifted down Gabrielle who was already in position to get down while Abigail inched past the tree, making her way towards the back of the wagon. Pa soon lifted Abigail down, and then it was time to take the tree from the wagon to the house. Needing help from both girls, Gabrielle wasn't by the wagon anywhere. Pa quickly turned to different directions, but he couldn't see her. "Where's your sister?" he asked Abigail. At that moment, he looked towards the house and saw her right when she was going inside, not knowing she had gone to the house to let Ma know they were back home. *Already at the house?* he thought. Just like months before, he was once again surprised at how fast her four-year-old legs could run, being that she was the fastest runner between all four daughters. With the wind blowing even stronger, something needed to be done immediately, so he turned back to Abigail and spoke loud enough to be heard. "I don't know what your sister is doing, but we need her help. Could you go get her for me while I stay here close to the horses?"

Almost immediately, Ma came hastening out the door. Abigail pointed towards the house. "Here comes Ma," she shouted above the sound of the storm.

Seconds later, Ma arrived at the back of the wagon. Snow was blowing into everyone's faces. By this time, Pa's and Abigail's noses and cheeks were numb in the bitter cold. With the strings of her bonnet grasping her neck through the strong wind, Ma took one end of the tree along with Abigail, and she helped carry the tree to the house, making the transporting of the tree go faster and easier than if Gabrielle were there to help.

After getting all the sleep that Mother Nature would allow, the Linstrom family and everyone else in River Town woke up the next morning to three feet of snow. Not only was it the biggest snowfall River Town had ever seen, but it was also still snowing outside. The citizens of the town were all stuck in their houses, and nobody could travel anywhere.

Close to the back door inside the Linstroms' house laid a few logs for the fireplace, which was enough to last through the morning. During the winter months each year, Pa had always brought in a few logs at a time for allowing them to dry out before adding them to the fireplace. The rest of the wood was piled in a large stack right behind the house close to the door, and now the entire stack was buried in the snow. But before Pa could make a pathway to the wood pile to bring in any more logs to dry out, he needed to wait until after breakfast to give Tabitha time to wake up before letting in the cold to where she slept.

Still in the early daylight hours of the morning, Pa wasn't looking forward to making a pathway to the barn, but he knew that the cow needed to be milked, so he bundled up as much as he could. Then he opened the front door, and it was no easy task just to get outside to close the door.

On his way from the house to the barn, Gabrielle stood on a chair right by the front window, looked outside, and watched her pa taking a long time to get there. Seeing it was a tough and challenging chore to go through three feet of snow, she remembered watching a video Mr.

Felding showed her about how snow blowers work, and she wondered why Pa was doing it the hard way.

By the time it stopped snowing the next day, River Town was buried under four feet of snow. Abigail was surprised it measured up to exactly how tall she was. The snow level went partly up the windows, and the only thing Gabrielle could see outside was the sky. The Linstrom family was grateful they had enough food to last for a few days. With freezing temperatures, everyone in River Town knew that the snow was not going to melt anytime soon. It was definitely a winter that would be written down in future history books for being known to future generations.

The morning of the following Saturday on Christmas Day, there were no presents under the tree. Not only had the snow kept the Linstroms from going to get any presents at the mercantile throughout that week, but they never had enough money to afford a lot of gifts. Because Abigail, Gabrielle, and Sabrina didn't know what it was like to get many gifts for Christmas, they were not the slightest bit devastated by the time they woke up and saw nothing besides empty floor space under the tree. All they knew was that it was Christmas Day and that the ultimate reason for the holiday was to celebrate the birth of Jesus Christ, which brought a degree of joy to their hearts that lasted throughout the day. It also filled the hearts of Ma and Pa when they saw their daughters expressing gratitude and joy for the holiday without expecting to unwrap anything.

Soon after breakfast, Ma walked into the room where she and Pa slept. She opened the wooden chest that was close to the bed, which was where she had placed Gabrielle's pink jeans and light blue t-shirt. One at a time, she pulled out four dolls that she had secretly made throughout the year. As soon as she pulled out the last one, she noticed a star that had been on their Christmas tree from the previous year, and she took that out as well. She carried the dolls and the star out to the main room where everyone else was trying to stay warm with the heat from the fireplace. Not having had enough money throughout the year to afford to wrap up the dolls, she started walking towards her daughters. "Merry Christmas!" she said right before handing a doll to each of the four girls.

"Thank you!" said Abigail with a smile.

"Yes, thank you!" said Gabrielle. "Merry Christmas, Ma!"

"Where did you get these?" Abigail asked Ma.

"I made them this year. I did it when you girls weren't around to see," answered Ma.

Gabrielle held her doll while keeping her eyes focused on it. Knowing that Ma had made it, it was more special to her than if it would have been purchased at the mercantile. It was also more than what she was expecting to get that day.

"Star!" said Sabrina while she pointed to it.

Abigail took a look at the star that Ma was still holding, and she recognized it. "That's the star we had on the tree last year," she said.

"Who wants to put it on the tree this year?" asked Pa.

"I do! I do!" Gabrielle quickly exclaimed.

Ma handed the star to Gabrielle. Then she and Pa walked to the tree. Pa lifted her up, and she carefully placed the star onto the top of the tree before Pa lowered her back down onto the floor.

Abigail watched as Gabrielle put the star on top, and she continued to look at the star afterwards. "It's the star of Bethlehem!" she said. "It brought the three wise men to the place where Jesus was born!"

Gabrielle thought about what her sister had just said. In addition to knowing she had a doll that was made by her ma, she also knew she was the one who had put up the star of Bethlehem. More joy filled her heart, and it was definitely a Christmas to remember.

Meanwhile, on Christmas Day in 2019, Mr. and Mrs. Felding had just finished opening the gifts to and from each other. Although they both had gratitude for the gifts they had received, they didn't feel much joy that day. They wondered where Gabby had gone. They had recently checked with Officer Gunwell, but he had no leads, no traces, no witnesses, and no evidence regarding Gabby's whereabouts.

Mrs. Felding held the crocheted doll she had finished making three weeks before that day, knowing she was planning on giving it to Gabby as a Christmas gift. With still no Gabby to give it to, her heart was overwhelmed with sorrow and despair. As much as she wanted to give the doll to her foster daughter, she decided to save it for a later day if Gabby were to ever be seen again. She reflected on the memory of when she and Mr. Felding first met Gabby. She remembered thinking of her as a sweet girl during that time, and those thoughts from months ago remained the same on that current Christmas Day.

Mr. Felding thought back to when he had a talk with Gabby by the front window. He remembered that day when he told her she had a precious heart. Thinking about so many good memories of her, he wondered how someone so precious could be so lost.

That previous Sunday, Mr. and Mrs. Felding had asked the preacher at church to pray that Gabby could return to them. After they explained the situation to him about how lost she was with no hope of being found, he told them that it sometimes takes a while for prayers to be answered.

Knowing what the preacher had said, Mr. and Mrs. Felding spent the majority of Christmas Day in prayer. They knew that God could perform miracles like He had done many times before—starting with the miracle in Bethlehem—and they wondered if there could possibly be a bright star to shine on Gabby for someone to find her. But no matter how their prayers would be answered, they always kept a prayer in their hearts that Gabby would eventually find her way back home.

# 13
## NOT A GOOD IDEA

Towards the beginning of January in the year of 1870, the snow finally melted enough to travel. The Linstrom family was almost out of food besides milk and eggs. It wasn't the season to start growing any crops, so the only other option for food was for Pa to go hunting for meat.

It was early on a cold morning when Pa started to prepare for a long day. At the break of dawn, he went to the barn to milk the cow and hitch up the team to the wagon.

A few minutes after sunrise, Pa returned to the house. Everyone besides Sabrina and Tabitha was awake at that time. Ma helped Pa get some food prepared to take with him on his hunting trip including sandwiches, nuts, and sunflower seeds.

After breakfast, Pa gave everyone a hug. Then he grabbed his rifle, and he made sure he had enough ammunition to last throughout the trip. He wasn't looking forward to a long day of being gone for so long, and neither did the womenfolk look forward to not having Pa around for most of the day. But everyone knew there were things that had to be done in order to survive.

While driving to a far-off pasture, Pa thought again about the future. He wondered what would happen when his four daughters would all be grown with no room for everyone in the house. With no way to build up enough savings, it wouldn't be possible to build on to the house, and buying a bigger house was far beyond consideration. His thoughts also led to that previous Christmas Day when he saw his wife holding four dolls that were not wrapped up because they couldn't even afford to do that.

Pa took a few minutes in wonder of how to prepare for the future, but he was unsuccessful at finding a solution. He thought about Mr. and Mrs. Walters who were the richest people in town. It seemed like they could afford almost anything they wanted. But how to be the owner of another mercantile in town with no money to even start building another one, Pa didn't think it was fair for some people to have more money than the cost of their basic needs while other people had no way to earn enough for what they needed. *What if everyone had the same amount of money?* he thought. *Then everyone would have enough to survive.*

Later that day just minutes before sunset, Pa returned home with one elk, one deer, and one rabbit. Now they had enough food to last for a while.

As soon as Pa entered the house, the three oldest girls immediately felt excited. "Pa!" they all shouted. They dashed over to him in the very short distance, and they all gave him a hug at the same time.

Feeling quite welcomed while giving three big hugs in return, Pa exclaimed, "Well, if this is the kind of recognition I get, then maybe I should go on hunting trips more often!"

Thinking he was serious about what he said, the three girls all shouted, "No!" In response, Pa gave a smile to let them know he was being silly.

"Did you get anything?" Abigail asked.

"I got one elk, one deer, and one rabbit. And since it's getting too dark outside, they'll keep until tomorrow, especially with how cold it is out there." Then he turned to face Ma. "How did things go around here?"

While holding Tabitha, Ma replied, "Oh, just be glad you weren't around!"

"Why? What happened?" asked Pa out of curiosity.

Abigail blurted out, "Gabrielle said you were doing it the hard way."

"Doing what?" Pa asked.

"Getting meat," said Ma. Right at that moment, she was at a loss for words because it was hard to explain.

Pa became confused. "Does Gabrielle know a better way to go hunting?"

Gabrielle replied, "You wouldn't be gone all day if you got the meat from the grocery store. You would have been home sooner."

Pa looked at Gabrielle. "Gabrielle, we already had a talk about this. There's no such thing as a grocery store in town, milk doesn't cost three dollars for one gallon, and nobody besides you has ever heard of something called a Pop-Tart."

In the afternoon of the following day, Pa took a look at different parts of the house while wondering where to build another room, and how it could be built at the cheapest possible cost. Instead of waiting for the future to come, he wanted to start preparing as soon as possible. He thought if he waited for the house to be too crowded, then it would be too late to prepare.

Gabrielle watched Pa for several minutes. In her eyes, it looked like Pa was acting mysterious. She wondered why he was examining every wall of the house. When it became too hard for any extra curiosity to be built up inside of her, she walked up to him. "What are you doing, Pa?" she asked.

"I'm trying to find out where to build an extra room," he said. "When the four of you girls grow up and get bigger, it's going to be too crowded in the back where Sabrina and Tabitha sleep, and there's no more space up in the loft for another bed. Not just that, but I'm also trying to think of the cheapest way to build in case we can't afford anything when the time comes."

"Oh," voiced Gabrielle. "Did you find out anything?"

"Well," said Pa, "if everything remains the same as it is, then I don't see how we're going to survive. We don't have enough money for every need, but other people have more than they need."

"Then they could give us the money we need," suggested Gabrielle.

"It's not that simple," said Pa. "People don't just give their money away. But if there was a law that could balance earnings for every household, then nobody would have any problems. So I've been thinking about running for president."

Immediately, Pa's last spoken word triggered Gabrielle's memory of what she heard from Mr. Felding, Mrs. Felding, and Sophie. She remembered hearing the name of Harold Linstrom being referred to as the worst president in history. Not knowing she had been in the future, all she knew was that the number of presidents was up to forty-five. And thinking of herself as the daughter of a future president, she grew somewhat excited. "You could be the 46th president!" she said. "And you'll be the second president with the name of Harold Linstrom!"

Again, the mystery of Gabrielle confused Pa. In correction to what his daughter said, he explained, "There was never a president with my name, and I'd have to live forever to be the 46th president. Why do you choose the number forty-six when we've only had eighteen presidents?"

"Mrs. Felding told me we've had forty-five presidents."

"Forty-five? Where did she get that idea?"

"I don't know. That's just what she said."

"If that's what she said, then who's the president right now?"

Gabrielle tried to remember the name she heard from Mrs. Linstrom, but as much as she tried to remember, her memory drew nothing besides a blank. "I can't remember his name."

"Then who were the presidents before him?"

Gabrielle took another moment to try to remember any name of any president, but was unsuccessful at remembering any name after the year of 1870. "I don't know. The last one I can remember is President Grant."

"That's because he's our current president," said Pa.

"But I heard he lived a long time ago."

"Maybe you heard wrong. Maybe you heard he was *born* a long time ago. After all, he's older than I am, and you once told me that *I'm* old."

At that point, it was Gabrielle's turn to be confused. Being left speechless, she wondered why she couldn't remember the name of any president after President Grant when she was so good at remembering. She remembered being at a grocery store, she remembered being at the cemetery in town that had hundreds of gravestones, she remembered seeing so many cars that didn't seem to exist anymore, and she remembered so many other things including her piano lessons with Mrs. Felding as well as the times that were spent with Molly.

A few days later while Abigail was at school, Gabrielle was deep in thought. Many things that were said regarding Harold Linstrom as the president had come to her remembrance. According to what Pa had said, why did Sophie and the Feldings say that Harold Linstrom was the worst president when there was never a president by that name? And who was telling the truth regarding how many presidents there were? Was the number of presidents eighteen, or was it up to forty-five? Gabrielle also wondered why everyone who said there were forty-five presidents also knew what a television, video camera, car, and many other inventions were. And everyone who said there were eighteen presidents didn't seem to know what anything was. Not being able to put everything together yet, she at least knew there was something she needed to find out. Not only that, but she also knew she was the only one left to find out why nothing made any sense. Nobody else seemed to have any answers including the whereabouts of Molly, Sophie, and the Feldings. There were so many questions that were unanswered, but the two biggest questions created a big challenge for Gabrielle. How was she going to solve this mystery of unanswered questions, and where could she possibly go to find the answers when there was nobody in town who could help?

Over the course of the next few weeks, Gabrielle overheard Pa a few different times when he mentioned the idea about running for president. Ma even thought it was a good idea. Gradually, the idea got all over town. During one of Gabrielle's piano lessons, Pa mentioned his plans to Mrs. Robinson. And when the Linstrom family was at the mercantile one day, he mentioned it to Mr. and Mrs. Walters. But he hadn't told the sheriff, and he would soon find out he didn't need to. That same day while at the mercantile, Sheriff Badger walked in and found Pa. "I heard you're planning on running for president, and I think the country needs someone like you," the sheriff said.

"But we haven't been to your office to tell you. How did you know?" Pa asked him.

"Mrs. Robinson told me," replied Sheriff Badger.

In Gabrielle's view, it seemed like Pa's plans were getting quite serious. During the time when the word was getting around the town, she constantly reflected on what was said months ago about a bad president who had the same name as Pa. She wondered why Pa had never heard of someone else with the same name, and she also started to wonder if perhaps the Feldings and Sophie had somehow known about Pa's plans before Pa even brought up the idea. Maybe they knew Pa better than he knew himself.

On a day towards the end of February, a similarity dawned on Gabrielle's memory what Mr. Felding and Pa both said. She remembered Mr. Felding explaining why President Linstrom was the worst president, and then she recalled Pa saying he wanted everyone to have an equal amount of money and, according to what Mr. Felding said, that's what caused the first of the two Great Depressions. Because there had never been a Great Depression by the year of 1870, according to what Pa had told her, she wondered whether Mr. Felding had the power to see into the future, especially since Pa had no idea what she was talking about after she mentioned the topic to him. But regardless of what the answers to this mystery were, the similarity was too great to ignore. Whatever a Great Depression would be like to live through, which sounded like something that would happen if Pa became the president, it didn't sound good, so Gabrielle didn't want to find out. Now she knew it was all up to her to get her pa to change his mind.

No matter what Gabrielle told anyone about things that didn't appear to exist, or about events nobody ever heard, everyone thought she was crazy. It seemed like she was the only one who knew about certain inventions and other things, and she was starting to feel quite discouraged with everyone calling her crazy. Eventually, she decided to start talking less about things that didn't appear to exist anymore. And the reason for the nonexistence of invented things was left totally up to her to find out.

While thinking about the comparison between Pa and President Linstrom, she remembered the library book Mr. Felding had checked out from the library about the life of President Linstrom. Even though she had known that the names of President Linstrom's daughters were the same as her and her sisters, she started thinking about it as being too much of a coincidence with knowing why Pa wanted to run for president. And knowing that President Linstrom lived right here in town, it was another big coincidence. Her thoughts soon led to thinking about where Mr. Felding had gotten the library book. She remembered being at the city library when the roads were paved, but she had never been to a library in town with dirt roads. She wondered who wrote the book, when it was written, and how to find the book with no library in town. This time, she was certain that the only way to find the answers to these specific questions was to ask Mr. Felding, but finding him was another task that only she could do. However, she didn't have a clue where to look or how to find anyone. *If only I could find that book,* she thought, *then I could show it to Pa and let him read what I want to tell him.*

During the next few days, Gabrielle tried to think of a good way to discourage Pa from wanting to run for president. In making sure that's what she wanted to do, she pictured herself as the president's daughter, and she wondered what it would be like to be famous. She imagined herself on national television—after the mystery of missing televisions would somehow be solved—and she thought of her name being written in future history books just like the other Gabrielle who had three sisters with the same names as her own sisters, and whose pa was the president of . . . something. In contrast, she envisioned what her life would be like if a Great Depression happened as a result from her pa being in the White House. In that case, every business would be going out of business including River Town Mercantile, and nobody would have any money to buy any food. In supposing that would happen, and still hoping to one day find the Feldings, she dreaded the thoughts of being too poor to afford any Pop-Tarts if she were to ever live with her foster parents again. In addition, if she were to be the daughter of a president who ruined the country, then the thoughts of being seen on television would be too hard to bear.

Thinking about every possible future situation, Gabrielle felt a great need to get Pa to change his mind. But what could a four-year-old girl say to her pa to get him to change his plans when he already had support for his decision from everyone else in town including everyone else in the Linstrom household? Even Abigail was excited about the thoughts of being the daughter of a president. So what could Gabrielle tell Pa without disappointing her sister?

All throughout the first weekend of the month of March, Gabrielle sensed the urgency in getting started with her attempt to explain something to Pa, but she was still clueless on what to say without being called crazy, and without shattering the hopes of everyone in town. It sounded like everyone at church that Sunday was talking about it and giving their full support to Pa. Nobody else knew what Gabrielle knew, so it was guaranteed that nobody would believe her no matter what she would say, and she especially didn't want to upset her older sister.

The first Monday in March was the 7th day of the month. On that day, Gabrielle waited for Abigail to be gone to school. She didn't want her sister to hear whatever she was going to say to Pa. She also didn't feel right about letting Ma listen, which would disappoint her too. So Gabrielle waited for an opportunity to be alone with Pa.

Towards the last of the morning right before noon, Pa left the house to go feed the cows in the barn while Gabrielle was up in the loft. She had no idea Pa was going anywhere until she heard the front door being closed. Then she looked down from the loft to see who went outside. She noticed Ma, Sabrina, and Tabitha still inside, but no sight of Pa. "Where did Pa go?" she asked aloud to Ma.

"He went out to the barn to feed the cows," answered Ma. Immediately, Gabrielle recognized an opportunity to talk with Pa without anyone else around to hear, but she didn't want Ma to know what she was going to do. "May I go help him?" she asked.

"I'm sure he won't mind some extra help. Yes, you may," Ma said.

Gabrielle quickly climbed down the ladder and hurried to the door. As soon as she got outside, she closed the door behind her, and she ran all the way to the barn. As serious as Pa was about his future plans, Gabrielle knew he wasn't going to take her advice right after the first word, so she knew it would take some time.

When she got to the barn door, Pa noticed her. "Hey, Gab!" he said. Every once in a while, he called his daughters by a shortened name—Ab, Gab, Sab, and Tab—but only on very rare occasions.

"Could I help feed the cows?" asked Gabrielle. Knowing that helping with work was generally appreciated, she wanted Pa to feel as high-spirited as possible.

Pa grabbed the pitchfork and started walking towards the supply of hay. "You need to be a bit bigger to use a pitchfork, but you can help carry handfuls of hay if you'd like."

Gabrielle walked over to the hay and started taking a handful of it to the cows while Pa carried a much larger amount. "Pa," said Gabrielle, seeing her pa in a good mood.

"What's on your mind?" asked Pa.

"Do you . . . uh . . ." Gabrielle stumbled with words. She wasn't quite sure what to say. She took a deep breath, and a question suddenly came to her thoughts. "Are you sure you want to run for president?"

"Why do you ask that? I wouldn't have let everyone in town know about it if I wasn't sure." At that instant, Pa thought about how Gabrielle had been acting compared to her older sister during the past few weeks. "And why haven't you been excited like Abigail? Don't you want to be the daughter of a president?"

"I don't know," replied Gabrielle. "What if you do something wrong, and what if it ruins the country? Do you really know how to be the president?"

Pa chuckled. "Is that what's been on your mind? Well, don't worry about it. Being the president can't be that hard. All I need to do is make a law that would give everyone the same amount of money. That way, everyone will be able to afford to live, and I might even be known in the future as the greatest president. But that's only if I get elected, so don't worry. I might not even get elected."

Gabrielle knew that nothing more could be said. She knew that if she talked about a certain library book without showing it to anyone, then nobody would believe her, and everyone would think she was just using her imagination to keep Pa from trying to help the country. The only thing left to do was hope Pa would one day reflect on her words and decide to change his mind before it would be too late.

# 14
# WHERE'S MOLLY?

*As long as you keep asking any questions you have, you'll keep getting smarter and smarter,* Gabrielle remembered from what Mrs. Felding once said.  Although she was determined to talk less about certain things to keep from being called crazy, there were so many questions that were piled up in her mind, and there was no way to get any answers unless she followed Mrs. Felding's advice.

On Saturday, the 19$^{th}$ day of March, Gabrielle went outside in the afternoon to take a walk.  Because the weather was distinctly warmer, she didn't need to bundle up anymore.  Walking away from the back of the house, she walked past the pond and eventually came to the tree stump.  She sat down on it just like she had done numerous times before.  She needed some time to herself to decide which questions to ask, how to ask them, and whom to ask.

Sitting on the stump, she found herself thinking about the day when she first met Mr. and Mrs. Felding as well as the day when she was reunited with her family.  Both days, she had been sitting on the tree stump, but she had no idea how so many trees either appeared or disappeared.  However, the mystery of the trees wasn't one of the questions she would soon be asking anyone.  For the next several minutes, she thought about which questions were ones that anyone might have an answer to, hoping the answers to those questions could somehow lead her to find the answers to the ones that would only put everyone in a state of bewilderment if she were to ask them to anyone.

"Where's Gabrielle?" asked Pa from inside the house.

Abigail replied, "I saw her about five minutes ago when I was outside. She's sitting on the tree stump."

"And she's probably still there," said Ma, knowing how much Gabrielle had been on the stump in times past.

"What's so fascinating about a tree stump to a four-year-old girl?" asked Pa, but nobody had a response. "Well, tell Gabrielle where I'm going if she asks. I need to go talk with Mr. Fredericks at the blacksmith shop about horseshoes. It's about time for our horses to get new ones again."

Two minutes after Pa started driving down the lane, Gabrielle entered the house. "Where did Pa go?" she asked.

"To the blacksmith shop to see about new horseshoes," said Ma. "You must like that tree stump."

Gabrielle looked at her ma with no reply. Without her pa there, it was one less parent to help answer her questions. However, she knew she could only ask one question at a time, and having multiple questions to ask, she knew that a large number of anything always started with the first one. "Ma," she said.

"Yes," replied Ma.

"What day is my birthday?"

"You were born on May 9th on the same day the Civil War ended," said Ma.

Remembering what her foster mom had said, Gabrielle replied, "But Mrs. Felding told me April 9th is when it ended."

"April 9th is when Robert E. Lee surrendered to Ulysses S. Grant, but it was on May 9th when President Johnson declared it to be over, and that's the same day you were born, although it wasn't the official end. There was one more battle called the Battle of Palmito Ranch that took place in Texas on the 12th and 13th of that month, but the Civil War wasn't officially over until the 20th of August of the following year when President Johnson finally issued a proclamation that stated the war to be over," explained Ma.

"Oh," said Gabrielle. "Mrs. Felding never told me that." Suddenly, she remembered Mrs. Felding reading the information to her compared to Ma telling her all by memory, which created another question in her mind. "How did you remember without reading it?"

"Without reading it?" repeated Ma, wondering yet again what Gabrielle was trying to ask. "I'm not aware of any books written about the Civil War. But I remember it because it seems like yesterday. It all happened less than five years ago. And when you're an adult, five years ago can seem like just yesterday."

"Only five years ago?" Gabrielle asked. "Then when were the two world wars, and when was the first Veterans Day?"

"World wars? Veterans Day? Gabrielle, what are you talking about?" Ma asked in a huge state of wonder.

Not wanting to be called crazy anymore, Gabrielle shrugged her shoulders. "Just something Mrs. Felding told me," she said. At that point, she wasn't sure what to believe anymore. Everything her foster parents told her was not what Ma and Pa were telling her, and she couldn't even ask questions anymore without anyone wondering what she was saying.

After Pa returned home, Ma told him what had been said. "Why is she making up names for wars?" asked Pa. "What have those Feldings done to her? And as for a holiday called Veterans Day, it sounds like a foreign holiday from another country." But regardless of how crazy Ma and Pa thought Gabrielle was acting, they hadn't heard the last of it.

The following Saturday on the 26th day of March, Pa and Gabrielle left a few minutes before noon to go to the Robinsons' house for another piano lesson.

As soon as they arrived, parked, and got down from the wagon, Mrs. Robinson came outside to talk to them. Pa noticed her coming out of her house, and he wondered why she was walking towards them. "Today's not a good day for piano lessons," she said. "My husband is not feeling too well. And let's cancel next week too. It looks like it will take a while for him to recover."

"Oh, no," sympathized Pa, referring to the news about Mr. Robinson. "Is there anything we can do for you?"

Mrs. Robinson shook her head. "Not right now. The doctor is here, so I'm sure Frank will be getting the best of care."

"Okay," Pa said to Mrs. Robinson. Then he turned to Gabrielle. "Let's go." He lifted her up onto the front seat of the wagon before he climbed up. When he was seated, he turned again to Mrs. Robinson. "Give him our love from the Linstrom family."

"Thank you! God bless you!" Mrs. Robinson cried out while they started driving away.

Minutes later, Ma looked towards the front door when she heard the sound of it opening. "Was she not home?" she asked immediately when she saw Pa and Gabrielle.

"She was home," said Pa, "but she sent us away because Frank was ill, and the doctor was taking care of him."

"Oh, I hope he recuperates soon," said Ma, feeling sorry to hear about the news.

The following Monday morning on the 28th day of March, Abigail was gathering eggs from the chickens outside while Gabrielle was helping Ma cook breakfast. Once again, Gabrielle had been asked to set the table. Halfway through setting the table, she heard a strange noise. "What was *that*?" she asked.

"What?" asked Ma.

"I heard a noise," said Gabrielle.

"Of course you did," said Ma. "I'm stirring the ingredients, the chickens are clucking, Pa is working in the barn, and it sounds like Sabrina is starting to wake up."

"No," said Gabrielle. "It was a different noise."

"What did it sound like?" asked Ma.

"I don't know. It was too quiet to tell what it was."

"Well, look at what you're doing. Setting the dishes onto the table makes a noise, your footsteps on the floor make a noise, and several other noises outside including a slightly blowing wind can be heard too."

"But it wasn't a regular noise."

"Then I don't know what to tell you," said Ma.

A second later, Abigail and Pa both walked into the house through the front doorway. "Here are the eggs," said Abigail. She set the basket gently onto the center of the table, and Gabrielle resumed placing the dishes down to finish setting the table.

A few minutes later, the Linstrom family was seated around the table and started eating breakfast. "I heard it again!" said Gabrielle, feeling somewhat startled.

"Heard what?" asked Pa.

"She heard a strange noise while you and Abigail were outside," Ma said, "but she didn't know what the noise was."

Immediately, a memory came to Pa. "It reminds me of the time when we all started hearing strange noises just weeks before we started hearing Gabrielle's voice while she was still lost."

Abigail spoke to Gabrielle. "Maybe you're going to start hearing someone's voice."

"But whose voice is it going to be?" asked Ma.

After breakfast, Pa drove Abigail into town to take her to school along with taking the eggs to the mercantile. While they were gone, Gabrielle heard the noise several more times, and it made her think about when she heard a noise while living with the Feldings, which later led to hearing Ma's and Pa's voices before finding the tree stump and seeing the surrounding trees disappear. Although it seemed like a similar situation, she had no idea what to think.

Right after breakfast on the morning of Sunday, the 3rd day of April, the Linstrom family made preparations for going to church. Ma helped the three youngest girls put on their Sunday dresses. Abigail fixed Sabrina's and Gabrielle's hair, and Ma fixed Abigail's hair as well

166

as her own. When they were all ready, they loaded up into the wagon and started the drive to church.

At the beginning of the church service, the preacher made an announcement. "I'd like to welcome everyone to church today. Before we begin, Edna Robinson has asked me to inform everyone. We are saddened to hear that Frank Robinson passed away last Thursday. His funeral service will take place at the River Town Cemetery this Tuesday at noon."

Throughout the following day, the quiet noise kept sounding in Gabrielle's ears, but no matter how many times she brought it to anyone's attention, nobody else could hear it. And having had this experience before, she soon decided to stop talking about it. She knew that anytime she mentioned it to anyone, it didn't help the situation. The only thing she could do was to just let the noise be heard, remembering what Mr. Felding said about noises not hurting anyone.

Shortly before noon on Tuesday, the Linstrom family arrived at the cemetery. After parking to the side of the street with other wagons, buggies, carriages, and stage coaches, Pa helped the three oldest girls down from the back of the wagon.

As soon as Gabrielle was standing on the ground, she turned to face the cemetery. Most of the land was empty with no gravestones, there was no gate around the edge of the cemetery, and there was no entrance with a sign above it that said River City Cemetery. It was definitely not where Mr. and Mrs. Felding had taken her.

When the Linstroms were all down from the wagon, they started walking to the gravesite where several people were standing. Gabrielle turned to Pa and asked, "Where's the other cemetery?"

"What other cemetery?" asked Pa. "There are other cemeteries in other towns and cities. Is there a certain one that you're asking about?"

"Where's the other one in town?"

"This is the only one in town."

"But the Feldings took me to one that had a gate around it with hundreds of gravestones, and I thought this is where they took me to. Did someone take down the gate and move lots of gravestones somewhere else?"

Ma and Abigail both heard the conversation. "What are you talking about?" asked Abigail.

"Gabrielle, you've been here before," said Ma, "and it hasn't changed much since then. There might be four or five more gravesites ever since you were last here, but it looks the same, and there was never a gate around this cemetery. You need to stop talking about things that don't exist."

Two weeks later, Gabrielle took a walk out to the pond. It was a bright, sunny day, and the weather felt nice for being outside. It had been two days since the last time she heard the noise, and she wondered if it was finally gone.

She arrived at the pond and stood at the edge of it. With a reflection of the sky and a few small clouds, she stared down at the pond for a minute until she heard someone whisper her name. As soon as she heard her name, she looked to the left, then to the right, and then turned around to look behind her to find out who said her name, but nobody was in sight. Again, just like before, the whisper was too quiet to know who spoke. With the whisper having no vocal sound, it was certainly not anyone hollering for her from the house. And knowing she had also lived through this experience when she was with the Feldings, she made it a point to never ask anyone who said her name anytime she would be hearing the whisper again.

Two more weeks went by, and the month of May arrived. During those two weeks, nobody had heard anything crazy from Gabrielle, and everyone was starting to wonder whether she had finally returned back to normalcy. However, she was still hearing the whisper that nobody else could hear, and it had gotten louder than the first time she heard it.

Thirty minutes before six o'clock in the morning on Monday, the 2nd day of May, Gabrielle awoke to the sound of Molly's voice. In no time at all, she grew excited and anxious to see her best friend, but where to look was another question. *She can't be inside the house,* Gabrielle thought. *My family never saw her before, and they wouldn't let in a stranger without waking me up first.* She sat up with the slightest amount of light from daybreak, and she saw Abigail still asleep. Not wanting to wake up her sister, she quietly got out of bed. Looking down from the loft, she couldn't detect any movement from anyone, and there were no sounds to be heard. Based upon the evidence as well as the lack of sunlight, she came to the conclusion that it must have been before six o'clock. *If Molly finally found my house, then why did she come this early?*

Still feeling anxious to see her best friend, she climbed down the ladder. While slowly walking to the front door, she thought about the time when she snuck out of the Feldings' house to go see Sophie. And having had the experience of sneaking out, she knew she could do it again, especially to see Molly. *I can't wait to finally introduce Molly to everyone!* she thought.

Slowly and quietly, she opened the door, stepped through the doorway, and closed the door behind her without making the slightest peep. She turned in all directions, but she couldn't see Molly. Wondering where to look, she thought to herself, *If she walked this far, maybe she had to go to the outhouse.*

After coming to the outhouse, she looked everywhere, but still no sight of Molly. *I heard her voice, so she can't be too far away. Maybe she's waiting for me in the barn.*

When Gabrielle got to the barn, she found Pa milking the cow. Pa turned to face the barn entrance, and he saw Gabrielle in her nightgown. "*You're* up early," he said. "There's still an hour until the time when you usually wake up. What got you up this early?"

Gabrielle recalled the time when she heard Ma's and Pa's voices while she was with the Feldings. At the time, nobody could hear what she heard. And knowing that Molly's voice didn't wake up Abigail, she assumed she would be called crazy again if she said anything about hearing a voice. "I had to go to the outhouse," she told Pa. Because she had just been to the outhouse, her answer to Pa wasn't a lie. She just simply didn't mention why she was at the outhouse.

Three days later, another thought came to Gabrielle. She remembered being on the tree stump when numerous trees suddenly appeared from out of the blue, and she was also on the stump when the missing house and the missing pond magically came back. She wondered if there was something magical about the stump. She had been hearing Molly's voice every day, and her desire to reunite with her best friend was increasing with every passing minute. With no luck in finding Molly or the Feldings throughout the past few months, was magic the only way to see them again?

While Abigail was at school, Gabrielle arrived at the stump and sat on it. She waited for the magic to happen. *This time, maybe the house and the pond will stay here when the trees appear,* she thought. *And as soon as I see Molly, I'm going to ask her where she was hiding. She's much too good at playing hide-and-seek!*

Twenty minutes later, Ma went outside to feed the chickens, and she brought Sabrina and Tabitha with her. Tabitha had learned to walk two months ago in March after having had her one-year birthday in February, and Sabrina was two months away from turning three years old.

After a few seconds of feeding the chickens, Sabrina looked past the pond, and she saw her sister. "Gabrielle on the stump," she said.

Ma turned to face the stump. Sure enough, Gabrielle was there. *I wonder why she likes that stump so much,* she thought. "I don't know why she's sitting there, but she needs to come inside soon to sweep the floor. I have a lot of laundry to wash today," she told the kids. Then she resumed feeding the chickens.

Ten minutes later, Gabrielle was still waiting for the magic to happen. Trees had not appeared, and there was no sight of Molly. While she waited and waited, she heard her name once more, but it wasn't Molly's voice. "Gabrielle!" hollered Ma who was close to the house. Gabrielle turned to face towards the house and saw Ma standing there. "You haven't swept the floors yet! We have a lot to do today! The stump can wait until later!"

Because the magic wasn't working, Gabrielle decided to remain obedient like Molly, so she stood up from the stump and started walking to the house. On the way, she wondered again how she was ever going to see Molly and her foster parents.

Four days later was Gabrielle's birthday. A party was scheduled for the afternoon right after school. Because Gabrielle didn't know any kids from school besides her sister, Abigail had invited some of her own friends at school on the previous Friday after making sure it was okay with Gabrielle.

At two o'clock when the students were dismissed from school, Abigail walked home with four of her friends, and they all arrived at the Linstrom house shortly before two-thirty. Abigail introduced them to Gabrielle. The four friends included Alice Jacobs, Mary Rogers, Hazel Williams, and Myrtle Edwards.

Much of the afternoon was spent playing games outside. Abigail got her game of *Graces*, and the six girls took turns playing.

Afterwards, one of the girls found a stick and used it to draw the game of hopscotch in the dirt. Then they used a small rock to throw onto the squares while they played.

Finally, they took turns counting while they played hide-and-seek. All throughout that game, Gabrielle thought of the times when she played hide-and-seek with Molly, and she wished Molly was there to play with them. It was fun playing with her older sister and four other girls, but not knowing the four girls besides just their names, she felt somewhat empty without her best friend there.

When they were done playing games, they all went inside the house where Ma had baked a birthday cake while they were outdoors. They all sat around the table and were each given a slice of cake.

"Did you make a birthday wish?" Alice asked Gabrielle.

Before Gabrielle could answer, Hazel interrupted. "Birthday wishes never come true! I once wished for a unicorn, but I never got one."

"They can come true if you wish hard enough," Mary said in a tone of confidence.

Alice nodded her head in agreement to what Mary said, and then she turned back to Gabrielle. "So did you make one yet?"

Gabrielle briefly thought about it. "There's something I've been wishing for, but it hasn't happened."

"See? They don't come true!" said Hazel.

"My pa always said that dreams can come true," Mary said to everyone, "and if dreams can come true, then wishes can too." Then she turned to face Gabrielle. "Just keep trying, and maybe your wish will come true."

After the party, Abigail's four friends needed to start heading back home. They stood up from the table and started walking to the door. On her way out, Myrtle turned to Gabrielle and said, "Happy Birthday!"

The same words were repeated three more times. "Happy Birthday!" said Alice, Mary, and Hazel, one right after another.

"Thank you," said Gabrielle while giving a half smile. Although there were no gifts besides the cake, she felt that her birthday was okay, but it would have been better if Molly were there.

"It was good to meet you," said Mary on her way out the door, speaking to Gabrielle.

"And I can't wait until your pa becomes the president!" said Hazel. "It will be fun having the president living right here in town!" Then she closed the door behind her.

At that moment, Gabrielle wondered about the two predicaments

171

she was still in.  One of them was how to get Pa to change his mind, and the other one was where and how to find Molly, Sophie, and her foster parents.  And knowing now that everyone in town was excited about Pa getting elected, she wondered what a five-year-old girl could possibly do to change that.  Not having the slightest clue, she was convinced that this situation was far beyond her control, and there was nothing she could do about it.  All that was left to do was to think about how to prepare for living through a Great Depression as well as preparing for the thoughts of being known as the daughter of the worst president.

That night while Gabrielle lay awake in bed, she remembered what Abigail's friends said about dreams and wishes. *They can come true if you wish hard enough.  Just keep trying, and maybe your wish will come true,* she recalled.  Once again, she reflected on the days of sitting on the tree stump when several trees either appeared or disappeared, and she remembered how hard she wished right before everything suddenly changed.

The next morning, Gabrielle awoke early.  Her longing to once again stand in the presence of her long-lost friends had grown stronger.  But even though she wanted to see them, the endless amount of questions wouldn't stop coming to her thoughts. *If the trees appear again, will the house and the pond disappear?* she thought to herself. *And if the house disappears again, then how are Ma and Pa going to meet Molly and the Feldings?*

Quietly, she got out of bed, climbed down the ladder, went outside, and walked back to the tree stump.  She sat down and started wishing to not only see Molly and her foster parents, but also for her house to not disappear again.  And keeping in mind what Abigail's friends said, she tried wishing as hard as she could.

After Ma started cooking breakfast, she saw Abigail climbing down the ladder from the loft, and she was all dressed for the day. "Where's your sister?"

"She's not up there," answered Abigail as soon as she got to the bottom of the ladder. "Maybe she went to the outhouse."

Well, it's time to start setting the table, so I hope she gets back soon," said Ma.

Abigail grabbed the empty basket from the table. "I'll go gather the eggs," she said.  Then she left the house from the front door to not disturb Sabrina and Tabitha who were both still asleep.

A minute later, Pa came inside from milking the cow. "Why is Gabrielle sitting on that stump again?" he asked Ma. "She's not even dressed for the day.  What's so important to her about that stump that makes her want to sit on it in her nightgown?"

"What?" asked Ma, finding it hard to believe what she heard. "Abigail said she might be at the outhouse. Is Gabrielle getting crazy again?" Feeling upset, she headed to the front door, went outside, and walked swiftly around the house to the back where she saw Gabrielle from a distance. "Gabrielle!" she hollered. Abigail was still gathering the eggs from behind the house, and she had just seen Gabrielle a few seconds before she heard Ma hollering. "You're not even dressed for the day, and it's time to set the table for breakfast! Come inside, and stop sitting on the stump!" Then Ma turned around and walked to the front of the house to go back inside.

Gabrielle wondered why wishing harder wasn't making her wish come true. Nevertheless, in obedience to her ma, she stood up and started walking to the house. On the way, additional thoughts came. Was it not true what Abigail's friends said about wishes coming true? Maybe Hazel was right. Maybe wishes don't come true. But if that was the case, then how did Gabrielle find the missing people in the first place, and how was she reunited with her family after the house was gone?

Inside the house, Gabrielle climbed up to the loft, got dressed for the day, climbed back down, and set the table for breakfast. Afterwards, she went towards the back of the house to wake up Sabrina, and she once again played peek-a-boo.

After breakfast, Pa drove Abigail into town for the same reasons as usual—to take her to school, and to take the eggs to the mercantile. While they were gone, Gabrielle wasn't giving up hope of making her wish come true. She wanted to try one more time. And assuming it would work this time, she started thinking that if she were to see Mr. and Mrs. Felding, then she wouldn't be returning the pink jeans and the light blue t-shirt that used to belong to one of their daughters. But where to find them was another question. While Ma was starting to clear off the table, Gabrielle quickly used the process of elimination to determine where the jeans and shirt might be. *They can't be in the barn,* she thought. *They aren't in the loft, they can't be outside, and they're not where Sabrina's and Tabitha's beds are located.* And knowing they weren't anywhere around the table, it eliminated all places besides Ma's and Pa's bedroom. Assuming they weren't under the bed, there was only one place to look. In a sneaky manner while Ma's head was turned away, she crept into the bedroom.

When she got to the wooden chest, she quickly and quietly opened the hinged lid. The first things she saw inside the chest did not include what she was looking for. Carefully, she reached down, moved a few things aside, found the clothes, and pulled them out before she slowly closed the lid of the chest without making a peep. Suspiciously, she inched her way back to the bedroom doorway until a slight glimpse of Ma was in sight. She stopped, peeked around the corner, and waited for Ma to turn her head away again.

When the time was perfect, Gabrielle started making her way. Carrying the jeans and the t-shirt, she quickly tiptoed past the table where Sabrina was still sitting. The two sisters made eye contact, and Gabrielle immediately motioned to her sister to stay quiet. Shortly thereafter, she came to the ladder, held the clothes close to her with one hand to hide them from Ma, carefully climbed up the ladder with the other hand, and successfully made it to the loft where she hid the clothes under the blankets on her bed.

Gabrielle looked down from the loft. Seeing Ma, Sabrina, and Tabitha, she looked in all directions at the rest of the house, and she soon came to the realization that half of what she had wished for had come true. She had wished the house would not disappear and, sure enough, it was still there. She also realized the only way for a wish to come true is for everything else to seem trivial.

Seconds later, Gabrielle heard Molly's voice again, which made her want nothing more than to see her best friend. However, she knew how Ma felt about the stump, and she didn't want to be caught sitting on it again.

Later that morning, Pa returned home and unhitched the team from the wagon. Because it was the season for planting crops, he hitched the team to the plow, took them to the field located out in front of the house, and began to plow the ground in preparation for planting.

Soon it was time to feed the chickens. "Let's go feed the chickens," Ma told Sabrina and Tabitha. Then she turned to Gabrielle and asked, "Gabrielle, are you coming with us?"

Suddenly, Gabrielle got an idea. "I want to go watch Pa plow the field," she replied.

"Okay. Come along, girls," Ma told the two youngest sisters while starting to take them to the back door.

As soon as the closing of the back door was heard, Gabrielle hurried to the ladder and climbed up to the loft. She uncovered the jeans and the t-shirt to take them with her, but she did not change into them. She intended to be obedient to her parents who taught her that girls don't wear trousers and that short sleeves are immodest. She grabbed her other everyday dress and matching bonnet in preparation for the possibility that the house would disappear again.

After carrying the clothes down the ladder, Gabrielle went out the front door, closing the door behind her. She didn't want to be dishonest in what she told Ma, so she watched Pa from a distance for a few seconds. Then she walked to the side of the house and stood around the corner from the back of the house until Ma and the two girls went back inside.

Thirty-eight seconds later, Gabrielle arrived at the stump and sat down. Once again, she heard Molly's voice. Just hearing Molly was enough to have no desire to wish for anything besides seeing her friends and foster parents again.

After a few more seconds of wishing as hard as she could, she looked all around her while hundreds of trees started to appear. They were faint and transparent, but they gradually became solid and opaque. She looked in the direction of the house and the pond, and neither one of them was there. She looked all around her once more, and everything looked exactly like it did when she was with Mr. and Mrs. Felding.

Feeling excited that Molly was not far away, Gabrielle stood up from the stump and rushed to the street where she eventually found it paved again. She looked down the street in both directions, and there were no cars. She remembered the roads to take, so she walked along the side of the road until she came to Main Street that veered off to the left. *The road is back!* she thought, knowing she had finally found the missing road.

After a while of walking the two-mile distance, she came to the Robinsons' house and looked at it from the sidewalk. She wanted so desperately to go ring the doorbell, but she first wanted to take the clothes to her foster parents, so she continued down the sidewalk until she arrived back home.

# 15
# WHAT GABBY FINDS OUT

Gabby came to the front door, but when she tried to open it, she learned that it was locked. *Where are Mom and Dad?* she wondered. She rang the doorbell and waited several seconds, but there was no sight or sound of anyone. *Did everyone leave the town?* Wanting to know if the house was empty, she remembered that the Feldings kept a key to the back door under the mat, so she walked around to the back of the house, found the key, unlocked the door, and went inside.

After entering the house, everything looked the same as it did the last time she was there. The furniture was not changed, the television was still there, and everything in her bedroom was also no different. But where were Mr. and Mrs. Felding?

While being back in her bedroom, she looked in the closet, and she found her other dress and bonnet she had left there. Because she had grown during the previous few months, the dress was now too small for her to fit into it. Next, she looked towards the floor and found her other boots. Suddenly, she realized she had left her shoes at her other home, so she was left with two pairs of laced boots.

Minutes later, Gabby heard the sound of the front door being unlocked and opened. Then she heard a familiar voice. "How much patience do we need?" Mom's voice sounded. "We've waited almost six months. What the preacher said about having patience with God's timing, I wish we knew how long it will take for his prayer to be answered."

Seconds later, Mr. and Mrs. Felding noticed Gabby coming from the hallway. "Mom! Dad!" shouted Gabby, excited to see her foster parents again while she ran to them to give them a big hug.

Joy immediately filled the hearts of Mr. and Mrs. Felding. "Gabby!" shouted Mrs. Felding joyfully with a full heart while crouching down with outstretched arms. Gabby and Mrs. Felding gave each other the biggest possible hug. "I missed you so much!"

"I missed you too," said Gabby.

"Well, that was fast!" said Mr. Felding. "We hardly had to wait at all for that prayer to be answered!"

Gabby moved over to her foster dad and gave him a hug. In response to what he said, she asked him, "What prayer?"

"The prayer from the preacher today," said Mr. Felding. "He asked God to bring you back home to us, and now you're back home. But how did you get into the house?"

"I remembered the key under the mat by the back door," said Gabby. "And why were you at church today? Today is Tuesday."

"No," said Mrs. Felding, "today is Sunday. What gave you the idea that today is Tuesday?" she asked while she took a look at how much Gabby had grown.

"Yesterday was Monday," said Gabby, "and it was also my . . ."

"My, you've grown so much ever since we last saw you," interrupted Mrs. Felding. "I'm sure you don't fit into the pink jeans or the light blue t-shirt anymore, but what did you do with them, and where did you get this dress?"

"I brought the jeans and the t-shirt back. They're in my bedroom. And this dress came from River Town Mercantile."

"I never heard of a mercantile around here," said Mr. Felding. "And did you say River *Town*?"

"That's what everyone else in town called it," said Gabby.

"Everyone in what town?" Mr. Felding asked.

"This one."

"But it's not called River Town," said Mrs. Felding. "Where we live is called River City."

"And I have a lot of questions to ask," Mr. Felding told Gabby. "I'm wondering who bought you this dress, and I'd also like to know who you stayed with during the past few months. But seeing how much you've grown, I'm mostly curious to know how old you are. I wish there was a way to find out."

"I'm five," said Gabby. "Yesterday was my birthday, and it was also Monday."

"No, yesterday was Saturday," said Mrs. Felding.

"But I went to church two days ago," said Gabby.

Mr. and Mrs. Felding looked at each other. They both shrugged their shoulders and shook their heads. "More mysteries," Mr. Felding said, knowing that churches everywhere were shut down because of the coronavirus pandemic.

Mrs. Felding turned back to face Gabby. "How do you know yesterday was your birthday, and who told you you're five?" she asked.

"My ma did. And my pa bought me this dress."

"You found your parents?" asked Mrs. Felding. Gabby nodded her head. "I'd like to meet them sometime."

"Is that who you've been living with?" Mr. Felding asked.

Gabby nodded her head again. "And my three sisters," she added.

"Then who brought you back here?" asked Mr. Felding.

"I walked back."

"Then that means they don't live far away. Can you show us where they live?"

Gabby shook her head. "I don't think so. The house disappeared when the trees came back," she said. "But I'm glad the roads are paved again. The dirt roads were too bumpy!"

"Disappeared? Paved again? What are you talking about?" Mr. Felding asked in great bewilderment.

Mr. and Mrs. Felding looked at each other again. "Mysteries!" said Mrs. Felding.

"And I have another word for you," Mr. Felding told his wife. "Imagination!"

*Huh?* thought Gabby, coming to the conclusion that it must have been adult talk that was too hard for kids to understand.

"Well, let's get you settled back in," Mrs. Felding told Gabby. "Let's get you into something more comfortable. I'll go find a bigger pair of jeans and another t-shirt," she said while starting to head to Gabby's bedroom.

"No," voiced Gabby. "My folks said those are too immodest. They said girls only wear dresses."

"Oh, I was starting to wonder why you were wearing a dress if you didn't think today was Sunday," Mr. Felding said.

"Why would your parents say that?" asked Mrs. Felding. "Girls have been wearing jeans and t-shirts for a long time including Molly and Sophie."

"But not Alice, Mary, Hazel, or Myrtle," said Gabby.

"Who are they?" Mrs. Felding asked.

"They're Abigail's friends from school. They came to my birthday party."

"Then they were probably dressed up for the party," said Mr. Felding.

"How did the party go?" asked Mrs. Felding. "Did you get a lot of gifts?"

"I had fun while I played with Abigail and her friends, but I didn't get anything besides a birthday cake. Ma and Pa couldn't afford to buy anything."

In Mrs. Felding's mind, what Gabby was saying did not make any sense. "How can they live in a city if they have no money for even a small gift? They could have bought something for just a dollar."

"A whole dollar?" expressed Gabby. "That would be an expensive gift!"

*She certainly has her opinions,* Mrs. Felding thought. "Well, no matter the price of a gift, it's sad you didn't get one for your birthday." At that point, she suddenly got an idea. "I know what I'll do." Then she started walking to the master bedroom. "I'll be right back."

Seconds later, Mrs. Felding came back with the crocheted doll she had made for Gabby for Christmas. But having had no chance to give it as a Christmas gift, she decided to give it as a late birthday gift instead, so she handed it to Gabby. "Happy Birthday! I made this for you. Even though it's a day late, you now have something for your birthday!"

Gabby took the doll from Mrs. Felding. She looked at it, and it reminded her about another doll. "This reminds me of the doll that Ma made me for Christmas."

*Two dolls were made for her for Christmas by two moms?* thought Mrs. Felding. However, she and Mr. Felding were both not sure Gabby had really found her parents if their house didn't even exist. Whoever took care of her while she was missing, she must have pretended they were her parents. "Where's your other doll?" Mrs. Felding asked.

"I left it at home . . . my other home. I forgot to get it because I really wanted to see Molly, Sophie, and both of you again."

"Aww, we're glad you wanted to see us again," said Mrs. Felding.

"But what about your parents?" asked Mr. Felding. "What if they wonder where you are?"

"Then it won't be any different than last time," said Gabby.

"It's not good to make your parents worry," said Mrs. Felding.

"But it was the only way I could see you," Gabby said.

"If they worry too much," said Mr. Felding, "then they might get Officer Gunwell to search for you again, and then we'll have to tell him where you are."

"Officer Gunwell is back?" asked Gabby. "Is Sheriff Badger still in town?"

"Who's Sheriff Badger?" Mr. Felding asked.

"He's the sheriff who tried to look for both of you and Molly."

"Why would a sheriff need to look for us? We were never lost," said Mr. Felding.

"I thought you were lost because I couldn't find you," Gabby replied. "This house wasn't here, and I couldn't even find Main Street. Lots of buildings weren't in the city, and I didn't see one single car. There were only horses pulling wagons, carriages, buggies, and stagecoaches. After we got Sheriff Badger to help find you, he said the only Feldings he could find were in Missouri."

Mr. and Mrs. Felding looked at each other again. They were both speechless and surprised at how much of an imagination a five-year-old girl could possibly have. Mrs. Felding turned back to Gabby and decided to change the subject. "Well . . . if your parents want you to only wear dresses, I think we have some more in your closet that might fit you."

"I saw them," said Gabby, "but those dresses have short sleeves."

"What's wrong with *that*?" asked Mrs. Felding.

"My folks said short sleeves are not modest. When I was living with them, I didn't see anyone else in town with short sleeves either."

Mr. and Mrs. Felding looked at each other once again. Amazed at Gabby's imagination, Mr. Felding tapped on his head with his index finger while making a facial expression. Mrs. Felding knew what he meant, and she nodded her head in agreement. Then she turned back to Gabby and resumed the conversation. "I don't think we have any dresses your size with long sleeves, and I don't think clothing stores sell them this time of year. It's getting close to summertime. If you won't wear short sleeves, then how are you going to wear the same dress every day?"

"I brought another one with me, and I brought a matching bonnet with it."

"Wagons, buggies, and bonnets? It sounds like you enjoy

history," said Mr. Felding. "And I'd love to hear what else happened during the past six months, but I need to go update the furniture store website." Then he left to go to his office room across the hallway from the master bedroom.

"What's history?" Gabby asked.

Mrs. Felding explained, "It's a time that was long ago. We learn about history when we read history books. Do you remember when I told you about the wars and how Veterans Day got started?"

Gabby nodded her head. "Yes, but my folks never heard about the world wars or Veterans Day, and my ma said I was born on the same day the Civil War ended, even though it wasn't the official end."

"Maybe she meant you were born on the same month and the same day of the month. But it couldn't have been the same year because the Civil War happened more than 150 years ago, and you're only five."

Gabby shook her head. "My ma said it was *five* years ago. She said it seemed like yesterday."

"Then she must have been talking about something else that was five years ago. History says it happened 150 years ago."

"Then how do my folks not know much about history?"

"Maybe they never read about it. Do they have any history books or the internet?"

"No, they don't. They don't even have a computer or a television. My pa can't afford much. He even had to sell one of our cows to buy me some new dresses."

"Oh, I didn't know your dad had any cows . . . and I don't remember any dairy farms around here."

"We just have a regular farm with our cows in the barn. Earlier today, my pa was plowing our field with our two horses."

"With horses? Why doesn't he just use a tractor?" asked Mrs. Felding.

"I don't think he knows what a tractor is, but he definitely couldn't buy one. He doesn't have enough money, and that's why he wants to run for president. He wants everyone to have the same amount of money so nobody will be too poor."

"Hmm, that sounds familiar," Mrs. Felding said. "And if you were really with your parents and you know what day your birthday is, then what's your last name?"

"It's Linstrom," said Gabby. "My full name is Gabrielle Anne Linstrom."

"That sounds like a pretty name! And you said your sisters are Abigail, Sabrina, and Tabitha?" Gabby nodded her head. "You also said your mother's name is Martha, and your father's name is Harold?"

Again, Gabby nodded her head. "You remembered their names!" she exclaimed with a smile.

*I suppose it's possible for there to be more than one Gabrielle Linstrom with the same number of sisters and all the same family names as President Linstrom's family,* Mrs. Felding thought, *but how can there be two families exactly alike with both dads running for president for the same reason?* "Did you know those are all the same names of President Linstrom's family?"

"Wow! All the same names?" expressed Gabby. "Maybe we're all twins!"

"No, twins can't be 150 years apart. And nobody can possibly travel through time. That's just an imaginary thing that only happens in movies and books," said Mrs. Felding while she started to wonder why President Linstrom's daughter named Gabrielle was the only one in the history book who didn't have a date of when she died. "But I'm wondering . . . did your parents or anyone else during the past six months ever mention what year it currently is?"

Gabby spent a few seconds to try to remember whether or not she had heard anyone say the current year. "I can't remember."

"Did anyone tell you the year on New Year's Eve or on New Year's Day?"

For a few more seconds, Gabby tried to remember. "I don't know. But I remember the new year came just a few days after the big snow storm."

"Last winter?"

Gabby nodded her head. "Uh-huh."

"We didn't have a big snow storm last winter. The most we got from any snow storm was two inches."

Gabby shook her head. "No, we got more than that. It snowed four feet. I could hardly see anything out the windows, and my pa had a hard time trying to get to the barn."

"Did you say *four feet?*"

Gabby nodded her head again. "Uh-huh."

"Are you sure?" asked Mrs. Felding.

"I'm sure," said Gabby in a tone of confidence. "The top of the snow was as tall as Abigail, and it took forever to melt! It was the longest time I ever stayed inside!"

"Uh, Sweetheart, the only time it ever snowed four feet in River City was back in December of 1869, and that was over 150 years ago. I remember reading about it just two or three months ago. So you couldn't have seen four feet of snow."

"But I did!" said Gabby. "It was taller than me, and we were trapped in the house!"

"Maybe you saw it in your imagination, but it never snowed that much around here since then. Like I said, it was way back in 1869."

"What year is it now?" asked Gabby, unaware that her question would lead to finally putting everything together.

"It's 2020. With the virus going around, I thought everyone knew what year it is."

"What virus?"

"The coronavirus called COVID-19 that caused this big shutdown."

"What's a shutdown?" Gabby asked.

"It's when a store or business needs to shut down for one reason or another. In this case, the pandemic is the reason that caused almost everything to shut down. Besides Walmart and a few grocery stores, everything else is closed including schools, restaurants, and churches for helping to keep the virus from spreading."

Hearing a year that she had never heard as well as hearing so much new information for the first time, Gabby thought about what the town looked like while she was living with Ma and Pa, and then she thought about what the city looked like while living with the Feldings. And recalling what her foster mom said regarding how long ago the big snowstorm occurred, she concluded that she was actually living in the future. However, according to what Mr. and Mrs. Felding said about movies and books, it didn't seem possible. *Maybe traveling through time only happens in movies and books because nobody else knows how to wish hard enough,* she thought. But just to make sure her conclusion was correct, she reflected on a few other things. *Pa said he never saw an airplane or a helicopter, and Dad said wagons, buggies, and bonnets are things in history. The school was small with just one room when I was with Ma and Pa, but the school that Molly and Sophie go to is much bigger. With Ma and Pa, the cemetery is always small with not many gravestones. With Mom and Dad, the cemetery has hundreds of gravestones. With Ma and Pa, horses always pull things like wagons, stagecoaches, and plows. With Mom and Dad, everyone uses cars, trucks, and tractors. With Ma and Pa, prices are a lot less than when I'm with Mom and Dad, but everyone has less money, and there are hardly any stores. With Ma and Pa, lots of people grow their own crops and milk their own cows. With Mom and Dad, everyone gets their food from the store. When I'm with Ma and Pa, nobody knows who Officer Gunwell is. Mom and Dad don't know who Sheriff Badger is, and I'm sure Molly and Sophie won't know him either. When I'm with Ma and Pa, I can't remember the name of any president after President Grant,*

*but now I remember there were two presidents with the last name of*
*Johnson, and the president right now is President Trump.*

After a while of many thoughts while staring off into space,
Gabby was convinced she had traveled through time. But not wanting to
be called crazy again, she made it a point to never tell anyone about it.

Mrs. Felding noticed Gabby staring off into space. "What are
you thinking about?" she asked.

"Too many things," replied Gabby, trying not to say anything
that might sound crazy. "And now I'm wondering something."

"What are you wondering?"

"If churches are closed, then how did you see the preacher
today?"

"We went to his house, but only one household at a time could
be there, and we had to sit apart from him outside on his front porch."

"Why couldn't you go into his house? Was the door locked?
And why did you have to sit apart?"

"Gabby, where have you been the last two or three months?
Haven't you ever heard of social distancing?" asked Mrs. Felding.
Gabby made an awkward expression while she shook her head. To
answer Gabby's question, Mrs. Felding replied, "We need to stay at least
six feet apart to decrease the chance of spreading the virus from one
person to another."

"Why is it six feet?" asked Gabby. "Can a virus not travel seven
feet?"

"I don't know, Sweetheart. Six feet is what our government told
us."

"But how do *they* know? If we can smell food from more than
six feet away, then can't a virus go as far as a smell in the air?"

For not knowing, Mrs. Felding shook her head. "You ask too
many questions. And I know I said you can be smarter by asking
questions, but I don't know the answer to that question any more than
you do."

Assuming that a virus was a complicated topic to talk about,
Gabby decided to stop asking questions about it, so she turned to face
away from Mrs. Felding. Then she noticed two matching objects that
were lying on the end table beside the couch, and they looked unfamiliar.
Wondering what they were, Gabby pointed to them and asked, "What are
those?"

Mrs. Felding turned to face the objects that Gabby was pointing
at. "Those are masks. I'm sure you've seen masks before, and I'm sure
your parents have worn them the last few times they've been out in
public."

Gabby shook her head. "No, they haven't. I never saw those things before."

"Then how do your parents go shopping when the wearing of masks in public is mandated?"

Suddenly, Gabby realized she had briefly forgotten about living in a different period of time. She knew that if she mentioned anything about living 150 years ago, then everyone would definitely be calling her crazy, so she shrugged her shoulders in response to Mrs. Felding's question.

To end the conversation regarding the pandemic, Mrs. Felding decided to change the subject. "Well, let's go have lunch. I'm hungry. Would you like something to eat?" Gabby nodded her head and started following her foster mom into the kitchen.

Although everything had appeared the same as when she was with the Feldings in 2019, Gabby was quickly sensing that what she thought she had returned to was actually a completely different period of time. Everything she was hearing was very strange. And knowing she wouldn't be attending church with her foster parents anymore, she was already longing for home and wanting to be back with Ma and Pa. *We might have been poor, but at least we lived,* she thought. *And whatever is happening here in these days, I'm not sure I'm going to like it.* But above any desire to leave again, her greatest wish was to be with Molly.

# 16
# GONE ARE THE DAYS

"May I have a Pop-Tart?" asked Gabby politely as soon as she entered the kitchen. She hadn't had a Pop-Tart in almost six months, and she was very eager to have one again.

"Yes, you may," said Mrs. Felding. She opened the door to the kitchen pantry and grabbed the box of Pop-Tarts from an upper shelf. "You seem so excited. Didn't your parents ever feed you any Pop-Tarts?"

*Pop-Tarts weren't even invented yet,* thought Gabby, *but I can't tell Mom, or she'll think I'm crazy.* In response, she shook her head. "My pa couldn't afford them," she said, knowing that her pa really wouldn't have been able to afford them at the current price.

"Can't even afford a box of Pop-Tarts?" asked Mrs. Felding confoundedly. "Then how does he even buy gasoline for his car? He can drive, can't he? Or does he not even have a car?"

*What will Mom think if I mention that Pa doesn't even know what a car is? She might think there's something wrong with my folks. But what can I say without telling any lies?* thought Gabby. Then she remembered what Mr. Felding once told her about how cars work. "My pa can drive," she said. "He has four wheels, but it only has two horsepower."

"Sounds like a clunker!"

*Well, it's over 150 years old by now,* Gabby thought, referring to Pa's wagon.

After eating her two Pop-Tarts, Gabby was quite anxious to see her best friend. "May I go see Molly?"

Mrs. Felding looked at the clock that was hanging on the wall by the back door. "They're probably back from the preacher's house by this time. But wait until I finish my lunch, and then I'll take you over there."

A few minutes later, Mrs. Felding and Gabby were almost ready to head over to the Robinsons' house. On their way to the front door, Mrs. Felding grabbed her mask. She also grabbed a spare one for Gabby and handed it to her while saying, "You need to put this on before we go."

Gabby took the mask, held it, and looked at it. "How do I put it on?" she wondered aloud.

Mrs. Felding explained, "You put the straps around your ears to hold it up, and the rest of it goes over your nose and your mouth."

Gabby made another awkward expression. "If it's over my nose and my mouth, then how do I breathe?"

"You can still breathe after you put it on."

"But we need air to breathe."

"You still have some air when you're wearing it."

Gabby was confused. "If air can get to our nose and mouth when we wear it, then why do we need a mask if there's a virus in the air?"

"It reduces the chance of catching it."

"Then why don't people who feel sick just stay home? That's what everyone else in town does."

"*Everyone* else?" repeated Mrs. Felding. "Sweetheart, I don't see how you can personally know over twelve thousand people."

*I forgot again,* Gabby thought to herself. "What I meant to say was that everyone in the old days in history always stayed home when they felt sick."

"How do you know?" asked Mrs. Felding, knowing that Gabby was too young to know how to read history books.

"That's what I heard somewhere," answered Gabby while remembering to not say when or where she heard it, nor whom she heard it from.

"Well, it's hard now days to tell who's sick. Anyone could be asymptomatic, which means they could be sick and not know it because they won't have any symptoms."

Again, Gabby made an awkward expression, having never heard such a thing. "In the old days, people who felt sick were sick, and people who didn't feel sick were not sick."

"But these aren't the old days," Mrs. Felding said.

*That's for sure,* Gabby thought.

Mrs. Felding and Gabby arrived at the front door to the

Robinsons' house. Gabby rang the doorbell. "Let's step back," Mrs. Felding said. "We need to be at least six feet away from the door."

When Molly answered the door, she saw Mrs. Felding standing next to a girl who was wearing a dress along with something on her head, but did not immediately recognize her behind the mask along with the extra six months of growth. "Molly!" muffled Gabby's voice.

Molly recognized the sound of the voice. "Gabby!" she hollered with excitement and a smile, yet both girls did not hurry toward each other for a hug like they would have done if they had not been taught about social distancing. "Where have you been all these months? Did Officer Gunwell find you? And why are you wearing a dress with something on your head?"

Seeing Molly who was not wearing a mask, Gabby was feeling too uncomfortable, so she took hers off, and Mrs. Felding noticed. "You need to keep your mask on. We're out in public," said Mrs. Felding.

"But Molly isn't wearing one," argued Gabby.

"Because she's inside her house."

Gabby turned to face Molly. "Are you sick?"

"No," said Molly. "I feel fine."

Then Gabby faced Mrs. Felding. "I'm not sick either. If Molly feels fine, then how can I catch anything?"

"Okay, but we can't stay long. We need to get back home before the neighbors come outside."

Gabby turned back to Molly to answer her questions. "What's on my head is called a bonnet. It keeps the sun out of my eyes, and it helps with modesty. My parents want me to wear dresses all the time because they said it's immodest for girls to wear trousers."

"What are trousers?" Molly asked.

"They're the same thing as pants," said Gabby.

Molly looked at Mrs. Felding, and then turned back to Gabby. "But your mom is wearing pants."

"She wasn't talking about me," said Mrs. Felding. "She was talking about her real, biological parents."

"Who's at the door?" asked Mrs. Robinson just before showing up at the doorway and noticing who was there. "Gabby? Is that you? Did Officer Gunwell finally find you?"

"No, Mom," said Molly. "She found her real parents."

Mrs. Robinson took a step forward to get a better look outside. She looked to the right and to the left. Seeing nobody else, she said to Gabby, "If you found your real parents, then where are they?"

"They live in another part of town," said Gabby.

"And why aren't they with you?" Mrs. Robinson asked.

"Because they had other things to do," replied Gabby, knowing that her folks were doing other things besides sitting on a stump and making wishes, "and I wanted to come see everyone again."

"So they brought you to the Feldings' house and dropped you off?" asked Mrs. Robinson.

"No, they didn't," said Gabby, wanting to remain truthful. "I walked by myself."

Mrs. Robinson couldn't believe her ears. "They let you go alone on these streets? They could get in trouble for neglect and child abuse if someone reports them to the police!"

Mrs. Felding turned to Gabby, wondering yet again. "I thought you said their house . . ."

"If you found your real parents, then what's your last name?" interrupted Molly right after she remembered asking Gabby that question before.

"It's Linstrom," said Gabby.

"Your name is Gabby Linstrom?" asked Molly. Gabby smiled and nodded her head.

"And why are you all dressed up?" asked Mrs. Robinson. "Was there a Sunday event that I missed?"

Molly looked upwards at her mom and answered, "She's dressed up because her real parents think it's the only way to be modest."

*Now I know where she gets her craziness from,* thought Mrs. Robinson while making an awkward expression of her own. Then she thought about Gabby's last name. "Linstrom? That name sounds familiar . . . Oh, that's the same last name as the worst president in history! I hope he's not one of your ancestors!" she told Gabby. "After what he did to my ancestors along with the rest of the country, he should be erased from every history book!"

With knowing she was in the future, Gabby now knew that this terrible president in history books was indeed her pa, and she thought about what Mrs. Robinson said. *He didn't listen to what I said?* she thought while reflecting on what she told her pa. *Or if he listened, then he didn't take my advice.*

"Talking about names," Molly told Gabby, "do you want to know how I got my name?" Curious to find out, Gabby nodded her head. "My mom told me she found some very old papers and some very old books inside a very old ancestry chest before I was born, and one of the books was an old diary that one of my ancestors wrote in, but I forget her name." Molly turned to face her mom who then added to what was said.

"Her name was Edna Robinson. She lived about five or six

generations ago . . . maybe seven generations from Molly. What she wrote was dated way back in December 1869.

"Oh, that's the same month as the big snow storm," said Mrs. Felding.

Mrs. Robinson continued. "She wrote in her diary that a girl named Gabrielle told her the name of Molly, and she thought it was the most beautiful name she ever heard. Then she wrote that it was her wish and her hope that one of her descendants would give the name of Molly to one of their daughters. She couldn't give that name to her own daughters because she was old by the time she wrote it, but that's how Molly got her name."

Not only was the name of Edna Robinson familiar to Gabby, but also the story that was just now told was all too familiar. *But Molly is older than I am, and it was only a few months ago when I said the name of Molly to Edna Robinson,* Gabby thought. And knowing she was the one whom Edna wrote about in her diary, it was more proof to her that she had definitely come from the past and was now in the future.

"And I wish I knew who that girl was who told her the name of Molly. Edna didn't write her last name," said Mrs. Robinson.

"But she had the same first name as you!" Molly said to Gabby.

"Edna also wrote in her diary that she was a piano teacher, and Gabrielle was her best student. She wrote that Gabrielle somehow learned more than what the piano lessons taught, and there were no other piano teachers in town."

"Mom," said Molly, "tell them what you found last week."

"I went through that ancestry chest again, and I found some papers that called this place River Town, which was the original name. And then it was changed to River City in 1898."

"Oh, I didn't know that," said Mrs. Felding. "But someone else must have known and told Gabby because she already knew before she came back to us today."

After arriving back home, Gabby headed to her bedroom to get reacquainted with everything again. When she was almost to her bedroom doorway, she glanced into the bathroom on her way past, and it didn't appear to look like it used to, so she turned back to the bathroom and stepped inside. What she saw was not what she expected to see, and she wanted to know the meaning of it. "Mom!" she hollered.

A few seconds later, Mrs. Felding was approaching the bathroom when she asked, "What's wrong?" Then she stepped into the bathroom and found Gabby.

"Why are there big stacks of toilet paper everywhere?" Gabby asked.

"When you were gone, there was a toilet paper shortage at stores."

Gabby took a good look at the multiple stacks that all appeared to reach almost to the ceiling, and it looked like there must have been one thousand rolls. "If everyone has this much toilet paper in their bathrooms, then no wonder there was a shortage! Who told you there was a shortage?"

"Before we stocked up, we heard about it on the news."

Gabby tried to put two and two together for making any sense of it. "The news talked about a shortage *before* everyone loaded up their bathrooms? It sounds to me like you were tricked!"

Later that night, Mrs. Felding tucked Gabby into bed. Gabby realized how much she had missed her bed as soon as her head hit the pillow. "This bed feels much better than my other bed."

"I'm glad you found your way back to us. When you were gone, there wasn't a single day when I didn't miss you," said Mrs. Felding. "But there's one thing I want to know, and I need you to tell me the truth."

"Okay," said Gabby.

"You said you found your real parents, but then you said their house disappeared. You should know that houses don't just disappear. Did you say it disappeared because you couldn't find it again after you left to come here, or were you using the finding of your parents as a way to keep from saying where you've really been these past few months?"

Gabby briefly gave it some thought on what she should say, but she quickly concluded that there was no way to explain it. "It's too complicated," she said. "I was honestly with my ma, my pa, and my three sisters, but I can't explain anything else."

"Why can't you explain anything? Can't you start by telling me where you slept last night?"

"I wish I could, but it's not that easy, Mom. I want you to trust me."

"How can I trust you if you can't even tell me where you slept last night? Did you already forget where?"

Gabby briefly gave it some thought again. "I didn't forget, but I promise the day will come when you'll find out why I couldn't explain it," she said, knowing she was the same Gabrielle in the history book who didn't yet have the date of when she died.

Mrs. Felding wasn't sure what else to say on this topic. "Well, goodnight," she said, leaning over to give Gabby a goodnight hug along with a kiss on her forehead. "I love you."

"I love you too, Mom."

Mrs. Felding sat beside her husband on the couch for getting ready to watch their late shows on television before going to bed. "I'm glad Gabby finally found her way back," she said, "but this imagination of hers is getting to be too much!"

"What did she tell you *this* time?" asked Mr. Felding. "And I overheard you talking about her last name earlier today. What did she say her last name is?"

"I hope you're ready for this. She said it's Linstrom."

"Linstrom?" repeated Mr. Felding out of surprise. "And she once said her parents are Harold and Martha, and her sisters are Abigail, Sabrina, and Tabitha?"

"Yeah, and she also said her pa wants to run for president to give everyone an equal amount of money for making sure nobody is too poor."

"Uh, I'm not too sure she actually found her parents. It sounds like she doesn't have a biological family, and she made an imaginary one from the information she learned from the history book. I bet she's pretending to be the same Gabrielle as President Linstrom's daughter."

"Why would she pretend such a thing?" asked Mrs. Felding.

"Because she probably feels bad about not having biological family members, and the reason why she left us last November was probably a plan to make us believe she found her family."

"But someone obviously fed her and sheltered her during the past six months."

As complicated as it seemed, Mr. Felding tried thinking of a reasonable explanation. "She probably knocked on random doors in the city to ask for food and shelter, and everyone probably welcomed her inside as cute as she is. And she probably moved from house to house to keep Officer Gunwell from finding her. I bet she asked everyone to keep her existence and whereabouts a secret, and nobody could say no to a cute face."

"Then she must have stayed with someone who knows a lot about history, and they probably knew how to sew, so they made the dresses and bonnets for her in addition to teaching her lots of history. Today, Gabby told me she was born the same day the Civil War ended, and she said it wasn't the official end. I later researched it, and she was right. There was a small battle that happened after that day in 1865."

Thinking about what they had said so far, Mr. Felding continued, "It all sounds logical. I think we have it figured out."

"All besides knowing how to teach her to tell the truth," added Mrs. Felding. "Even though she's been telling lies, it probably makes her feel better to believe in an imaginary, biological family. If we try to debunk those lies, then she might go back to feeling bad about having no family members."

In the meantime, Gabby was still awake. While thinking about the shutdowns, the masks, and the social distancing, she wondered if she was ever going to have a chance to play with Molly again. And with schools shut down, she couldn't look out the window in the mornings to see Sophie anymore. For seeing Molly, her wish when she sat on the stump had come true, but not in the way she had expected. She could only see her best friend from a distance, and it seemed like the days of playing together were all gone.

# 17
# IT JUST GETS CRAZIER!

On the morning of Monday, the 11th day of May, Gabby woke up early enough to help Mrs. Felding prepare breakfast. Once again, she set the table. Mrs. Felding watched her and noticed how perfectly detailed and meticulous she was at placing every dish, and she even did it faster than before. "You're getting even better at that. You must have had lots of practice these past few months," said Mrs. Felding right when Mr. Felding walked into the kitchen.

One of the first things he noticed upon entering the kitchen was the last dish being placed onto the table right when Gabby was finished. "Good morning, Precious!" he told her.

Gabby looked towards the kitchen entryway where Mr. Felding was standing. "Good morning, Daddy!" Temporarily fixing her eyes on his apparel, she wondered what he was planning to do that day. "Why aren't you dressed in your business attire? Don't you need to go to work at the furniture store?" she asked.

Mr. Felding walked towards the table. "Nobody works there right now. The store is shut down like most other stores. Several employees got laid off, but I was lucky enough to be placed in charge of updating the website. The only sales we're getting are orders from the website, and the shipping department ships off those orders. And since the website is all I'm doing, then I'm working from home now."

During breakfast, Gabby wondered what there was to do in these days of so many shutdowns and restrictions. "May I go play with Molly today?" she asked her foster parents.

"No, not today," answered her foster mom.

"Then what day may I go to her house to play?"

Mr. Felding replied, "We need to wait until the government lifts the mandates, and there's no telling when that will happen."

"So I can't go see Sophie either?" Gabby asked.

Mrs. Felding shook her head. "I'm afraid not, Sweetheart," she said.

"Then what's there to do?"

"Well," said Mrs. Felding, wanting to give Gabby as many options as possible, "you can play with your toys, color in your coloring books, practice the piano, watch television, or we can get out some board games or card games."

"Only five things to do?" Gabby asked, feeling and sounding a bit bummed that life in this period of time had become unrecognizable.

"Unless you want to go to Walmart or a grocery store," said Mr. Felding.

"But then you would need to wear your mask," added Mrs. Felding, but Gabby had no response.

Thinking about one of the five options that were mentioned, Gabby got an idea. "If I can't go see Molly or Sophie, then could I play with them next Saturday when they come for piano lessons?"

"They aren't coming for piano lessons anymore," said Mrs. Felding. "Because of social distancing, they're both practicing on their own pianos at home while we wait for the mandates to be lifted."

"Then how am I ever going to see them again?"

"Just wait for the mandates to be lifted," Mr. Felding said. "I'm sure this pandemic won't last forever."

In the morning of the following day, Gabby was in her bedroom when she heard the sound of the mail truck just seconds before she heard the lid of their mailbox being closed. She rushed to the living room where she found Mrs. Felding. "May I go check the mail?" she asked.

Mrs. Felding turned to get a view of the mailbox through the front window. Then she turned to Gabby. "Yes, but come right back and don't go anywhere else. I'll be watching you from right here."

As soon as Gabby opened the mailbox, she found a package along with an envelope. She pulled them out, closed the mailbox, and carried the mail to the house.

"We got a package!" said Gabby as soon as she stepped into the house.

"Let's see," said Mrs. Felding while reaching out her hand in a manner of telling Gabby to bring the package to her.

Gabby closed the front door. She walked over to Mrs. Felding and handed her the mail. "Here you go, Mom."

195

Mrs. Felding looked at the envelope. "Another bill to pay," she said. Taking a look at the label on the package, she saw it was addressed to George Felding. "This is for your dad. He must have ordered something."

"What's in it?" Gabby asked about the package.

"I don't know," said Mrs. Felding right when Mr. Felding entered the room from the hallway.

"I heard someone mention a package," he said.

"I got it from the mailbox!" exclaimed Gabby while Mrs. Felding handed the package to her husband who took ahold of it.

"Oh, my book came!"

"What book did you order?" Mrs. Felding asked.

Mr. Felding replied, "Since the libraries are all shut down, I bought the book called *The Life of President Linstrom* after I looked online and found a chapter in the book that I couldn't remember from when I checked it out at the library."

During dinnertime that evening while Gabby and her foster parents sat at the table, Mr. Felding brought up the topic of what he had learned that afternoon. "Earlier today, I read through the unfamiliar chapter in the book about President Linstrom. The rest of the chapters looked the same as the book from the library, so I don't know why the library book was missing this other chapter. But the extra chapter told about what happened after President Linstrom first thought about running for president."

"Oh, really?" asked Mrs. Felding. "What happened?"

Mr. Felding continued. "When Harold Linstrom thought about running for president, the news traveled quickly, and everyone in River Town soon knew about it. Almost everyone including the sheriff instantly thought it was a good idea for him to be the president. And this chapter even said the sheriff's name was Sheriff Badger."

"Seriously?" Mrs. Felding asked.

"And this is the only source I could find that mentions the sheriff's name," added Mr. Felding.

"Then whoever told Gabby the name of the sheriff obviously has a copy of that book."

Listening to the conversation, the name of Sheriff Badger sounded more than just familiar to Gabby. Not only did she know Sheriff Badger personally, but this was also more proof to her that she was now in the future. However, to avoid being called crazy, she didn't say a single word about it, and she refrained from correcting Mrs. Felding's last comment.

"And you said it was almost everyone who thought it was a good idea," said Mrs. Felding. "Who didn't think it was a good idea for him to run for president?"

Mr. Felding replied, "There was only one person in the entire town who didn't like the idea, and that was one of his own daughters . . . his second daughter named Gabrielle. She didn't want to disappoint her mom or her sisters, so she waited for a chance to talk alone with her dad in the barn. She tried to talk him out of it, but his plan on being the president was greater to him than taking the advice of a four-year-old kid."

"Gabrielle was only four years old?" exclaimed Mrs. Felding. Then she faced Gabby. "That's the same age you were before your recent birthday!" With nothing to say, Gabby gave a half smile in response. Mrs. Felding turned back to face her husband. "But how would a four-year-old girl not be interested in her dad being the president? Four-year-old kids don't know anything about politics!"

*How did this story get into a book?* Gabby wondered. *There was nobody in the barn besides Pa and me.* She turned to Mr. Felding. "Dad," she said, "does the book say how the author knew about it when there were only two people in the barn?"

As a matter of fact, it does," answered Mr. Felding. "Towards the end of the chapter, it mentions an interview that was done soon after President Linstrom's presidential term. He and Gabrielle were both interviewed at the same time for a newspaper article, and the article is obviously where the information for the book came from. After President Linstrom's term, he said he looked at the harm he caused for the entire country, and he deeply regretted his decision to not take the advice of his daughter."

"If he regretted what he did," said Mrs. Felding, "then it sounds like he was a good guy, but he must have not known what he was doing while he was the president. What else did you find out?"

Mr. Felding thought for a second. "Before Gabrielle tried to convince her dad to change his mind, she went missing for a few months until she came back to her family. Nobody ever found out where she stayed during those few months, but then she went missing again a few months later. The book doesn't say when she returned again, but she must have eventually returned before doing the interview with her dad."

"With an extra chapter, maybe you found an updated edition of the book," said Mrs. Felding. "Does it list the date of when Gabrielle died?"

"No, it doesn't. It's my guess that Gabrielle went missing for a third time and was never found."

"Unless the author accidentally missed putting in that

# 18
# ANOTHER ATTEMPT

"What happened to your shoes, your coat, and your teddy bear?" Mrs. Felding asked Gabby in the morning of the 29th day of May after realizing she hadn't seen them in a long time.

"I left them at the other house."

"What other house?"

"Where my folks and my sisters live."

"Is that the house that doesn't exist?" asked Mrs. Felding. Gabby nodded her head. "Then how are we going to get them?"

"I'll have to get them next time I go back there," Gabby said.

"If you're going back there, then why can't you show me where it is?"

"Because it doesn't exist right now."

"But if the house doesn't exist, then how are you going back?"

No matter what she would say, Gabby made sure to not mention anything about her travel through time. "It's too complicated to explain right now, but I promise you'll eventually find out."

*I definitely have something to talk about tonight after I put Gabby to bed,* Mrs. Felding thought right when she gave up on trying to make any sense out of anything. The only thing she could do was trust Gabby's promise and just wait to find out why Gabby was the only one who could go to a house that didn't exist.

Having been back to these future days for about three weeks, Gabby was feeling lonely and bored. The only thing she could do was be with her foster parents, and there were not many places to go that weren't shut down. She couldn't see Molly or Sophie anymore unless she were to cross paths with either of them at Walmart or a grocery store. But even if paths were crossed, would she recognize them behind the mask? And even if she recognized them, then there would be no hugs to give or smiles to be seen.

On Monday, the 1st day of June, Gabby felt ready to return back to the days of history to be with her biological family, and she wondered if any of her sisters or folks had caught the virus. She knew the differences between the two periods of time, but it only made sense to her that a virus spreading through the air would remain in the air regardless of time travel.

By this time, Gabby had gotten used to wearing a facemask out in public places, and because she and her foster parents hadn't caught any virus, she was convinced that masks help reduce the spread of diseases. However, she had never seen a facemask in the old days of River Town, and she was sure her sisters and folks did not have any masks, which caused her to worry about them having a greater chance of catching COVID.

The next morning, Gabby awoke at the break of dawn. As soon as she opened her eyes, her thoughts turned to her family, and she started feeling too worried about them to get back to sleep. She had heard people saying COVID could be deadly in some cases, and she wanted to see her family before any possible chance that it would be too late.

Quickly and quietly, she got out of bed. She hurried over to the light switch, turned on her bedroom light, and changed out of her nightgown into one of her two dresses.

Knowing she would soon be back with her family, she tried thinking of everything she needed to take with her. From her closet, she grabbed the dress, pinafore, bonnet, and boots that had been stored in that closet for several months. Not including the bonnet, they were all too small for her, but she didn't want to leave them in the future forever. *I don't know what I'm going to say to Ma and Pa when they ask where I got these from, but Sabrina will eventually need them when she grows bigger,* Gabby thought. *And I'll need more than one everyday dress to wear.* She grabbed her other dress in her current size as well as the matching bonnets for each dress, and she soon found herself at the bedroom door. She turned off the light, slowly opened the door with as little noise as possible, and came to the living room in a matter of seconds. She walked over to the piano where an opened box of facemasks was lying on top, and she pulled out six of them after placing the clothes on a nearby chair. Knowing she would be going outside in the virus-infested air, she put on one of the six facemasks, and she placed the other five of them with the clothes to take with her. She then put on her bonnet, grabbed everything from the chair, and headed on her way out the door.

It had crossed Gabby's mind to save the trouble of walking back to the tree stump if she were to simply stay in the home of her foster parents while wishing to go back in time, but she didn't think it would work. *If I stay here,* she had thought when she was still in the house, *and the house disappears, then I might disappear with it just like my dress did. The tree stump is the only thing that doesn't disappear in either of the two time periods.*

When Gabby arrived at the stump once again, she sat down on it, and she placed the masks and outfits onto her lap. Then she started thinking about the two periods of time. *In these days, I can't see Molly or Sophie, and there's hardly anywhere to go with almost everything shut down. In the old days, I wonder if River Town Mercantile is shut down, and I hope nobody in town caught COVID. I hope it's not too late to start introducing these masks to everyone.*

Sitting on the tree stump, she waited for the surrounding trees to disappear while she constantly wished harder and harder and harder to go back in time. With every minute that passed while still in the presence of hundreds of trees, she tried putting more effort into wishing.

After several minutes, Gabby got to the point of wishing so hard that everything else seemed trivial. However, she still saw hundreds of trees when she turned her head in all directions. *Why aren't the trees disappearing?* she wondered. *I really want to see Ma, Pa, Abigail, Sabrina, and Tabitha again. I can't wish any harder than this! Am I stuck in these days with no way to get back?*

As much as she wanted to return to her family, Gabby felt as though the future days would not let go of her. She wanted to push her way to the past, but it seemed like something in the future was pulling her back. As exhausted as she felt through all the effort of wishing, she let go of her efforts and started focusing her thoughts back to her best friend. *I never said a final goodbye to Molly,* she realized. *Maybe she will miss me too much.* Not wanting to return to the future that had so many restrictions, she somehow felt a need to be in the future, but she first wanted to be with her family to see how they were doing. Because of how she felt, she made plans in advance to return to River City after she would see River Town again.

Once more, her thoughts turned back to the days of history. At the same time, she felt as though the force of the future was letting go of her immediately after she decided to eventually come back, but for what reason of coming back, she did not know. Thinking about her family while looking at the masks on top of the outfits on her lap, she wanted so desperately to help everyone survive the deadly disease, and it quickly became her only desire. Finally, she looked up and noticed the trees starting to fade away.

After a few seconds, the trees were gone. Both the house and the pond were back in sight. She took ahold of everything on her lap while she stood up and started walking to the house. Still unaware of how she was going to explain anything to her folks, she decided to wait to find out what questions she would be asked, and then just let the explanation come to mind when the time would come.

"Ma! Pa!" shouted Abigail who was gathering eggs from the chickens behind the house. "Gabrielle is back!"

Gabrielle looked towards the chicken coop and saw Abigail. *I'm glad Abigail is still alive!* she thought. *And she shouted for Ma and Pa, so they must be alive too, but I wonder how Sabrina and Tabitha are doing.*

Ma and Pa hurried out the front door to not awaken Tabitha, and they soon turned the corner at the side of the house to see Gabrielle in sight. "Oh, *now* what? Has that child gone out of her mind?" asked Ma in a tone of utmost displeasure and disgust as soon as she saw her daughter's face—part of her face—and wondered why Gabrielle seemed to be suffocating herself.

"Maybe it's a bandage," said Pa. "Maybe she broke her nose."

When the folks and Gabrielle approached each other, Pa asked out of concern, "Are you okay? What happened?"

"I'm okay," answered Gabrielle in a muffled voice. "I was going to ask if *you're* okay."

"If we're what?" asked Ma. "I can hardly understand you. Take that thing off your face."

"But then I might catch the . . ."

"Gabrielle Anne Linstrom, you heard what I said," interrupted Ma in a firm tone of voice. Then she looked at what her daughter was holding while Gabrielle took off her mask. "And where did you find your missing dress?"

"Did you finally find where the Feldings live?" added Pa.

Gabrielle assumed her folks would be asking the same questions her foster parents asked. "I did, but it's very hard to find, and I can't take you there. Please don't ask me why. I can't explain it."

"Can't explain it?" repeated Ma. "Then explain to us why you were suffocating yourself."

"What I was wearing is called a facemask. It helps protect from the virus," Gabrielle explained. "And I brought five more of them for each of you."

"What do you mean *the virus*?" asked Pa. "There's more than one virus going around."

"The new one," said Gabrielle. "It's called COVID."

Ma and Pa both looked at each other, and they both shrugged their shoulders while shaking their heads out of unfamiliarity. "I never heard the name of COVID for any disease," said Ma. "The diseases that are going around include scarlet fever, pneumonia, and typhoid fever."

"And there's a cholera pandemic that's killed thousands of people so far," continued Pa.

"But suffocating yourself isn't going to protect you from anything. We all need plenty of oxygen to survive," Ma said.

"I *do* get plenty of oxygen with the mask," Gabrielle said.

"Look at it this way," Pa started to explain. "If you're getting plenty of oxygen from the air when you wear the mask, then you're also getting plenty of anything else that's in the air."

Gabrielle sensed no chance of changing the minds of her folks, so she moved to a somewhat different topic. "Is River Town Mercantile shut down?"

Ma couldn't believe what she had just heard. "What in Heaven's name are you talking about? Mr. and Mrs. Walters haven't shut down anything, and the mercantile is the only store in town. Where do you get these crazy ideas?"

Hearing the word "crazy" again, Gabrielle decided to stop asking questions about anything she had learned in the future during the past few weeks, so she shrugged her shoulders in response. It was now apparent to her that COVID only existed in the future days, and facemasks in the days of history had not yet been invented.

Ma turned to face the house right when Abigail was quietly entering through the back door with the basket of eggs. Then she turned to face Gabrielle. "We need to go back to the house. Breakfast is ready, so enough of this nonsense!"

When Ma, Pa, and Gabrielle entered the house, Sabrina looked towards the door and saw who was coming. "Gabrielle!"

Already knowing who was coming, Abigail faced Gabrielle. "Why did you leave us this time?" Immediately, she looked at the outfits her sister was holding. "Just to get your dress?" she assumed. "You must have found the Feldings. Did you also find your friend named Molly?"

It's a long story," Gabrielle said, thinking of how many years there were between then and the future days. "It's longer than you think!"

"But you don't need to tell me the whole story, and it doesn't take long just to tell me if you saw Molly or not," argued Abigail. "Did you see her, or did you not?"

Still thinking of the number of years that separated the two periods of time, Gabrielle shook her head while everyone started to get seated at the table. "Not anytime recently," she replied.

"But you said she lives close to the Feldings, and it looks like you found their house, so why didn't you go see Molly?"

"Abigail," said Pa, "I don't think your sister's in the mood to explain anything right now. For some reason, she couldn't even tell us where the Feldings live. Let's just focus on eating breakfast, and we'll talk about this another time."

During breakfast, Gabrielle wondered when she should attempt to talk with Pa again about running for president. She knew she had already talked alone with him, but it didn't seem to help. *Maybe he'll listen if other people are around us,* she thought. She also figured there would be no better time than right then to bring up the subject. She turned her head to face her pa. "Pa," she said for getting his attention. "Are you still thinking about running for president?"

"Of course I am," said Pa. "Seeing people work so hard and never having enough for their needs while other people who don't work as hard seem to have more than they need, there's something not right about that. If I'm the president, then things will be better for everyone."

"But what if it makes things worse when everyone has the same amount of money?" asked Gabrielle.

"Gabrielle," said Ma, "your pa is a good man, and he won't ever make things worse for anyone."

"That's right," said Pa. "And Sheriff Badger even said he would put in a good word to the state representatives for me. I don't see how anything can be made worse."

At that moment, Gabrielle couldn't think of a better way to explain things to Pa other than telling him what she learned from the future. However, she knew the risk of being called "crazy" again, but she wasn't ready to give up on trying. Deciding to take the risk, she asked, "What if it turns out that big businesses don't have enough money for what they need, what if the small businesses have so much money that they go bankrupt after spending too much, and what if everyone else goes broke after paying so much on taxes that stores and the government would both need to raise?"

"Where on earth do you come up with these silly ideas?" asked Ma.

"You're only five years old," said Abigail, "and *I* don't even know anything about businesses and taxes!"

"That's just crazy," said Pa, referring to what Gabrielle said. "If I don't run for president, then we won't have enough room in this house for everyone when you four girls grow bigger."

"And speaking about Sheriff Badger," said Ma, "he still couldn't find you after you went missing again. We even let him keep your interesting shoes, your unique coat, and your stuffed bear for a few days for him to find out where they came from or where they were made, but he never had any success at finding out anything."

"When you're ready to tell us, I'd sure like to know where you went," said Pa. "And one more thing . . . your ma and I don't want you to ever go running off again. You need to stay with us and stop disappearing for weeks or months at a time. Before the next time you want to wander off somewhere, please tell us first, and we will be happy to go with you to make sure we know where you are."

That night when Ma was down from the loft after putting the two oldest girls to bed, Gabrielle reflected on what Pa had said, and then she remembered the pulling force she had felt in the future. *I need to go back,* she thought, *but how do I remain honest to Pa when he doesn't want me to go anywhere without him or without Ma? And why did that force want me to go back? Do my foster parents, Molly, or Sophie miss me too much? Maybe I need to say my goodbyes to them. But how can I go back if Pa comes with me? He would have to wish as hard as I do, but it won't work if he doesn't believe in time travel. It's not possible to wish for something that you don't believe in. Even if he said a wish, words alone won't make it come true.*

For the next few days, Gabrielle constantly contemplated her two dilemmas. One of them was how to return to the future while remaining honest and obedient to what her pa said, and the other one was how to get her pa to change his mind about running for president. She still felt disgusted at the thoughts of doing a newspaper interview that she was not looking forward to in the slightest degree, and the only way to keep the interview from happening was to find a better way to change her pa's mind. Temporarily, she tried thinking of a way to keep Sheriff Badger from passing the word on to the state representatives, but how does a five-year-old girl stop a sheriff?

Eventually, Gabrielle came to a conclusion. She thought about the time when she heard her folks calling her name while she was in the future, and she never would have seen them again if she would have remained obedient to her foster mom by not wandering off to the tree stump alone. She wanted to be as obedient as possible for being like Molly as well as Abigail, but she also knew that staying perfectly honest with her folks and her foster parents would not make it possible to do what adults don't believe in. *The only way to get back is to be disobedient,* she thought. However, before making the final decision about leaving once again, she wondered how life in the future would turn out if she chose to stay in the past and was dishonest to herself in the promise she had made with the future force to one day return. At that point, she got another idea.

While Officer Gunwell was attempting another useless search for Gabby, Mrs. Felding had been doing research on Mr. Felding's ancestors. She was curious to know where his ancestors came from after she remembered what Gabby had said.

Over time, the research created another mystery. As soon as she found the answer to her curiosity, she wondered how Gabby could have possibly known about a piece of Felding history that she and her husband hadn't even known.

Mr. Felding walked into the master bedroom after he was finished updating the furniture store website, and he found Mrs. Felding at the computer. "Did you find anything?" he asked.

"I just now found another mystery," Mrs. Felding said.

"What's so mysterious about family history?"

"It's not a mystery about ancestors. It's another mystery to add to our collection."

"Oh, let me guess," said Mr. Felding. "My ancestors really did come from Missouri like Gabby said?"

Mrs. Felding nodded her head. "The only ancestors with the last name of Felding who lived in the 1800s lived in Missouri. The first Feldings to live in Tennessee came here in 1921, which was one hundred years after Missouri became a state."

Mr. Felding was quite surprised. "And Gabby knew about my ancestors before we did? Who's been researching my family history, and why?"

"Maybe Gabby stayed with a relative. Do you have any cousins or distant relatives around here?"

"Not that I'm aware of," said Mr. Felding. "And since Gabby seems to have no ancestors, maybe we should pass this story of Felding ancestry on to Officer Gunwell, and then he could try looking for other Feldings around this part of Tennessee to see if that's where Gabby went."

# 19

# GABBY SAVES MOLLY

On Tuesday, the 9th day of June in the year 2020, Mrs. Felding was sitting in the living room when she heard the doorbell about fifteen minutes before noon. She stood up, walked to the front door, and started to open it, unaware of who was standing outside. She opened the door, and she immediately recognized who had come. "Gabby!" she shouted out of joy. "Come in!" Gabby stepped into the house while carrying her shoes and her coat that she had brought back from the past.

From the office room, Mr. Felding heard the shout, and he hurried to the living room. "Gabby!" he said right when he saw her while Mrs. Felding was giving her another big hug after Gabby had dropped the shoes and coat onto the floor. However, Gabby didn't seem to be too happy. Mr. Felding looked into her eyes and could sense something was wrong. "What's wrong, Precious?"

Mrs. Felding stopped hugging and took a look at Gabby's expression that had the appearance of feeling worried about something. "What is it, Sweetheart?"

"What day is it today?" asked Gabby in a worried tone of voice.

"It's Tuesday, and it's the 9th day of June," said Mrs. Felding. "Why are you worried about what day it is?"

Without answering, Gabby asked, "Is Molly at her house?"

"I think so, but her mom called me this morning to ask about you, and she also said they would be leaving this morning to pick up Molly's dad."

"What time of the day are they leaving?" Gabby quickly asked, still sounding worried.

"They're picking him up at noon," said Mrs. Felding while turning to look at her watch, "and it's almost ten minutes 'till noon, so they're probably leaving right about now."

Suddenly, Gabby dashed to the front door, swiftly opened it, and darted outside, giving no time for Mr. or Mrs. Felding to even wonder what was happening. Immediately upon stepping outside in a hurry, Gabby looked towards the Robinsons' house and noticed their car slowly backing out of the driveway. With no time to lose, Gabby sprinted down the Feldings' driveway and down the sidewalk faster than her five-year-old legs had ever taken her. At the same time, she shouted, "Molly! Molly! Molly! Wait! Stop!"

The car started to back onto the street when Molly heard a faint noise through the rolled-up windows. She turned to look down the sidewalk and noticed Gabby running towards them. "Mom, stop!" Molly abruptly said.

Mrs. Robinson quickly put on the brakes. "Why?"

Molly pointed at Gabby out the window on the driver's side. "It's Gabby!"

Mrs. Robinson pulled the car forward to get off the street, and she rolled down the front and back windows on the driver's side for both herself and Molly. "Molly!" hollered Gabby, quickly finishing the distance to the car while in her dress and bonnet.

"You came back again!" said Molly, feeling happy to see her best friend again. "We're picking up my dad. Are you coming with us?"

Mrs. Robinson quickly intervened. "We don't have an extra car seat, and we need to get going. We're already late." Then she put the car in reverse once again and slowly backed up. Facing Gabby, she said, "We'll see you after we get back."

"Don't go!" said Gabby. But Mrs. Robinson ignored her, and she and Molly were soon on their way.

When the car was out of sight, Gabby started walking back to the home of her foster parents. Throughout the entire distance of three houses, the memory of what she had seen earlier that morning haunted her to the point that tears filled her eyes.

Mr. and Mrs. Felding were still standing in the living room when Gabby opened the front door and stepped inside. She was still teary-eyed. As soon as she saw her mom, she ran over to her with a saddened heart while she burst out into many more tears. Mrs. Felding hugged her and tried to calm her down.

After a minute, Mr. Felding asked, "What's wrong?"

With no response, Mrs. Felding calmly asked, "Can you tell us what that was all about? Why did you need to leave so fast?"

"It's Molly," Gabby said sadly.

"What about Molly? She's just going with her mom to pick up her dad, and then they're going shopping afterwards, but they'll be back later today," Mrs. Felding said.

"No, they won't," said Gabby.

"How do you know?" Mr. Felding asked.

Gabby figured there was only one way to explain. And knowing this would be the last day to see her foster parents, it didn't matter to her anymore how crazy she would sound. "I went to Molly's house in 2023, and the Robinsons weren't living there."

"Are you sure you know what you're saying?" asked Mrs. Felding. "That year hasn't come yet. It's three years from now."

"I know it's in the future," said Gabby. "I'm also in the future right now. I was born in 1865, and that's why my folks haven't heard about a lot of inventions. In my time, the year right now is 1870."

"Sweetheart, time travel only happens in movies and books. It doesn't happen in real life."

"But I'm the same Gabrielle in the book about President Linstrom."

"President who?" asked Mr. Felding.

"President Linstrom. He was the president right after President Grant."

"You definitely don't know what you're talking about," said Mrs. Felding. "The president right after President Grant was Rutherford B. Hayes."

"It wasn't Harold Linstrom?" asked Gabby.

"No," said Mrs. Felding, "but the name of Harold Linstrom is a well-known name. After you told us your last name, I recently found a book called *The Life of Harold Linstrom* that I've been reading. He lived about two miles away from here when this city was called River Town. He loved to go hunting, and he became famous for making bear skin rugs as well as rugs from other animal skins. When I first saw the book, I was surprised he had the same last name as you, but you can't be mentioned in that book. He lived in the 1800s."

"Does the book mention the names of his kids?" asked Gabby.

"As a matter of fact, it does," replied Mrs. Felding. "He had four daughters, and their names from oldest to youngest were Abigail, Gabrielle, Sabrina, and Tabitha."

*I wonder what finally got Pa to change his mind,* thought Gabby. *But how am I going to tell Mom and Dad who I am before I need to go back?* "It doesn't sound like those names are familiar to you," Gabby told Mrs. Felding.

"Well, besides the second daughter having the same name as you, are they supposed to sound familiar?"

"Don't you remember when I told you the names of my three sisters?"

"No, I don't. I didn't even know you had three sisters," said Mrs. Felding.

Suddenly, it dawned on Gabby that a book about the life of President Linstrom didn't exist anymore, and it was from that book that her foster parents had learned the names of her sisters. And without the book in existence, there was also no knowledge about it anymore. However, the other book about Harold Linstrom also mentioned his four daughters, and Gabby soon became curious as to whether other information in it was the same as the one that was never written because of her pa choosing to not run for president. "I'm the same Gabrielle in the book, and the other three girls are my sisters. But before you start thinking I'm crazy, does the book list the dates of when the four girls were born and when they died?"

"I don't know," said Mrs. Felding.

"Let me go get the book," Mr. Felding said on his way to another room to find it.

"If this silly conversation about living in the 1800s is going to take too much longer," said Mrs. Felding to Gabby, "then let's get you settled back in, and we can continue this tomorrow. By the way, did you not bring an extra dress? And where's your mask?"

"I didn't bring another dress because I need to go back home today," said Gabby. "My folks don't want me to be away for a long time by myself. And between oxygen and a virus that are both in the air, my folks also said it's not possible for a man-made thing to keep only one of the two away from breathing it in. They said whoever came up with that idea is tricking everyone, and it's not even Halloween!"

Mr. Felding came back into the living room with the book. "I found it," he said. Then he started to open it to find the needed page.

"I'm sure it doesn't have the date of when Gabrielle died," said Gabby.

Mr. Felding found the page. He read the dates of when each of the four girls was born. Afterwards, he started reading the dates of when they died, but there was no date for Gabrielle.

"How did you know?" asked Mrs. Felding to Gabby.

"Because I'm the same Gabrielle in the book."

"Precious, even though she has the same name and birthday, you're 150 years apart," said Mr. Felding. "But what's this about Molly?"

"When I went to her house in the future, someone who lived there—or someone who *will* live there—said they died in a car accident. Then I walked to the cemetery, and I found a gravestone that had the name of Molly Robinson with the date of June 9, 2020 on it."

"Sweetheart," said Mrs. Felding, "your imagination has been getting you too emotional. But just to go along with what you're saying, how do you go to other years?"

"I go to the tree stump in the field of trees, and I wish very hard. When I go back to history, the trees all around me disappear, and when I come to the future, the trees appear again. All I need to do is wish hard enough. One of Abigail's friends said that if dreams can come true, then wishes can too."

"Yes, dreams and wishes can come true," said Mr. Felding, but there are still things that are not possible, and time travel is one of them."

Wanting her foster parents to believe her, Gabby wondered what else there was to say. While wondering, she faced the book that Mr. Felding was still holding, and she got an idea. "After I go back home to my folks today, open the book, and you'll see the date of when Gabrielle died." Changing the subject, she continued, "I just hope something will keep Molly from getting hurt, and I'm really going to miss her."

"You don't need to miss her so much if you come visit her . . . either at a distance, or whenever the mask mandate is ever lifted," said Mrs. Felding.

Gabby shook her head. "My folks don't want me to leave again, and I want to be obedient by doing what they say. And this mask mandate won't last forever. I didn't see anyone in 2023 who was wearing one."

Mr. and Mrs. Felding both looked at each other, surprised that Gabby was pretending to know about the future. Mrs. Felding then looked at her watch. Feeling the desperate need to change the subject, she said, "It's getting close to lunchtime."

*Lunchtime already?* thought Gabby. "I need to go back home before Ma and Pa wonder where I am. But before I go, may I have one more Pop-Tart?"

"Yes, you may," said Mrs. Felding while she started to head to the kitchen. Gabby followed. "And it's not safe for kids your age to be alone outside, especially along a busy street. I don't know how you left us twice all by yourself without something happening to you, but we need to take you home this time." Arriving at the pantry door, she opened it, grabbed the box of Pop-Tarts, and handed a package of two to Gabby.

"I'm going to miss these Pop-Tarts," said Gabby. "In my day, these weren't invented yet." Mrs. Felding continued to wonder about Gabby's mentality. She had never heard anything more ridiculous in her life. At the same time, another thought came to Gabby from what her foster mom said. "Speaking about busy streets, I think I know why I never see a lot of cars. It's because my time hasn't met up with their time. I remember when Dad took me into the police station, and I couldn't see Officer Gunwell until my time and his time finally came together."

Gabby started eating her Pop-Tart when Mr. Felding walked into the kitchen. He had been listening to the conversation from the other room. "As soon as you're done with your Pop-Tart, we'll drive you back to the field of trees, and we'll take you to the tree stump," he said. "But I'm afraid it's going to end up like it did last time we took you there. You won't find a pond, and you won't find a house." Then he moved back to the topic that Gabby had last mentioned. "And what's this idea about two different times coming together? If that were true, then adults would be the first ones to see you because they were born closer to the old days than the kids, but your mom once told me Molly saw you from the very start."

"I guess everyone has their own time," said Gabby, "and it's up to my time and their time to decide when to come together, but I think a lot of it also has to do with believing. Adults don't believe as much as kids do."

Being left speechless once again, Mr. and Mrs. Felding looked at each other in silence. Turning back to Gabby, Mr. Felding changed the topic. "Well, finish your Pop-Tart, and then we'll take you back to the field of trees just to show you again that there's nothing besides trees."

A few minutes later, Mr. Felding parked the car on the side of Cherry Street right next to the field of trees. He, Mrs. Felding, and Gabby all got out and started walking to the tree stump.

After two minutes of walking, they arrived at the stump. "Here we are," said Gabby. She turned to look at her foster parents. Realizing the time was drawing nigh when she would soon not be seeing them anymore, a tear fell down her cheek. "Thank you both for loving me and taking care of me. I'll never forget you!"

Mr. Felding turned his head in different directions to look for a pond or a house. "Why are we saying goodbye when there's nowhere to go? I still don't see a house."

"That's because it doesn't exist in these days. I'll see it when I go back to the old days."

"Back to the old days?" repeated Mrs. Felding. "I never heard an imagination quite like yours! When you're done imagining, we'll take you back home."

Gabby shook her head. "I need to get back to my folks, but I need to do it alone," she said in a sincere voice.

Mrs. Felding didn't want to stay in the field of trees all afternoon, and she wasn't about to leave her foster daughter alone outside. "Remember what I said about being alone?" she asked Gabby.

Suddenly, Mr. Felding thought of something after having heard the sincerity in Gabby's voice. He faced his wife and quietly said, "I have an idea. Let's start walking back, and I'll tell you on the way."

Curious to know what the idea was, Mrs. Felding agreed. "Okay," she said. And just to play along with Gabby's imagination, she leaned down to Gabby and gave her one last kiss on her forehead while Gabby started to shed one more tear. "I love you."

"I love you too, Mom," said Gabby. "Thank you for everything you've done for me." Then Mrs. Felding turned away and started walking back with her husband. Gabby sat down on the stump to start getting ready to wish. She turned to face her foster parents once more.

By this time, they were about twenty feet away. "Don't forget to look at the dates in the book when you get back," she hollered.

Seconds later, Mr. Felding stopped. "Let's stop right here," he said quietly. Mrs. Felding stood beside him. Now they were sixty feet away from Gabby behind several trees. Speaking in a low volume, Mr. Felding said, "I think Gabby made plans with her parents to meet at the stump. Let's wait right here until they come. Maybe she didn't want us to meet them. But if we stay out of sight right here, then we can peek between the trees to make sure she doesn't get lost again."

At the stump, Gabby assumed her foster parents had finally trusted her to be alone and had gone back home. Although she thought she was alone, it was hard for her to leave that period of time. She had enjoyed learning so much about so many inventions, and she was the only person from the 1800s who knew about the latest technology as of 2020. She also enjoyed making new friends, yet she knew it would not have mattered to many of them whether or not she would have had a chance to say goodbye. She wondered if the main purpose for this last return to the future was successful or not, but she knew she had tried her best. Only the people in these future days would know the results of her attempt to save her best friend.

Minutes passed. After struggling to find it in her heart to leave what she would miss, Gabby remembered what her pa had told her as well as how obedient Molly had always been, and there was only one way to be just like her best friend. Her ultimate purpose for coming to the future that was predestined for her to get her pa to change his mind was now complete. It felt good to be relieved from the thoughts of being interviewed for a newspaper article along with letting go of worrying about being one of the daughters of the worst president. But she didn't know what got Pa to change his mind, and she didn't know how the rest of her family and the entire town would react to his change of plans. She also didn't know where her pa would get the idea of making rugs from animal skins, but there was only one way to find out. Curious to know the answer to all these questions, she started wishing to return back to history.

After three more minutes, the trees started to fade away, according to what Gabby saw. However, through the eyes of Mr. and Mrs. Felding, nothing was happening to the trees, but it was Gabby that was fading away.

In a few seconds, Gabby was back to June 9, 1870. Mr. and Mrs. Felding couldn't believe their eyes. "Did you just see what I thought I saw?" asked Mrs. Felding.

"I don't know," replied Mr. Felding. "If you're asking about something that's not believable, then I think I did." A brief pause followed while he thought about what had been said at home. "Maybe this is why Gabby said adults don't believe as much as kids do. I saw it, and I still don't believe it!"

Soon after arriving back home, Mr. Felding found the book about Harold Linstrom. Remembering Gabby's reminder to look at the dates, he opened the book to the page that he had read before leaving to go to the field of trees, and there on the page was listed Gabrielle Linstrom's death date. "This book has the date of when Gabrielle died," said Mr. Felding to his wife, "and I know for sure this wasn't here before."

Mrs. Felding was quite surprised. "You can't be serious! Are you sure it's the same book and the same Gabrielle?"

"It's definitely the same book, and the same birth date of May 9, 1865 is still here."

Both Mr. and Mrs. Felding were completely flabbergasted at what they had been seeing and hearing. "Maybe we need to start believing in things that seem impossible," Mrs. Felding said. Then they both started thinking about every experience with Gabby that happened ever since they first found her wandering lost beside the street.

"What if everything Gabby ever told us is all true?" thought Mr. Felding aloud. "When we first found her, she only saw one building on the way to the police station, and she thought we were driving onto the grass.  Perhaps her time hadn't all come together with River City. Maybe some of her time was still in River Town."

"If she really came from the 1800s, then it would make sense as to why she didn't know what a car was, but she knew about horses and buggies."

"And that's probably why she was wearing an old-fashioned dress with a bonnet when we first saw her.  It wasn't for a party or any other occasion."

"Also, she was scared of Halloween because she personally knew what it was like in the old days, and it also might answer how she knew about Thanksgiving occurring on different Thursdays in November as well as not knowing any president after President Grant."

"What about the mystery of how she was advanced on her piano lessons after she came back from being lost?  I'm sure her other piano teacher was just as perplexed as you were when you wondered who else was teaching her," said Mr. Felding.  "And now we know why Gabby and Gabrielle were both lost for months at a time.  Maybe she really *was* the same girl."

Mrs. Felding had no response to Mr. Felding's last comment. Her mind was starting to focus on something else.  "But what about earlier today when she told us about the Robinsons in a car accident?  I didn't believe her at the time, but what if what she said was true?  I might be losing one of my piano students."

A moment of silence occurred while Mr. and Mrs. Felding both dreaded the thoughts of a horrific catastrophe.  They knew that Gabby wasn't able to keep the Robinsons from driving away that day.  Then Mrs. Felding spoke with a touch of sadness.  "Now I've lost both Gabby *and* Molly.  I don't know if I can continue teaching piano lessons."

"There's nothing we could have done about losing Gabby.  She went back to where she came from, and we were fortunate to be the ones to raise her while she was here in these days for whatever reason.  But as for Molly, let's wait to find out what happened."

# 20
# I'LL ALWAYS REMEMBER YOU

Mrs. Felding's cell phone started ringing. "I don't think I'm in the mood to answer phone calls right now. Someone in the neighborhood might be calling to inform us about a car accident, and I don't want to hear about it."

"But what if it's not someone in the neighborhood, and what if it's important? It won't hurt to at least see who it is."

Mrs. Felding gloomily grabbed her nearby phone, and she looked to see who was calling. "It's Mrs. Robinson's phone! Maybe someone recovered it and they're calling people in the contact list." She answered it. "Hello."

"Hi, Mrs. Felding. This is Mrs. Robinson. Molly is now finished with the last piano assignment you gave her. Can you tell us what she's supposed to do in the next lesson?"

Mrs. Felding felt every ounce of gloom depart from her heart. "You're still alive?" she asked excitedly.

"Well, if that isn't the stupidest question I ever heard in my life!" said Mrs. Robinson. "And what does being alive have to do with the next piano lesson?"

"It's what Gabby said after she came back from trying to stop you from leaving this morning."

"Who's Gabby?" asked Mrs. Robinson.

"Don't you remember my foster daughter? She's best friends with Molly. Why are you asking who Gabby is?"

"I didn't know you had a foster kid, and I think Molly would have told me about a girl named Gabby, especially if they were really best friends. But I don't know anyone named Gabby, and what makes you think anyone tried to stop us from leaving? Have you gone crazy?"

"Well," Mrs. Felding said slowly while she started to wonder, "I'm not quite sure." *Does Mrs. Robinson have amnesia, or is this just weird like a book with a missing date that later showed up on the page?* she thought. *I wonder what Gabby saw in the future.* "So nobody tried to stop you from leaving this morning, and you weren't in a car wreck?"

"Was I supposed to be in a car wreck? I have no idea what you're trying to say! But now that you mention it, I was almost in a wreck earlier today. Someone ran through a stop sign at a high speed, and they went right in front of me. If I were just a few feet ahead of where I was, then we would have been in a wreck that might have been deadly. And now that I think about it, Molly thought she heard something while we were backing out of the driveway this morning, so I stopped for a second, but I couldn't see anything. If it weren't for Molly hearing something that wasn't there, then we might have been right in front of the speeding car. But why did you bring up the topic of a car wreck? Were you following us on the road?"

*Oh, now when it seems all the mysteries are finally solved, here comes another mystery,* Mrs. Felding thought. Quickly, she tried to make up a believable answer to Mrs. Robinson's question. "Maybe I got mixed up with another car wreck that I heard on the news. But it's good to hear you're safe."

"That's nice of you, but what about my reason for calling?"

Mrs. Felding immediately got an idea. "May I talk to Molly to explain the next lesson to her?"

"Okay. Here she is."

"Hello," said Molly.

Mrs. Felding told Molly the next step of the lessons. Afterwards, she asked, "Do you remember Gabby?"

"Who's Gabby?" asked Molly.

"Oh, never mind. Just remember to practice every day."

"What was that all about?" Mr. Felding asked after the phone call.

"The Robinsons are safe at home, but Mrs. Robinson said they would have been in a car wreck if Molly hadn't thought she heard something while they were backing off their driveway, which made Mrs. Robinson stop for a second. But I talked with both Molly and her mom, and neither one of them could remember Gabby."

"Is this turning out to be the strangest day ever?" asked Mr. Felding. "First, we see Gabby disappear after she starts to fade away, and then we see a date on the page of a book that wasn't there before, and now we have neighbors who can't remember our foster daughter after seeing her plenty of times?"

"Well, she *is* from the past," said Mrs. Felding. "If the Robinsons never heard of her, then could she have just been a figment of our imaginations?"

"How do you kiss an imagination on the forehead?" Followed by another brief pause, Mr. Felding continued, "If Officer Gunwell ever finds out we aren't fostering Gabby anymore, then he might do an investigation, and we might get into trouble. We should go talk to him and tell him that Gabby is with her biological parents, and then he could update his records."

When Gabrielle opened the front door, her parents looked to see her coming. "You're just in time for dinner," said Ma while she placed the last dish onto the table.

"We were starting to wonder again where you went because we hadn't seen you ever since breakfast," said Pa.

"It's already dinner?" asked Gabrielle. "You didn't wonder where I went when you had lunch?"

"What's lunch?" asked Ma.

"Oh, I forgot that's not what we call it," replied Gabrielle. "That's the word the Feldings said to describe the midday meal, and they said the evening meal was dinner." However, she knew that's what everyone in River City called it, but she mentioned the Feldings to her folks instead of mentioning the name of a city that didn't yet exist.

"That's strange!" said Abigail. "I thought everyone referred to the midday meal as dinner, and the evening meal as supper."

Ma turned back to Gabrielle for a different topic. "While you were gone this morning, I couldn't find your interesting coat or shoes. Where did you put them?"

"I took them back to the Feldings," Gabrielle said in honesty.

"So that must be where you went this morning," said Pa. "I really wish you would show us where they live. I'd like to meet them. Are you ready to show us?"

Gabrielle shook her head. "I can't," she said. "They're moving far away." *They're 150 years away,* she thought.

"In that case," said Ma, "I assume you won't be leaving us to go see them anymore."

"And when we couldn't find you this morning," said Pa, "I was hoping you would remember what I said about not wandering off and getting lost again."

Gabrielle nodded her head. "I remember. That's why I came back as soon as I could. I'm always going to remember what you told me, and I'm never going to leave again . . . unless it's just for an hour or two to go into town," she said, knowing these were the days when it was safe for children to be alone outside.

"That's good to know," said Ma.

Throughout the remainder of the day, Gabrielle didn't think it was a good time to ask Pa what changed his mind about running for president. It was just the previous day when he was still looking forward to campaigning, and she didn't figure he would change his mind in just one day. *He's going to change his mind sometime, so I better wait to find out what will change his mind. Otherwise, if I talk to him about it, then he might not change his mind, and then the future will change again, and I'll have to do that interview.*

In the morning of June 10, 2020, Mr. and Mrs. Felding arrived at the police station. They found Officer Gunwell sitting at the same, usual desk, and he was busy doing paperwork once again.

When the Feldings came to the desk, Mr. Felding spoke. "Pardon me, officer."

Officer Gunwell looked up to face them. "What can I do for you?"

"We came to tell you about Gabby. She found her biological parents, so she's not living with us anymore," said Mr. Felding.

"Now, let's back up a bit," Officer Gunwell said. "First, I need to know who you are, so if you'll just sign your names on this guest sheet, and then you'll need to tell me why you want to talk about a girl who's with her biological parents. If she was missing, then we can't do anything about it right now if she's not missing anymore, and I don't think we have anyone named Gabby on our list of missing children to update.

"But don't you remember who we are? I'm George Felding, and this is my wife, Linda. We brought in a missing girl named Gabby a little over a year ago. Then you sent her with us after we got licensed for foster care, and you later tried searching for her twice when she went missing from our home two different times."

"I never sent a foster child home with anyone. According to the law, nobody is supposed to do that besides the agency that you're licensed through. And you must have me mixed up with an officer in another city, county, or state. Now, is there anything else I can help you folks with?"

"No," said Mrs. Felding. "We're sorry to bother you, officer."

"That's okay," Officer Gunwell said. "I'm sure lots of people have misunderstandings about foster agencies or get two different officers mixed up."

After leaving the police station, Mr. and Mrs. Felding both couldn't believe what they had just heard. "It's almost like the Robinsons not remembering Gabby, but Officer Gunwell also couldn't remember *us*! What in the world is going on?" asked Mrs. Felding. "Did everyone suddenly lose their memory?" Throughout the rest of the way home, they both tried to think of any logical explanations for this big mystery.

When they stepped into their house, Mr. Felding finally pieced his thoughts together, much like a jigsaw puzzle. "Maybe I know the reason for all this madness. If Gabby is from the 1800s, then it would make sense why the book didn't have the death date until recently."

"What do you mean?" Mrs. Felding asked.

"When Gabby was missing, she was back in the 1800s with her family, and that's why Officer Gunwell could never find her. But the people these days who knew her could still remember her because she was still connected to these days somehow. And now that she went back to her own time again, assuming she's never coming back, then it broke the connection to *our* time, and that's how the date appeared in the book."

"And with the connection broken, it's as though she was never here at this point in time, and that's why nobody can remember her," added Mrs. Felding.

Mr. Felding nodded his head. "Exactly!" he exclaimed.

"Then how do *we* still remember her when nobody else does?"

Mr. Felding tried for a few seconds to think of an answer. "I don't know, but Gabby mentioned something about a book about President Linstrom, and there was never any president by that name. I wonder if her dad would have been the president, and maybe she got him to change his mind, which changed the future. Assuming that's what happened, there might have been a book in existence about someone named President Linstrom like what she mentioned, and maybe we can't remember it just like nobody can remember Gabby."

"That's a possibility, and I never thought I'd actually believe in such ridiculous things," said Mrs. Felding. "I still wouldn't believe any of this if it wasn't actually happening, but there's one more thing I'm wondering. If we can still remember Gabby, then I wonder if she still remembered us after the last time she went back to the past."

"I don't think there's any way to find out," said Mr. Felding.

Sunday morning came. On June 12, 1870, the Linstrom family

arrived at church.  They took a seat and waited for more people to arrive. While they waited, Gabrielle's thoughts were constantly on Molly, wondering what had happened on that frightful day, and wondering whether Molly would be living past the age of six.  Although Molly wasn't yet born at that time, Gabrielle's memory would forever remain tied to the days of her best friend, knowing they would have been best friends if Gabrielle had been born 150 years later.  Nevertheless, she wondered how she could ever know whether or not the life of her best friend would be cut short.

After the preacher got started, part of what he taught was about sacrifice.  "How many of us have had to sacrifice something for something else?  I'm sure we all have.  Some of us have sacrificed our time for something important when we could have used that time for something else.  Some of us have sacrificed an opportunity to be somewhere in order to be somewhere else.  If any of you are ever placed in a situation where you need to decide between two choices, which one are you going to sacrifice, and which one are you going to choose? Would you not choose the one that's more important?  Or if they're equally important, then perhaps the one to choose is the one your heart is more set on.  Which one do you love the most?  Or let's suppose your heart is not in the right place.  In that case, which one would the Greatest Example of sacrifice want you to choose?" the preacher said.

For the next few days, Gabrielle's words kept repeating in her pa's mind.  *I'm always going to remember what you told me,* he kept thinking to himself.  And quite often, he also reflected on what the preacher said, knowing he was in a situation that was much like what the preacher described.

On Tuesday, the 21st day of June, Pa made an announcement to the family right after breakfast that he needed to go into town and would be gone for a good part of the day, but he didn't want to say the reason why he needed to go.  Ma helped him get ready by making some food for him to take, and he was soon on his way after hitching up the team.

A few hours later, Pa was back home.  Ma was in the house when she saw him coming inside, and she asked, "Will you tell us why you went to town?"

"Did you get us something?  Is there a surprise?" asked Abigail.

"No," said Pa, "I didn't get anything."

Abigail couldn't think of any other reason why Pa needed to go when he ended up coming back with nothing.  "Then why did you go?" she asked.

Briefly, Pa turned to face Ma, then to Abigail, and then turned to face Gabrielle who was looking back at him.  "Let's sit down, and I'll explain."

When everyone was gathered around the table, Pa began his explanation. "The past several days, I had a few thoughts. What the preacher said about making choices, it got me thinking about my choice to run for president. He also talked about sacrifices, and if I become the president, then I would be doing a lot of traveling all over the country, and I wouldn't have as much time to spend with any of you. I won't even get to see my four girls grow up for at least four years, and that would be a sacrifice that I would need to make. But as for the country, if I don't campaign, then there might be another candidate who will do a good job. Therefore, after giving it a lot of thought, I left today to tell everyone in the entire town that I won't be running for president."

The news was a big surprise to Ma in a shocking way. "But what about the size of this house when the girls grow bigger? What are we going to do when that time comes?"

"I don't know, but we still have a few years. Maybe something will happen between now and then," said Pa.

"This means I won't be the daughter of a president," said Abigail in a somewhat disappointing way after she had been looking forward to it for quite some time.

"I'm afraid so," said Pa.

As soon as Pa had finished explaining, Gabrielle somehow sensed in his voice that he was leaving something out, and she wondered what else he wasn't saying.

That evening while Pa was milking the cows in the barn, Gabrielle showed up. Pa raised his head to see her. "Would you like to help?" he asked.

Gabrielle shook her head. "I wanted to talk with you."

"About what?"

"What else made you change your mind about running for president?"

"What do you mean?" asked Pa. "I explained it in the house."

"Pa," said Gabrielle, sounding serious, "if spending more time with the family was the only reason for changing your mind, then you wouldn't have ever thought about running at all."

Getting ready to explain everything, Pa stood up, walked over to Gabrielle, crouched down, and put his arm around her. "What really helped me change my mind was you."

"Me?" asked Gabrielle.

Pa nodded his head. "Each time you went missing, I became more and more worried about you, and it wasn't until later when I realized how much I love you, and the time spent without you when you were gone made me think of more time that would be spent without you if I were to be the one who was gone. But that's not all. I also remember the words you said to me several days ago when you said you're always going to remember what I told you, and then I got to thinking it should go both ways. I also need to remember what you told me when you tried to discourage me from being the president. Ever since you last tried to talk me out of it, I wondered what I would do as the president if something really did go wrong, and just in case I wouldn't know how to handle it, I wouldn't want to be known to future generations as the worst president in history. But the only problem with this change of mind is not knowing how to earn enough money to make more space for when we'll need it when you girls are more grown."

Gabrielle remembered the book about the life of her pa that was read to her by the Feldings when she was in the future. "Have you thought about making animal skin rugs?" she asked her pa.

"Now, what gave you that idea?"

Gabrielle shrugged her shoulders while refraining from mentioning where the idea came from. "I just thought you might be interested in doing that as much as you like to go hunting."

"But the only way to make enough money would be to sell them, and suppose they don't sell. What if nobody wants to buy them?"

"You need to look on the positive side, Pa. I bet you'll sell lots of them, and you might even be famous!" said Gabrielle.

The words went through Pa's mind once again. *I'm always going to remember what you told me.* "Since it's a good idea, I'll give it a try, and we'll see what happens," he said.

As the years went by, Gabrielle grew old. At age ninety-six, she was fortunate to still be living in the same house where she grew up. Abigail, Sabrina, and Tabitha had all passed away, and she was the only original resident of the house who was still alive. The house was twice as big as what it was when she was a little girl, and it had been decades ever since her pa built extra rooms onto it. Her husband had been deceased for a few years, and her two children would often come to take care of her.

The time eventually came when she could not live alone because she needed constant care. When it was time to move out of the house to go live with her daughter, she found her wooden chest that she had been using to keep important things. She opened the lid of the chest, and she pulled out two things. One of them was a letter, and one of them was a note. She had written both of them many years ago when she was much younger. She read through the letter while reflecting on good memories, and then she placed it back into the chest. The note was only one page. Right before she stepped out of the house for the final time, she taped the note to the front window so the words could be seen from outside. Then she looked around at the empty house including the extension to the loft as well as the stairs her pa had built. It wasn't easy to leave so many memories behind, but she was grateful for her grandchildren to be there to help her walk out the door for the last time.

After she was seated on the passenger seat in the car, she took one more look at the house and the pond as well as the tree stump where she always used to sit to make her wishes. Then her daughter slowly drove down the paved lane until they got to Cherry Street before continuing on to their destination.

In the morning of Monday, June 22, 2020, an idea finally came to Mr. Felding. "If Gabby was really the same girl in the book who was born in 1865, then she's obviously deceased, according to her death date. There's no record of where she lived when she was in her later years, but going on the assumption that she lived in River City her entire life, what if she's buried in the local cemetery?"

"It won't hurt to take a look," said Mrs. Felding. "She might have a different last name on the gravestone if she was married, but we could try looking for any name of Gabrielle with the same birth and death dates that are in the book."

Later that day, they arrived at River City Cemetery. Not knowing exactly where to look, they parked to the side of one of the roads in the area that had older gravestones.

After getting out of the car and searching for a while, they found themselves back in the section where both sets of their grandparents were buried, which brought back memories. "I remember bringing Gabby here," said Mr. Felding.

"That was after we learned that Gabby knew how to play *Graces*, and now we know where she learned how to play it," Mrs. Felding added.

"Well, let's keep searching," said Mr. Felding.

Turning their heads from side to side in their search for any gravestone that had the name of Gabrielle, it was only a matter of seconds before Mr. Felding turned his head again and noticed something very strange. Then he stopped walking. "That's strange," he said.

"What's strange?"

Mr. Felding pointed in the direction. "Two sections over there. It doesn't look like there's any empty spot like there used to be when we were here with Gabby."

After coming to the specified section, they both searched each gravestone while trying to find where the empty spot used to be. Suddenly, Mrs. Felding caught sight of a gravestone a short distance away with the name of Gabrielle. "Over here," she said loud enough to be heard. Mr. Felding turned to see where his wife was at, and they both walked quickly to where the name on the gravestone was located.

Facing the headstone that stood above the ground, they found the last name of Robbins at the top of the two carved names. Taking a look at the wife's name, carved on the headstone was shown:

GABRIELLE ANNE LINSTROM
MAY 9, 1865
MAR. 28, 1962

"Those are the same dates in the book," Mr. Felding said. Then he glanced around the section of gravestones. "And this is exactly where the empty spot used to be."

Mrs. Felding stared at the gravestone while trying to put a few unorganized thoughts together. "She died before we were even born," she said while starting to be disbelieving again. "Is this really the same Gabrielle who stayed with us?"

In response, Mr. Felding said, "I've never seen anyone else disappear by fading away. And how many times have you seen a missing piece of information suddenly show up in a book all by itself?"

"Maybe there are things in life that can't be explained. But how is it possible that we remember seeing someone who died before we were born?"

Mr. Felding took a second to think about it. Slowly, he shook his head. "I don't know. But if we can remember her, then I wonder how to find out whether she remembered us, especially since we weren't born yet."

Mrs. Felding had no response. Wanting to take a look at the entire headstone, she slowly walked around to the back of it. As soon as she saw what was carved, she placed her hand over her mouth while her eyes grew wide. Her heart was quickly filled with emotions, and a tear fell down her cheek. Mr. Felding noticed her expression. "What's wrong?" he asked. Mrs. Felding was too chocked up to speak, so she pointed to the back side of the headstone. Curious to know what had gotten his wife to become tearful, he walked around to where she stood. Then he read the words that said:

OUR CHILDREN
GEORGE AND LINDA

NAMED AFTER THE BEST FOSTER PARENTS
IN THE WORLD

I'LL ALWAYS REMEMBER YOU

The following day, Mrs. Felding was starting to prepare lunch in the kitchen when she heard the doorbell. Not knowing who had come, she walked to the front door while thinking, *I wonder who that could be. I don't suppose it's Gabby.*

While Mr. Felding was on his way to the door, Mrs. Felding turned the doorknob and opened the door. They both saw a young lady who was holding an envelope. She was twenty years of age. "May we help you?" Mrs. Felding asked.

"My name is Emily Robbins. I live out of town. I was going through some old things from my ancestors, and I found this envelope from an ancestor named Gabrielle who was five generations before me. Written on the envelope, she asked for a descendant to deliver this letter to this address when the summer of 2020 comes. The envelope is dated back in 1889. Not only was that a few years before River Town became River City, but I found out that Main Street didn't exist back then, so I don't know how she came up with this address when she wrote it." Emily handed the envelope to Mrs. Felding who was speechless. "I better not take any more of your time, and I need to get back home."

"It's good to have met you," said Mr. Felding.

"Same here," said Emily. "But before I go, I also found several papers that were written by my ancestor that sounded mysterious. It was almost like she was writing to keep herself from forgetting how things work, but the things she wrote about weren't even invented at the time she wrote about them. I know it's hard to believe, but I hope whatever she wrote in that letter isn't too mysterious."

"I think I can believe everything you said," Mrs. Felding told her, "and I'm sure the letter won't be mysterious at all. Thank you for delivering it."

After Emily left, Mrs. Felding opened the envelope and took out the letter. She and Mr. Felding read it together.

*Dear Mom and Dad,*

*I'm very grateful for the chance I had to get to know you. I couldn't have asked for better foster parents. Although I'm twenty-four years old while writing this letter to you, I still remember you as though it were just yesterday when I was with you.*

*Assuming one of my descendants will deliver this letter to you, I'm sure there are several things you're both wondering including why I came to the future and how it all got started. I don't want to keep you wondering, so that's why I'm writing this letter.*

*Before I was four years old, I wanted to learn about the future. After I turned four, I sat on my favorite tree stump while I made a birthday wish to be in the future, and that's when my wish came true, but I couldn't remember where I came from because it was 150 years ago. Not many kids can remember things after 150 years.*

*Although you can't remember, Sophie told me who the worst president in history was, and I learned more about him from you. I later found out he was my pa. After I discovered how to get back to my days, I tried to get him to not run for president, and he eventually took my advice. If it were not for you, he would have taken office right after President Grant, and we would have gone through the First Great Depression.  But in your history books, there was only one Great Depression that I'm not looking forward to while writing this letter.  And because my pa changed his mind, that's why you can't remember anyone by the name of President Linstrom.*

*I'm sure I will be deceased a long time ago by the time you read this.  I will never forget you, and I know you haven't forgotten me.  I still remember Molly and Sophie even though they can't remember me. The last time you took me to the stump on the last day when we were together, I made one last wish to come back to what you would refer to as the days of history, but it wasn't just a wish.  I couldn't wish to go back unless my time remained connected to your time.  Right before I left your days, I felt a connecting force that tied us together, and that's how I know we will never forget each other.  I also stayed connected to Molly and Sophie in my memory when I left, but I couldn't hold on to the force that tied me to them, and that's why they can't remember me.*

*I know there have been too many mysteries about me that were hard for you to believe, especially the things I told you on our last day together. Once you start believing, please don't ever stop. If you ever stop believing, then it could break the connection between us. Please look after Molly and Sophie when you can as soon as the government mandates are lifted. I love you both, and I'll always remember you!*

*Your foster daughter from a different time,*
*Gabrielle*

After they finished reading the letter, Mrs. Felding thought of an idea. "Let's go see that old house on the other side of Cherry Street."

"Are you talking about the one on the other side of the pond that's close to the tree stump?" asked Mr. Felding.

Mrs. Felding nodded her head. "I know we've taken Gabby to the stump twice, but I never took a close look at the house, and I don't think anyone lives there."

On Wednesday, the 24th day of June, Mr. and Mrs. Felding arrived at the old house. Mrs. Felding looked on the other side of the pond and found the tree stump. "I remember the first time we brought Gabby to the stump," she said. "She kept hearing the voices of her parents, but none of us ever saw them anywhere."

"Hey, look here," said Mr. Felding who was standing in front of the house. "I don't remember seeing this note taped to the window."

Mrs. Felding walked to the window and found the note. As soon as she took a look at it, something seemed familiar, and she said, "After reading the letter from Gabby yesterday, that sure does look like her handwriting." Then she read the note that said:

*Please don't ever demolish this house. It was once the home of Harold Linstrom who was well known for making animal skin rugs.*

"Now we know this was definitely her house," said Mr. Felding.

"And now I feel bad for not believing her when she told us."

"It's not like we were keeping her away from her parents," said Mrs. Felding. "This house was abandoned with nobody living here at the time."

"That's true," Mr. Felding agreed. "I'm going to take a walk to the stump for memories sake."

On his way to the stump, Mrs. Felding followed. "It's strange that a note like that would be taped to the window of an old house," Mrs. Felding said.

Mr. Felding gave it some thought. "Maybe it's like the book she started to mention that was about President Linstrom. If her dad had been the president, then that book might have been in existence. And with a note that says not to demolish the house, it might have been torn down by now if the note wasn't there."

"When Gabby was with us, maybe the house didn't exist, and maybe that's why she left the note after she returned to the past in order to make sure it wouldn't turn out like how she saw it in our time," Mrs. Felding said.

"Depending on what we do can change the future, but it's funny that it depended on what we did that changed the past. And when the past changed, then it also changed the future, and that's why we can't remember telling Gabby about a president who was never the president," said Mr. Felding.

They soon came to the stump. "Here's where Gabby loved to sit," Mr. Felding said.

"And this is where she made her wishes that somehow came true," added Mrs. Felding right when she turned her head and noticed an old object lying on the ground beside the stump. She bent down and picked it up, and it was only a matter of seconds before she recognized what it was.

"That's not just a teddy bear," said Mr. Felding. "That looks like the same one Gabby got from the police station."

"She must have taken it with her to the past and forgot to bring it back. It looks like it's well over one hundred years old."

After looking at it momentarily, Mr. Felding mentioned, "Maybe we should leave it right here where it was lying just in case one of Gabby's descendants knows about its whereabouts." Mrs. Felding agreed, and she placed the shabby, timeworn teddy bear back onto the ground beside the stump. "And I had another idea," said Mr. Felding. "Now that our foster daughter is gone, I'm back to feeling old. What would you think if we tried doing foster care again?"

"I like that idea," Mrs. Felding said. "But next time, let's get a foster child who isn't so full of mysteries."

❖

In the morning of June 9, 2020, Mrs. Robinson and Molly both got ready to pick up Mr. Robinson from the airport, knowing he was coming back from another business trip. When they were ready, they left the house and were soon getting into the car.

After Mrs. Robinson got Molly buckled into her booster seat, she sat on the driver's seat and started the car. About ten minutes 'till noon, she started backing the car on the driveway towards the street.

At that point, Gabrielle was sent down from Heaven as an angel, unseen by mortal eyes. She sat in the back seat of the car right next to Molly. She knew what would happen if they didn't briefly stop, and Gabrielle was determined to keep it from happening. She then started to holler as loud as she could with full trust that Molly would have enough faith to hear her.

Right when the back of the car reached the street while they were next to the sidewalk, Molly heard a faint noise that was too quiet to tell what it was, but hearing something that did not sound familiar was enough to startle her. "Mom, stop!" she abruptly said.

Mrs. Robinson quickly put on the brakes. "Why?"

"I thought I heard something."

"What did you hear?"

"I don't know. It was too quiet to tell what it was."

Mrs. Robinson took one more look in all directions to make sure she would not hit anything with the car. "I don't see anything, and we're already late." Then she resumed backing off the driveway, and they headed on their way.

From that day, Molly had constant protection throughout the rest of her life. Although she would not know it, Gabrielle would always be by her side.

# 21
## SEVERAL MORE WISHES

At the beginning of the school year towards the fall of 1871, Gabrielle started attending school. On many school days including her very first day, she walked to school with Abigail who enjoyed having her younger sister for company in comparison to walking alone.

Having lived in both the future and the past, Gabrielle wasn't ready to leave the future alone, but she still intended to obey her folks.

On rare occasions when the members of her family were elsewhere, she didn't pass up an opportunity to sit on the stump just to take a quick peek into the future to see what was happening.

Years passed, and Gabrielle knew how to read. One day while she was temporarily in the future, she learned about something she considered as worse than anything related to COVID. She was reading through a history book with information that took place in the period of time that she had come from, but the information didn't sound familiar.

Several weeks were spent going between the two periods of time whenever she got a chance, and she eventually learned that the information in the history book was not true according to what actually happened while she was learning about it back in the days. *Why are people writing things in a history book that aren't true?* she wondered.

After continuing to search in different years by way of time travel through wishing, Gabrielle discovered the same history book in a more previous year in the future, and it contained information that was all true. Immediately, she came to the conclusion that history was being rewritten, and the truth was being erased. Knowing what was happening in the future days, she tried thinking of what she could do to stop it, but there was only one possible option.

Back in her days, she wrote a message, hoping the day would come when someone in the future would read it. In the message, she wrote:

> *The day will come when history books will change, but history itself will not. To anyone trying to change history, it can't be done by rewriting a book. If you want history to change, you have to go back and do it yourself, but only if you can wish hard enough.*
>
> *Gabrielle Anne Linstrom*

# ABOUT THE AUTHOR

Writer, piano tuner, woodworker, and chip carver Jeffrey Higginson is the author of *Jenny's Unordinary Story*. As a kid, he wrote several short, silly stories just for fun, but was not planning on becoming an author at the time. His first published book started out as a short story, but the story eventually became the first chapter of the book while adding on to it.

He grew up in Granby, Missouri and now lives in Pocatello, Idaho with his wife, two children, and a third child on the way. In the summers, he works a lot in the garden for growing fruits and vegetables. He enjoys traveling to other states for vacations although current situations have turned it into a rare occasion. He's also been making videos for YouTube with his daughter as well as ones of just himself on their channels called *E for Emily* and *D for Daddy*. He's had several years of camera experience with both video and photography along with years of experience in creating his own designs for chip carving, which led to also creating designs for his book covers.

# Also written by this author:

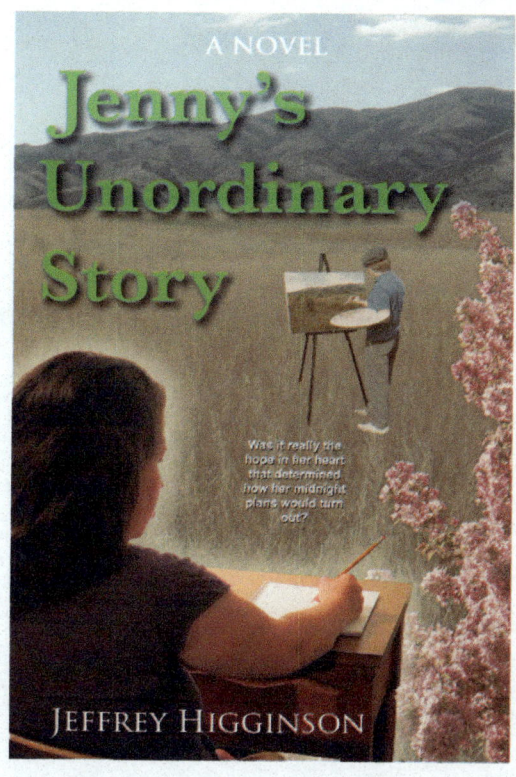

Made in the USA
Columbia, SC
09 November 2024

45711498R00137